TYPE 2 DIABETE

COOKBOOK FOR

BEGINNERS

500 Delicious and Healthy Recipes for the Newly
Diagnosed. 28 Day Meal Plan to Manage Type 2
Diabetes And Prediabetes included

TABLE OF CONTENTS

8

INTRODUCTION

Diabetes is a common disease that leads to metabolic disorders of carbohydrates and water balance. As a result of that, pancreatic functions are impaired. It is the pancreas that produces an important hormone called insulin.

Insulin regulates the level of blood sugar that is supplied with food. Without it, the body cannot convert sugar into glucose, and sugar starts accumulating in the body of a person with the disease.

Apart from the pancreas disorders, the water balance is impaired as well. As a result of that, the tissues do not retain water, and the kidneys excrete much fluid.

So What Happens When A Person Has Diabetes?

When the condition develops, the body produces too little insulin. At the same time, the level of blood sugar increases, and the cells become starved for glucose, which is the main base of energy.

Types of Diabetes

There are two types of diabetes.

- **Type 1 diabetes.** This condition is also known as insulin-dependent. It usually affects young people under 40. Individuals with type 1 diabetes will need to take insulin injections for the rest of their lives because their body produces antibodies that destroy the beta-cells which produce the hormone.

Type 1 diabetes is hard to cure. However, it is possible to restore pancreatic functions by adhering to a healthy diet. Products with a high glycemic index such as soda, juice, and sweets should be excluded.

- **Type 2 diabetes.** This happens as a result of the lack of sensitivity of the pancreas cells towards insulin because of the excess of nutrients. People with excess weight are the most susceptible to the disease.

What's The Difference?

	TYPE 1	TYPE 2
Who it affects	Represent up to 5 to 10 percent of all cases of diabetes. It was once called "juvenile-onset" diabetes because it was thought to develop most often in children and young adults. We now know it can occur in people of any age, including older adults.	Accounts for 90 to 95 percent of all diagnosed cases of diabetes. It used to be called "adult-onset" diabetes, but it is now known that even children—mainly if they're overweight—can develop type 2 diabetes.
What happens	The pancreas makes little if any insulin.	The pancreas does not develop enough insulin or the body doesn't respond properly to the insulin that is produced.
Risk factors	Less well-defined, but autoimmune, genetic, and environmental factors are believed to be involved.	Obesity, older age, family history of diabetes, physical inactivity, and race/ethnicity.

13

Treatment	Individualized meal plans, insulin therapy (usually several injections a day), self-monitoring glucose testing several times a day, regular physical activity, and a healthy diet.	A healthy diet, weight loss (if overweight), regular exercise, and monitoring blood glucose levels. Some individuals can manage blood sugar through diet and exercise alone. However, diabetes tends to be a progressive disease, so oral medications and possibly insulin may be needed at some point.

Food to Eat

Vegetables

Fresh vegetables never cause harm to anyone. So, adding a meal full of vegetables is the best shot for all diabetic patients. But not all vegetables contain the same amount of macronutrients. Some vegetables contain a high amount of carbohydrates, so those are not suitable for a diabetic diet. We need to use vegetables that contain a low amount of carbohydrates.

- Cauliflower
- Spinach
- Tomatoes
- Broccoli
- Lemons
- Artichoke
- Garlic
- Asparagus
- Spring onions
- Onions
- Ginger etc.

Meat

Meat is not on the red list for the diabetic diet. It is fine to have some meat every now and then for diabetic patients. However certain meat types are better than others. For instance, red meat is not a preferable option for such patients. They should consume white meat more often whether it's seafood or poultry. Healthy options in meat are:

- All fish, i.e., salmon, halibut, trout, cod, sardine, etc.
- Scallops
- Mussels
- Shrimp
- Oysters etc.

Fruits

Not all fruits are good for diabetes. To know if the fruit is suitable for this diet, it is important to note its sugar content. Some fruits contain a high amount of sugars in the form of sucrose and fructose, and those should be readily avoided. Here is the list of popularly used fruits that can be taken on the diabetic diet:

- Peaches
- Nectarines
- Avocados
- Apples
- Berries
- Grapefruit
- Kiwi Fruit
- Bananas
- Cherries
- Grapes
- Orange
- Pears
- Plums
- Strawberries

Nuts and Seeds

Nuts and seeds are perhaps the most enriched edibles, and they contain such a mix of macronutrients which can never harm anyone. So diabetic patients can take the nuts and seeds in their diet without any fear of a glucose spike.

- Pistachios
- Sunflower seeds
- Walnuts
- Peanuts
- Pecans
- Pumpkin seeds
- Almonds
- Sesame seeds etc.

Grains

Diabetic patients should also be selective while choosing the right grains for their diet. The idea is to keep the amount of starch as minimum as possible. That is why you won't see any white rice in the list rather it is replaced with more fibrous brown rice.

- Quinoa
- Oats
- Multigrain
- Whole grains
- Brown rice
- Millet
- Barley
- Sorghum
- Tapioca

Fats

Fat intake is the most debated topic as far as the diabetic diet is concerned. As there are diets like ketogenic, which are loaded with fats and still proved effective for diabetic patients. The key is the absence of carbohydrates. In any other situation, fats are as harmful to diabetics as any normal person. Switching to unsaturated fats is a better option.

- Sesame oil
- Olive oil
- Canola oil
- Grapeseed oil
- Other vegetable oils
- Fats extracted from plant sources.

Diary

Any dairy product which directly or indirectly causes a glucose rise in the blood should not be taken on this diet. Other than those, all products are good to use. These items include:

- Skimmed milk
- Low-fat cheese
- Eggs
- Yogurt
- Trans fat-free margarine or butter

Sugar Alternatives

Since ordinary sugars or sweeteners are strictly forbidden on a diabetic diet. There are artificial varieties that can add sweetness without raising the level of carbohydrates in the meal. These substitutes are:

- Stevia
- Xylitol
- Natvia
- Swerve
- Monk fruit
- Erythritol

Make sure to substitute them with extra care. The sweetness of each sweetener is entirely different from the table sugar, so add each following the intensity of their flavor. Stevia is the sweetest of them, and it should be used with more care. In place of 1 cup of sugar, a tsp. of stevia is enough. All other sweeteners are more or less similar to sugar in their intensity of sweetness.

Foods to Avoid

Knowing a general scheme of diet helps a lot, but it is equally important to be well familiar with the items which have to be avoided. With this list, you can make your diet a hundred% sugar-free. Many other food items can cause some harm to a diabetic patient as the sugars do. So, let's discuss them in some detail here.

Sugars

Sugar is a big NO-GO for a diabetic diet. Once you are diabetic, you would need to say goodbye to all the natural sweeteners which are loaded with carbohydrates. They contain polysaccharides that readily break into glucose after getting into our body. And the list does not only include table sugars but other items like honey and molasses should also be avoided.

- White sugar
- Brown sugar
- Confectionary sugar
- Honey
- Molasses
- Granulated sugar

Your mind and your body, will not accept the abrupt change. It is recommended to go for a gradual change. It means start substituting it with low carb substitutes in a small amount, day by day.

High Fat Dairy Products

Once you are diabetic, you may get susceptible to several other fatal diseases including cardiovascular ones. That is why experts strictly recommend avoiding high-fat food products, especially dairy items. The high amount of fat can make your body insulin resistant. So even when you take insulin, it won't be of any use as the body will not work on it.

Saturated Animal Fats

Saturated animal fats are not good for anyone, whether diabetic or normal. So, better avoid using them in general. Whenever you are cooking meat, try to trim off all the excess fat. Cooking oils made out of these saturated fats should be avoided. Keep yourself away from any of the animal-origin fats.

High Carb Vegetables

As discussed above, vegetables with more starch are not suitable for diabetes. These veggies can increase the carbohydrate levels of food. So, omit these from the recipes and enjoy the rest of the less starchy vegetables. Some of the high carb vegetables are:

- Potatoes
- Sweet potatoes
- Yams etc.

Cholesterol Rich Ingredients

Bad cholesterol or High-density Lipoprotein tends to deposit in different parts of the body. That is why food items having high bad cholesterol are not good for diabetes. Such items should be replaced with the ones with low cholesterol.

High Sodium Products

Sodium is related to hypertension and blood pressure. Since diabetes is already the result of a hormonal imbalance in the body, in the presence of excess sodium—another imbalance—a fluid imbalance may occur which a diabetic body cannot tolerate. It adds up to the already present complications of the disease. So, avoid using food items with a high amount of sodium. Mainly store packed items, processed foods, and salt all contain sodium, and one should avoid them all. Use only the 'Unsalted' variety of food products, whether it's butter, margarine, nuts, or other items.

Sugary Drinks

Cola drinks or other similar beverages are filled with sugars. If you had seen different video presentations showing the amount of sugars present in a single bottle of soda, you would know how dangerous those are for diabetic patients. They can drastically increase the amount of blood glucose level within 30 minutes of drinking. Fortunately, there are many sugar-free varieties available in the drinks which are suitable for diabetic patients.

Sugar Syrups and Toppings

A number of syrups available in the markets are made out of nothing but sugar. Maple syrup is one good example For a diabetic diet, the patient should avoid such sugary syrups and also stay away from the sugar-rich toppings available in the stores. If you want to use them at all, trust yourself and prepare them at home with a sugar-free recipe.

Sweet Chocolate and candies

For diabetic patients, sugar-free chocolates or candies are the best way out. Other processed chocolate bars and candies are extremely damaging to their health, and all of these should be avoided. You can try and prepare healthy bars and candies at home with sugar-free recipes.

Alcohol

Alcohol tends to reduce the rate of our metabolism and take away our appetite, which can render a diabetic patient into a very life-threatening condition. Alcohol in a very small amount cannot harm the patient, but the regular or constant intake of alcohol is bad for health and glucose levels.

THE BASICS OF DIABETES

Diabetes Mellitus is a disease that affects our metabolism. The predominant characteristic of diabetes is an inability to create or utilize insulin, a hormone that moves sugar from our blood cells into the rest of our bodies' cells. This is crucial for us because we rely on that blood sugar to power our body and provide energy. High blood sugar, if not treated, can lead to serious damage to our eyes, nerves, kidneys, and other major organs. There are 2 main types of diabetes, they are type 1 and type 2, with the second being the most common of the two with over 90 percent of diabetics suffering from it.

Type 1 Vs Type 2 Diabetes

- **Type 1 diabetes** is an autoimmune disease. In cases of type 1 diabetes, the immune system attacks cells in the pancreas responsible for insulin production. Although we are unsure what causes this reaction, many experts believe it is brought upon by a gene deficiency or by viral infections that may trigger the disease.

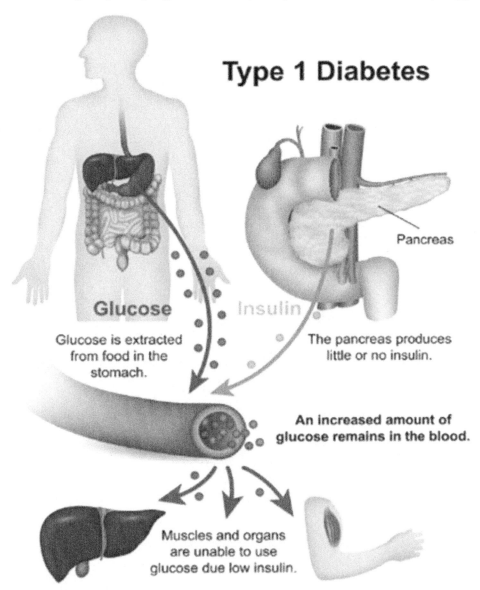

Type 1 Diabetes

Glucose

Insulin

Pancreas

Glucose is extracted from food in the stomach.

The pancreas produces little or no insulin.

An increased amount of glucose remains in the blood.

Muscles and organs are unable to use glucose due low insulin.

- **Type 2 diabetes** is a metabolic disorder, although research suggests it may warrant reclassification as an autoimmune disease as well. People who grieve from type 2 diabetes have a high resistance to insulin or an inability to produce enough insulin. Professionals believe that type 2 diabetes is a result of a genetic predisposition in many people, which is further aggravated by obesity and other environmental triggers.

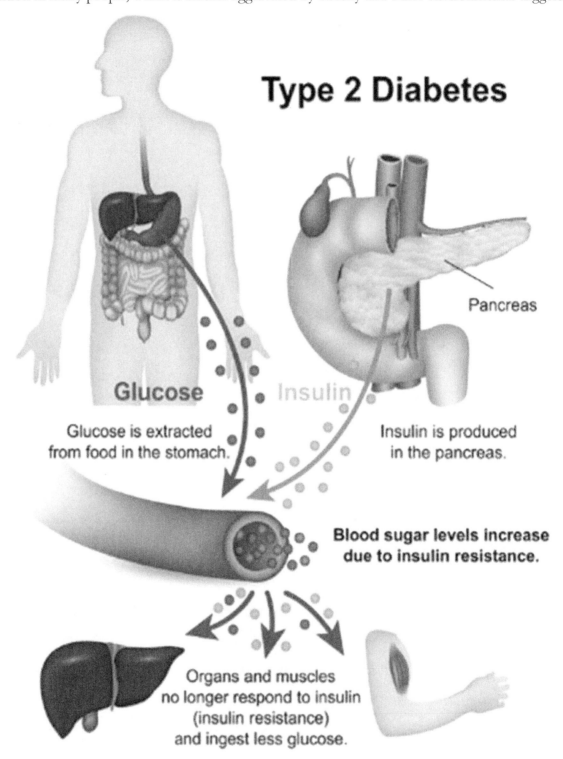

Diagnosis

Diabetes diagnosis has come incredibly far in the last few decades. Currently, there are two primary tests for diagnosing diabetes: the fasting plasma glucose (FPG) test and the hemoglobin A1c test.

The FPG test takes your blood sugar levels after an eight-hour fasting period; this helps to show if your body is processing glucose at a healthy rate.

The A1c test shows your blood sugar levels over the last three months. It does this by testing the amount of glucose being carried by the hemoglobin of your red blood cells. Hemoglobin has a lifespan of roughly three months; this allows us to test them to see how long they have been carrying their glucose for and how much they have.

Symptoms & Risk Factors

In type 1 diabetes, the list of symptoms can be extensive with both serious and less obvious indicators. Below, I will list the most common symptoms as well as other potential complications of type 1 diabetes:

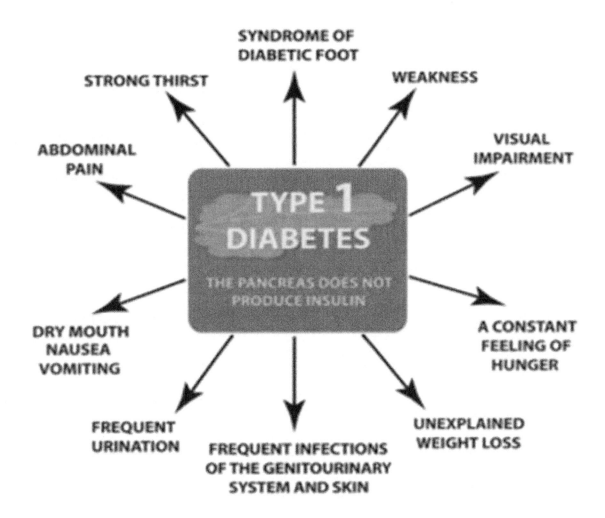

- **Excessive thirst:** Extreme thirst is one of the less noticeable indicators of type 1 diabetes. It is brought upon by high blood sugar (hyperglycemia).
- **Frequent urination:** Frequent urination is caused by your kidneys failing to process all of the glucose in your blood; this forces your body to attempt to flush out excess glucose through urinating.

- **Fatigue:** Fatigue in type 1 diabetes patients is caused by the body's inability to process glucose for energy.
- **Excessive hunger:** Those suffering from type 1 diabetes often have persistent hunger and increased appetites. This is because the body is desperate for glucose despite its inability to process it without insulin.
- **Cloudy or unclear vision:** Rapid fluctuations in blood sugar levels can lead to cloudy or blurred vision. Those suffering from untreated type 1 diabetes are unable to naturally control their blood sugar levels, making rapid fluctuations a very common occurrence.
- **Rapid weight loss:** Rapid weight loss is probably the most noticeable symptom of type 1 diabetes. As your body starves off glucose, it resorts to breaking down muscle and fat to sustain itself. This can lead to incredibly fast weight loss in type 1 diabetes cases.
- **Ketoacidosis:** Ketoacidosis is a potentially deadly complication of untreated type 1 diabetes. In response to the lack of glucose being fed into your muscles and organs, your body starts breaking down your fat and muscle into an energy source called ketones, which can be burned without the need for insulin. Ketones are usually perfectly fine in normal amounts. But, when your body is starving, it may end up flooding itself with ketones in an attempt to fuel itself; the acidification of your blood that follows this influx of acid molecules may lead to more serious conditions, a coma, or death.

In cases of type 2 diabetes, the symptoms tend to be slower to develop, and they tend to be mild early on. Some early symptoms mimic type 1 diabetes and may include:

- **Excessive hunger:** Similar to type 1 diabetes, those of us with type 2 diabetes will feel constant hunger. Again, this is brought on by our bodies looking for fuel because of our inability to process glucose.
- **Fatigue and mental fog:** Depending on the severity of the insulin shortage in type 2 sufferers, they may feel physical fatigue and a mental fogginess during their average day.
- **Frequent urination:** Another symptom of both type 1 and 2 diabetes. Frequent urination is simply your body's way of attempting to rid itself of excess glucose.
- **Dry mouth and constant thirst:** It is unclear what causes dry mouth in diabetic sufferers, but it is tightly linked to high blood sugar levels. Constant thirst is brought on not only by a dry mouth but also by the dehydration that frequent urination causes.
- **Itchy skin:** Itching of the skin, especially around the hands and feet, is a sign of polyneuropathy (diabetic nerve damage). As well as being a sign of potential nerve damage, itching can be a sign of high concentrations of cytokines circulating in your bloodstream; these are inflammatory molecules that can lead to itching. Cytokines are signaling proteins and hormonal regulators that are often released in high amounts before nerve damage.

SYMPTOMS OF TYPE 2 DIABETES

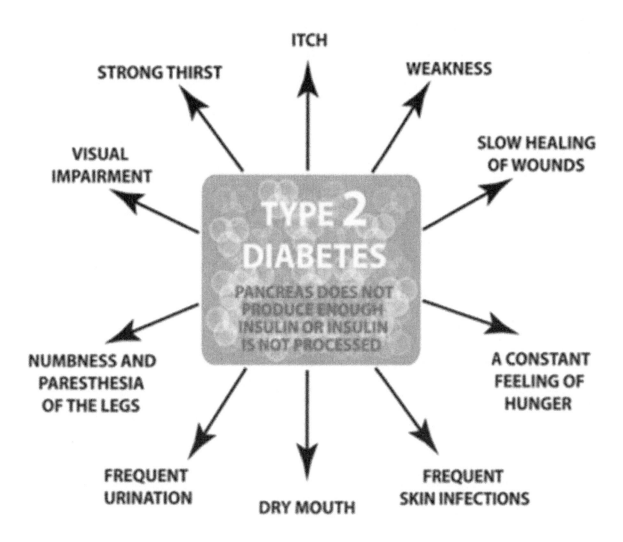

As type 2 diabetes progresses and becomes more serious, the symptoms can become highly uncomfortable and dangerous. Some of these advanced symptoms include:

- **Slow healing of bruises, cuts, and abrasions:** Many people suffering from type 2 diabetes have impaired immune systems due to the lack of energy available to the body. As well as a lack of energy, many diabetics have slowed circulation brought upon by high blood glucose levels. Both of these factors lead to a much slower healing process and far greater risks of infection.

- **Yeast infections:** Women with type 2 diabetes, the chances of yeast infections are far higher than in non-diabetic women. This is due to high blood sugar levels and a lowered immune system response.

23

- **Neuropathy or numbness:** Long-term high blood sugar levels can lead to severe nerve damage in adults with diabetes. It is believed around 70 percent of people with type 2 diabetes have some form of neuropathy (Hoskins, 2020). Diabetic neuropathy is characterized by numbness in the extremities, specifically around the feet and fingers.
- **Dark skin patches (acanthosis nigricans):** Some people with type 2 diabetes may have far above normal levels of insulin in their blood, as their body is unable to utilize it due to insulin resistance. This rise of insulin in the bloodstream can lead to some skin cells over reproducing and cause black patches to form on the skin.

Complications

Severe complications of diabetes can be debilitating and deadly. Both type 1 & type 2 diabetes can cause serious neurological, cardiovascular, and optical conditions. Some of the most common complications of advanced diabetes are as follows:

- **Heart attacks:** Diabetes is directly linked to a higher rate of heart attacks in adults. High blood glucose levels damage the cells and nerves around the heart and blood vessels over time, which can cause a plethora of heart diseases to form.
- **Cataracts:** People with diabetes have a nearly 60 percent greater chance of developing cataracts later in life if their diabetes is left unchecked (Diabetes.co.uk, 2019a). Doctors are not sure of the real reason for cataracts forming at a higher rate in diabetes patients, but many believe it has to do with the lower amounts of glucose available to the cells powering our eyes.
- **Peripheral artery disease (PAD):** This is a very common diabetes complication and this causes decreased blood flow, which leads to serious issues in the lower legs, often resulting in amputation.
- **Diabetic nephropathy:** Diabetic nephropathy happens when high levels of blood glucose damage parts of your kidneys, which are responsible for filtering blood. This causes your kidneys to develop chronic kidney diseases and break down over time, leading to failure.
- **Glaucoma:** Diabetes can cause glaucoma in sufferers due to high blood sugar levels and this directly damages blood vessels in the eyes. When your body attempts to repair these vessels, it may cause glaucoma on the iris where the damage was caused.

10 Tips to Control Diabetes

- **Eat less salt:** Salt can increase your chances of having high blood pressure, which leads to increased chance of heart disease and stroke.
- **Replace sugar:** Replace sugar with zero-calorie sweeteners. Cutting out sugar gives you much more control over your blood sugar levels.
- **Cut out alcohol:** Alcohol tends to be high in calories, and if drunk on an empty stomach with insulin medication, it can cause drastic drops in blood sugar.
- **Be physically active:** Physical action decreases your risk of cardiovascular issues and increases your body's natural glucose burn rate.
- **Avoid saturated fats:** Saturated fats like butter and pastries can lead to high cholesterol and blood circulation issues.
- **Use canola or olive oil:** If you need to use oil in your cooking, use canola or olive oil. Both are high in beneficial fatty acids and monounsaturated fat.

- **Drink water:** Water is by far the healthiest drink you can have. Drinking water helps to regulate blood sugar and insulin levels.
- **Make sure you get enough vitamin D:** Vitamin D is a crucial vitamin for controlling blood sugar levels. Eat food high in this vitamin or ask your doctor about supplements.
- **Avoid processed food:** Processed foods tend to be high in vegetable oils, salt, refined grains, or other unhealthy additives.
- **Drink coffee and tea:** Not only are coffee and tea great hunger suppressants for dieters, but they contain important antioxidants that help with protecting cells.

UNDERSTANDING TYPE 2 DIABETES

Insulin resistance is the most popular cause of type 2 diabetes. Because muscle, fat, and liver cells no longer respond to insulin, the pancreas secretes a lot of it to keep blood sugar levels in check. Insulin resistance is exacerbated by being overweight and physically sedentary.

Prediabetes and glucose intolerance both cause insulin resistance. Prediabetes affects an estimated 79 million Americans. According to studies, decreasing 7% of your body weight and exercising regularly can reduce your risk of type 2 diabetes by 58 percent. Insulin resistance can be reduced by decreasing weight, exercising regularly, eating carbohydrates in moderation, and eating a nutritious diet once you've been diagnosed with diabetes. As a result, better blood sugar control will be achieved.

The Importance of Insulin

Diabetes is a serious condition caused by a deficiency of insulin. Insulin is a hormone that is necessary for the proper functioning of the body. When a person develops diabetes, the cells in the body do not respond to insulin properly. The result is that the cells do not get the energy and nutrients they need, and then they start to die

Diabetes treatments differ depending on the kind, number, and severity of complications as well as the patient's overall health. Fortunately, diabetes has been studied extensively by the medical community, and as a result, there are numerous resources and treatments accessible.

For type 1 diabetes, insulin supplements are essential. Type 1 diabetics rely on daily insulin injections; some prefer a costlier but easier-to-use insulin pump. Insulin needs in type 1 diabetics will vary throughout the day as they eat and exercise. This means many type 1 diabetics will regularly test their blood sugar levels to assess whether their insulin needs are being met.

Some type 1 diabetics develop insulin resistance after years of injections. This means that oral diabetes medication such as metformin is becoming increasingly more commonly prescribed to type 1 diabetic to help prevent insulin resistance.

In some circumstances, type 2 diabetes can be managed without the need for medication. Many type 2 diabetic individuals can control their blood sugar levels by watching what they eat and doing some modest exercise. The majority of type 2 diabetics are advised to stick to low-fat, high-fiber, and low-carbohydrate diets.

Medication is required for some persons with type 2 diabetes. Type 2 diabetes, unlike type 1, does not demand the use of insulin as frequently. Some type 2 diabetics, however, require insulin to complement their pancreas' production

Metformin is the most widely given type 2 diabetic medication. This prescription medication aids in the reduction of blood glucose levels and the improvement of insulin sensitivity. Other drugs prescribed to type 2 diabetics include sulfonylureas, thiazolidinediones, and meglitinides, which all help increase insulin production or sensitivity.

Diabetes
Blood Sugar Level

HBA-1C Test Score	Mean Blood mg/dl	Glucose mmol/l
14.0	380	21.1
13.0	350	19.3
12.0	315	17.4
11.0	280	15.6
10.0	250	13.7
9.0	215	11.9
8.0	180	10.0
7.0	150	8.2
6.0	115	6.3
5.0	80	4.7
4.0	50	2.6
3.0	35	2.0

Action Suggested

Good

Excellent

Very high
A little high to very high depending on patient
Maximum after meal in nondiabetics
Normal before meal in nondiabetics
Normal
Low
Extremely low

The normal range of blood sugar according to the glucose levels chart is between 70 and 100 mg/dl

Causes of Type 2 Diabetes

Although some of the causes are completely unclear, even trivial viral infections are recognized, which can affect insulin-producing cells in the pancreas, such as:

- Measles.
- Cytomegalovirus.
- Epstein-Barr.
- Coxsackievirus.

For Type 2 Diabetes, however, the main risk factors are:

- Overweight and obesity.

- Genetic factors: family history increases the risk of developing type 2 diabetes.
- Ethnicity: the highest number of cases is recorded in the populations of sub-Saharan Africa and the Middle East and North Africa.
- Environmental factors are especially related to incorrect lifestyles (sedentary lifestyle and obesity).
- Gestational diabetes, which is diabetes that happens during pregnancy.
- Age: type 2 diabetes increases with increasing age, especially above the age of 65.
- Diet high in fat that promotes obesity.
- Alcohol consumption.
- Sedentary lifestyle.

1. Bacon and Chicken Garlic Wrap

Preparation Time: 15 minutes
Cooking Time: 10 minutes
Servings: 4
Ingredients:

- 1 chicken fillet, cut into small cubes
- 8–9 thin slices bacon, cut to fit cubes
- 6 garlic cloves, minced

Directions:

1. Preheat your oven to 400°F
2. Line a baking tray with aluminum foil
3. Add minced garlic to a bowl and rub each chicken piece with it
4. Wrap bacon piece around each garlic chicken bite
5. Secure with toothpick
6. Transfer bites to the baking sheet, keeping a little bit of space between them
7. Bake for about 15–20 minutes until crispy
8. Serve and enjoy!

Nutrition: Calories: 260; Fat: 19g; Carbohydrates: 5g; Protein: 22g

2. Salty Macadamia Chocolate Smoothie

Preparation Time: 5 minutes
Cooking Time: 0 minutes
Servings: 1
Ingredients:

- 2 tbsp. macadamia nuts, salted
- 1/3 cup chocolate whey protein powder, low carb
- 1 cup almond milk, unsweetened

Directions:

1. Add the listed ingredients to your blender and blend until you have a smooth mixture
2. Chill and enjoy it!

Nutrition: Calories: 165; Fat: 2g; Carbohydrates: 1g; Protein: 12g

3. Buckwheat Grouts Breakfast Bowl

Preparation Time: 5 minutes, plus overnight to soak
Cooking Time: 10 to 12 minutes
Servings: 4
Ingredients:

- 3 cups skim milk
- 1 cup buckwheat grouts
- ¼ cup chia seeds
- 2 tsp. vanilla extract
- 1/2 tsp. ground cinnamon
- A pinch salt
- 1 cup water
- 1/2 cup unsalted pistachios
- 2 cups sliced fresh strawberries
- ¼ cup cacao nibs (optional)

Directions:

1. In a large bowl, stir together the milk, groats, chia seeds, vanilla, cinnamon, and salt. Cover and refrigerate overnight.
2. The next morning, transfer the soaked mixture to a medium pot and add the water. Bring to a boil over medium-high heat, reduce the heat to maintain a simmer, and cook for 10 to 12 minutes, until the buckwheat is tender and thickened.
3. Transfer to bowls and serve, topped with the pistachios, strawberries, and cacao nibs (if using).

Nutrition: Calories: 340; Total Fat: 8g; Saturated Fat: 1g; Protein: 15g; Carbs: 52g; Sugar: 14g; Fiber: 10g; Cholesterol: 4mg; Sodium: 140mg

4. Peach Muesli Bake

Preparation Time: 10 minutes
Cooking Time: 40 minutes
Servings: 4
Ingredients:

- Nonstick cooking spray
- 2 cups skim milk
- 11/2 cups rolled oats
- 1/2 cup chopped walnuts
- 1 large egg
- 2 tbsp. maple syrup

- 1 tsp. ground cinnamon
- 1 tsp. baking powder
- 1/2 tsp. salt
- 2 to 3 peaches, sliced

Directions:
1. Preheat the oven to 375°F. Spray a 9-inch square baking dish with cooking spray. Set aside.
2. In a large bowl, stir together the milk, oats, walnuts, egg, maple syrup, cinnamon, baking powder, and salt. Spread half the mixture in the prepared baking dish.
3. Place half the peaches in a single layer across the oat mixture.
4. Spread the remaining oat mixture over the top. Add the remaining peaches in a thin layer over the oats. Bake for 35 to 40 minutes, uncovered until thickened and browned.
5. Cut into 8 squares and serve warm.

Nutrition: Calories: 138; Total Fat: 3g; Saturated Fat: 1g; Protein: 6g; Carbs: 22g; Sugar: 10g; Fiber: 3g; Cholesterol: 24mg; Sodium: 191mg

5. Steel-Cut Oatmeal Bowl with Fruit and Nuts

Preparation Time: 5 minutes
Cooking Time: 20 minutes
Servings: 4
Ingredients:
- 1 cup steel-cut oats
- 2 cups almond milk
- ¾ cup water
- 1 tsp. ground cinnamon
- ¼ tsp. salt
- 2 cups chopped fresh fruit, such as blueberries, strawberries, raspberries, or peaches
- 1/2 cup chopped walnuts
- ¼ cup chia seeds

Directions:
1. In a medium saucepan over medium-high heat, combine the oats, almond milk, water, cinnamon, and salt. Bring to a boil, reduce the heat to low, and simmer for 15 to 20 minutes, until the oats are softened and thickened.
2. Top each bowl with 1/2 cup of fresh fruit, 2 tbsp. of walnuts, and 1 tbsp. of chia seeds before serving.

Nutrition: Calories: 288; Total Fat: 11g; Saturated Fat: 1g; Protein: 10g; Carbs: 38g; Sugar: 7g; Fiber: 10g; Cholesterol: 0mg; Sodium: 329mg

6. Whole-Grain Dutch Baby Pancake

Preparation Time: 5 minutes
Cooking Time: 25 minutes
Servings: 4
Ingredients:
- 2 tbsp. coconut oil
- 1/2 cup whole-wheat flour
- ¼ cup skim milk
- 3 large eggs
- 1 tsp. vanilla extract
- 1/2 tsp. baking powder
- ¼ tsp. salt
- ¼ tsp. ground cinnamon
- Powdered sugar, for dusting

Directions:
1. Preheat the oven to 400°F.
2. Put the coconut oil in a medium oven-safe skillet, and place the skillet in the oven to melt the oil while it preheats.
3. In a blender, combine the flour, milk, eggs, vanilla, baking powder, salt, and cinnamon. Process until smooth.
4. Carefully remove the skillet from the oven and tilt it to spread the oil around evenly.
5. Pour the batter into the skillet and return it to the oven for 23 to 25 minutes, until the pancake puffs and lightly browns.
6. Remove, dust lightly with powdered sugar, cut into 4 wedges, and serve.

Nutrition: Calories: 195; Total Fat: 11g; Saturated Fat: 7g; Protein: 8g; Carbs: 16g; Sugar: 1g; Fiber: 2g; Cholesterol: 140mg; Sodium: 209mg

7. Mushroom, Zucchini, and Onion Frittata

Preparation Time: 10 minutes
Cooking Time: 20 minutes
Servings: 4
Ingredients:
- 1 tbsp. extra-virgin olive oil
- 1/2 onion, chopped
- 1 medium zucchini, chopped

- 11/2 cups sliced mushrooms
- 6 large eggs, beaten
- 2 tbsp. skim milk
- Salt
- Freshly ground black pepper
- 1-ounce feta cheese, crumbled

Directions:

1. Preheat the oven to 400°F.
2. In a medium oven-safe skillet over medium-high heat, heat the olive oil.
3. Add the onion and sauté for 3 to 5 minutes, until translucent.
4. Add the zucchini and mushrooms, and cook for 3 to 5 more minutes, until the vegetables are tender.
5. Meanwhile, in a small bowl, whisk the eggs, milk, salt, and pepper. Pour the mixture into the skillet, stirring to combine, and transfer the skillet to the oven. Cook for 7 to 9 minutes, until set.
6. Sprinkle with the feta cheese, and cook for 1 to 2 minutes more, until heated through.
7. Remove, cut into 4 wedges, and serve.

Nutrition: Calories: 178; Total Fat: 13g; Saturated Fat: 4g; Protein: 12g; Carbs: 5g; Sugar: 3g; Fiber: 1g; Cholesterol: 285mg; Sodium: 234mg

8. Berry-Oat Breakfast Bars

Preparation Time: 10 minutes
Cooking Time: 25 minutes
Servings: 2
Ingredients:

- 2 cups fresh raspberries or blueberries
- 2 tbsp. sugar
- 2 tbsp. freshly squeezed lemon juice
- 1 tbsp. cornstarch
- 11/2 cups rolled oats
- 1/2 cup whole-wheat flour
- 1/2 cup walnuts
- ¼ cup chia seeds
- ¼ cup extra-virgin olive oil
- ¼ cup honey
- 1 large egg

Directions:

1. Preheat the oven to 350°F.

2. In a small saucepan over medium heat, stir together the berries, sugar, lemon juice, and cornstarch. Bring to a simmer. Reduce the heat and simmer for 2 to 3 minutes, until the mixture thickens.
3. In a food processor or high-speed blender, combine the oats, flour, walnuts, and chia seeds. Process until powdered. Add the olive oil, honey, and egg. Pulse a few more times, until well combined. Press half of the mixture into a 9-inch square baking dish.
4. Spread the berry filling over the oat mixture. Add the remaining oat mixture on top of the berries. Bake for 25 minutes, until browned.
5. Let cool completely, cut into 12 pieces, and serve. Store in a covered container for up to 5 days.

Nutrition: Calories: 201; Total Fat: 10g; Saturated Fat: 1g; Protein: 5g; Carbs: 26g; Sugar: 9g; Fiber: 5g; Cholesterol: 16mg; Sodium: 8mg

9. Spinach and Cheese Quiche

Preparation Time: 10 minutes, plus 10 minutes to rest
Cooking Time: 50 minutes
Servings: 4
Ingredients:

- Nonstick cooking spray
- 8 ounces Yukon gold potatoes, shredded
- 1 tbsp. plus 2 tsp. extra-virgin olive oil, divided
- 1 tsp. salt, divided
- Freshly ground black pepper
- 1 onion, finely chopped
- 1 (10-ounce) bag fresh spinach
- 4 large eggs
- 1/2 cup skim milk
- 1-ounce gruyère cheese, shredded

Directions:

1. Preheat the oven to 350°F. Spray a 9-inch pie dish with cooking spray. Set aside.
2. In a small bowl, toss the potatoes with 2 tsp. of olive oil, 1/2 tsp. of salt, and season with pepper. Press the potatoes into the bottom and sides of the pie dish to form a thin, even layer. Bake for 20 minutes, until golden brown. Remove from the oven and set aside to cool.

3. In a large skillet over medium-high heat, heat the remaining 1 tbsp. of olive oil.
4. Add the onion and sauté for 3 to 5 minutes, until softened.
5. By handfuls, add the spinach, stirring between each addition, until it just starts to wilt before adding more. Cook for about 1 minute, until it cooks down.
6. In a medium bowl, whisk the eggs and milk. Add the gruyère, and season with the remaining 1/2 tsp. of salt and some pepper. Fold the eggs into the spinach. Pour the mixture into the pie dish and bake for 25 minutes, until the eggs are set.
7. Let rest for 10 minutes before serving.

Nutrition: Calories: 445; Total Fat: 14g; Saturated Fat: 4g; Protein: 19g; Carbs: 68g; Sugar: 6g; Fiber: 7g; Cholesterol: 193mg; Sodium: 773mg

10. Spicy Jalapeno Popper Deviled Eggs

Preparation Time: 5 minutes
Cooking Time: 5 minutes
Servings: 4
Ingredients:
- 4 large whole eggs, hardboiled
- 2 tbsp. Keto-Friendly mayonnaise
- ¼ cup cheddar cheese, grated
- 2 slices bacon, cooked and crumbled
- 1 jalapeno, sliced

Directions:
1. Cut eggs in half, remove the yolk, and put them in a bowl
2. Lay egg whites on a platter
3. Mix in the remaining ingredients and mash them with the egg yolks
4. Transfer yolk mix back to the egg whites
5. Serve and enjoy!

Nutrition: Calories: 176; Fat: 14g; Carbohydrates: 0.7g; Protein: 10g

11. Blueberry Breakfast Cake

Preparation Time: 15 minutes
Cooking Time: 45 minutes
Servings: 4
Ingredients:
For the topping

- ¼ cup finely chopped walnuts
- 1/2 tsp. ground cinnamon
- 2 tbsp. butter, chopped into small pieces
- 2 tbsp. sugar

For the cake
- Nonstick cooking spray
- 1 cup whole-wheat pastry flour
- 1 cup oat flour
- ¼ cup sugar
- 2 tsp. baking powder
- 1 large egg, beaten
- 1/2 cup skim milk
- 2 tbsp. butter, melted
- 1 tsp. grated lemon peel
- 2 cups fresh or frozen blueberries

Directions:
To make the topping
1. In a small bowl, stir together the walnuts, cinnamon, butter, and sugar. Set aside.
To make the cake
2. Preheat the oven to 350°F. Spray a 9-inch square pan with cooking spray. Set aside.
3. In a large bowl, stir together the pastry flour, oat flour, sugar, and baking powder.
4. Add the egg, milk, butter, and lemon peel, and stir until there are no dry spots.
5. Stir in the blueberries, and gently mix until incorporated. Press the batter into the prepared pan, using a spoon to flatten it into the dish.
6. Sprinkle the topping over the cake.
7. Bake for 40 to 45 minutes, until a toothpick inserted into the cake, comes out clean, and serve.

Nutrition: Calories: 177; Total Fat: 7g; Saturated Fat: 3g; Protein: 4g; Carbs: 26g; Sugar: 9g; Fiber: 3g; Cholesterol: 26mg; Sodium: 39mg

12. Lovely Porridge

Preparation Time: 15 minutes
Cooking Time: Nil
Servings: 2
Ingredients:
- 2 tbsp. coconut flour
- 2 tbsp. vanilla protein powder
- 3 tbsp. Golden Flaxseed meal
- 1 and 1/2 cups almond milk, unsweetened
- Powdered erythritol

Directions:

1. Take a bowl and mix in flaxseed meal, protein powder, coconut flour and mix well
2. Add mix to the saucepan (placed over medium heat)
3. Add almond milk and stir, let the mixture thicken
4. Add your desired amount of sweetener and serve
5. Enjoy!

Nutrition: Calories: 259; Fat: 13g; Carbohydrates: 5g; Protein: 16g

13. <u>Basil and Tomato Baked Eggs</u>

Preparation Time: 10 minutes
Cooking Time: 15 minutes
Servings: 4
Ingredients:

- 1 garlic clove, minced
- 1 cup canned tomatoes
- ¼ cup fresh basil leaves, roughly chopped
- 1/2 tsp. chili powder
- 1 tbsp. olive oil
- 4 whole eggs
- Salt and pepper to taste

Directions:

1. Preheat your oven to 375°F
2. Take a small baking dish and grease it with olive oil
3. Add garlic, basil, tomatoes chili, olive oil into a dish and stir
4. Crackdown eggs into a dish, keeping space between the two
5. Sprinkle the whole dish with salt and pepper
6. Place in oven and cook for 12 minutes until eggs are set and tomatoes are bubbling
7. Serve with basil on top
8. Enjoy!

Nutrition: Calories: 235; Fat: 16g; Carbohydrates: 7g; Protein: 14g

14. <u>Whole-Grain Pancakes</u>

Preparation Time: 10 minutes
Cooking Time: 15 minutes
Servings: 4
Ingredients:

- 2 cups whole-wheat pastry flour

- 4 tsp. baking powder
- 2 tsp. ground cinnamon
- 1/2 tsp. salt
- 2 cups skim milk, plus more as needed
- 2 large eggs
- 1 tbsp. honey
- Nonstick cooking spray
- Maple syrup, for serving
- Fresh fruit, for serving

Directions:

1. In a large bowl, stir together the flour, baking powder, cinnamon, and salt.
2. Add the milk, eggs, and honey, and stir well to combine. If needed, add more milk, 1 tbsp. at a time, until there are no dry spots and you have a pourable batter.
3. Heat a large skillet over medium-high heat, and spray it with cooking spray.
4. Using a ¼-cup measuring cup, scoop 2 or 3 pancakes into the skillet at a time. Cook for a couple of minutes, until bubbles form on the surface of the pancakes, flip, and cook for 1 to 2 minutes more, until golden brown and cooked through. Repeat with the remaining batter.
5. Serve topped with maple syrup or fresh fruit.

Nutrition: Calories: 392; Total Fat: 4g; Saturated Fat: 1g; Protein: 15g; Carbs: 71g; Sugar: 11g; Fiber: 9g; Cholesterol: 95mg; Sodium: 396mg

15. <u>Whole-Grain Breakfast Cookies</u>

Preparation Time: 20 minutes
Cooking Time: 10 minutes
Servings: 18 cookies
Ingredients:

- 2 cups rolled oats
- 1/2 cup whole-wheat flour
- ¼ cup ground flaxseed
- 1 tsp. baking powder
- 1 cup unsweetened applesauce
- 2 large eggs
- 2 tbsp. vegetable oil
- 2 tsp. vanilla extract
- 1 tsp. ground cinnamon
- 1/2 cup dried cherries
- ¼ cup unsweetened shredded coconut

- 2 ounces dark chocolate, chopped

Directions:
1. Preheat the oven to 350°F.
2. In a large bowl, combine the oats, flour, flaxseed, and baking powder. Stir well to mix.
3. In a medium bowl, whisk the applesauce, eggs, vegetable oil, vanilla, and cinnamon. Pour the wet mixture into the dry mixture, and stir until just combined.
4. Fold in the cherries, coconut, and chocolate. Drop tbsp.-size balls of dough onto a baking sheet. Bake for 10 to 12 minutes, until browned and cooked through.
5. Let cool for about 3 minutes, remove from the baking sheet, and cool completely before serving. Store in an airtight container for up to 1 week.

Nutrition: Calories: 136; Total Fat: 7g; Saturated Fat: 3g; Protein: 4g; Carbs: 14g; Sugar: 4g; Fiber: 3g; Cholesterol: 21mg; Sodium: 11mg

16. Cinnamon and Coconut Porridge

Preparation Time: 5 minutes
Cooking Time: 5 minutes
Servings: 4
Ingredients:
- 2 cups water
- 1 cup 36% heavy cream
- 1/2 cup unsweetened dried coconut, shredded
- 2 tbsp. flaxseed meal
- 1 tbsp. butter
- 1 and 1/2 tsp. stevia
- 1 tsp. cinnamon
- Salt to taste
- Toppings as blueberries

Directions:
1. Add the listed ingredients to a small pot, mix well
2. Transfer pot to stove and place it over medium-low heat
3. Bring to mix to a slow boil
4. Stir well and remove the heat
5. Divide the mix into equal servings and let them sit for 10 minutes
6. Top with your desired toppings and enjoy!

Nutrition: Calories: 171; Fat: 16g; Carbohydrates: 6g; Protein: 2g

17. An Omelet of Swiss Chard

Preparation Time: 5 minutes
Cooking Time: 5 minutes
Servings: 4
Ingredients:
- 4 eggs, lightly beaten
- 4 cups Swiss chard, sliced
- 2 tbsp. butter
- 1/2 tsp. garlic salt
- Fresh pepper

Directions:
1. Take a non-stick frying pan and place it over medium-low heat
2. Once the butter melts, add Swiss chard and stir cook for 2 minutes
3. Pour egg into the pan and gently stir them into Swiss chard
4. Season with garlic salt and pepper
5. Cook for 2 minutes
6. Serve and enjoy!

Nutrition: Calories: 260; Fat: 21g; Carbohydrates: 4g; Protein: 14g

18. Cheesy Low-Carb Omelet

Preparation Time: 5 minutes
Cooking Time: 5 minutes
Servings: 3
Ingredients:
- 2 whole eggs
- 1 tbsp. water
- 1 tbsp. butter
- 3 thin slices salami
- 5 fresh basil leaves
- 5 thin slices, fresh ripe tomatoes
- 2 ounces fresh mozzarella cheese
- Salt and pepper as needed

Directions:
1. Take a small bowl and whisk in eggs and water
2. Take a non-stick Sauté pan and place it over medium heat, add butter and let it melt
3. Pour egg mixture and cook for 30 seconds
4. Spread salami slices on half of egg mix and top with cheese, tomatoes, basil slices

5. Season with salt and pepper according to your taste
6. Cook for 2 minutes and fold the egg with the empty half
7. Cover and cook on LOW for 1 minute
8. Serve and enjoy!

Nutrition: Calories: 451; Fat: 36g; Carbohydrates: 3g; Protein: 33g

19. Yogurt and Kale Smoothie

Preparation Time: 10 minutes
Cooking Time: 0 minutes
Servings: 1
Ingredients:

- 1 cup whole milk yogurt
- 1 cup baby kale greens
- 1 pack stevia
- 1 tbsp. MCT oil
- 1 tbsp. sunflower seeds
- 1 cup water

Directions:

1. Add listed ingredients to the blender
2. Blend until you have a smooth and creamy texture
3. Serve chilled and enjoy!

Nutrition: Calories: 329; Fat: 26g; Carbohydrates: 15g; Protein: 11g

20. Grilled Chicken Platter

Preparation Time: 5 minutes
Cooking Time: 10 minutes
Servings: 3
Ingredients:

- 3 large chicken breasts, sliced half lengthwise
- 10-ounce spinach, frozen and drained
- 3-ounce mozzarella cheese, part-skim
- 1/2 a cup roasted red peppers, cut in long strips
- 1 tsp. olive oil
- 2 garlic cloves, minced
- Salt and pepper as needed

Directions:

1. Preheat your oven to 400°F
2. Slice 3 chicken breast lengthwise

3. Take a non-stick pan and grease with cooking spray
4. Bake for 2–3 minutes on each side
5. Take another skillet and cook spinach and garlic in oil for 3 minutes
6. Place chicken on an oven pan and top with spinach, roasted peppers, and mozzarella
7. Bake until the cheese melted
8. Enjoy!

Nutrition: Calories: 195; Fat: 7g Net Carbohydrates: 3g; Protein: 30g

21. Parsley Chicken Breast

Preparation Time: 10 minutes
Cooking Time: 40 minutes
Servings: 4
Ingredients:

- 1 tbsp. dry parsley
- 1 tbsp. dry basil
- 4 chicken breast halves, boneless and skinless
- 1/2 tsp. salt
- 1/2 tsp. red pepper flakes, crushed
- 2 tomatoes, sliced

Directions:

1. Preheat your oven to 350°F
2. Take a 9x13 inch baking dish and grease it up with cooking spray
3. Sprinkle 1 tbsp. of parsley, 1 tsp. of basil, and spread the mixture over your baking dish
4. Arrange the chicken breast halves over the dish and sprinkle garlic slices on top
5. Take a small bowl and add 1 tsp. parsley, 1 tsp. of basil, salt, basil, red pepper and mix well. Pour the mixture over the chicken breast
6. Top with tomato slices and cover, bake for 25 minutes
7. Remove the cover and bake for 15 minutes more
8. Serve and enjoy!

Nutrition: Calories: 150; Fat: 4g; Carbohydrates: 4g; Protein: 25g

22. Mustard Chicken

Preparation Time: 10 minutes
Cooking Time: 40 minutes
Servings: 2
Ingredients:

- 4 chicken breasts
- 1/2 cup chicken broth
- 3–4 tbsp. mustard
- 3 tbsp. olive oil
- 1 tsp. paprika
- 1 tsp. chili powder
- 1 tsp. garlic powder

Directions:

1. Take a small bowl and mix mustard, olive oil, paprika, chicken broth, garlic powder, chicken broth, and chili
2. Add chicken breast and marinate for 30 minutes
3. Take a lined baking sheet and arrange the chicken
4. Bake for 35 minutes at 375°F
5. Serve and enjoy!

Nutrition: Calories: 531; Fat: 23g; Carbohydrates: 10g; Protein: 64g

23. **Balsamic Chicken**

Preparation Time: 10 minutes
Cooking Time: 25 minutes
Servings: 3
Ingredients:

- 6 chicken breast halves, skinless and boneless
- 1 tsp. garlic salt
- Ground black pepper
- 2 tbsp. olive oil
- 1 onion, thinly sliced
- 14 and 1/2 ounces tomatoes, diced
- 1/2 cup balsamic vinegar
- 1 tsp. dried basil
- 1 tsp. dried oregano
- 1 tsp. dried rosemary
- 1/2 tsp. dried thyme

Directions:

1. Season both sides of your chicken breasts thoroughly with pepper and garlic salt
2. Take a skillet and place it over medium heat
3. Add some oil and cook your seasoned chicken for 3–4 minutes per side until the breasts are nicely browned
4. Add some onion and cook for another 3–4 minutes until the onions are browned
5. Pour the diced up tomatoes and balsamic vinegar over your chicken and season with some rosemary, basil, thyme, and rosemary

6. Simmer the chicken for about 15 minutes un they are no longer pink
7. Take an instant-read thermometer and check the internal temperature gives a reading 165°F
8. If yes, then you are good to go!

Nutrition: Calories: 196; Fat: 7g; Carbohydrates: 7 Protein: 23g

24. **Greek Chicken Breast**

Preparation Time: 10 minutes
Cooking Time: 25 minutes
Servings: 4
Ingredients:

- 4 chicken breast halves, skinless and boneles
- 1 cup extra virgin olive oil
- 1 lemon, juiced
- 2 tsp. garlic, crushed
- 1 and 1/2 tsp. black pepper
- 1/3 tsp. paprika

Directions:

1. Cut 3 slits in the chicken breast
2. Take a small bowl and whisk in olive oil, sa lemon juice, garlic, paprika, pepper, and whi for 30 seconds
3. Place chicken in a large bowl and po marinade
4. Rub the marinade all over using your hand
5. Refrigerate overnight
6. Pre-heat grill to medium heat and oil the gra
7. Cook chicken in the grill until the center is r longer pink
8. Serve and enjoy!

Nutrition: Calories: 644; Fat: 57g; Carbohydrates: 2 Protein: 27g

25. **Chipotle Lettuce Chicken**

Preparation Time: 10 minutes
Cooking Time: 25 minutes
Servings: 3
Ingredients:

- 1 pound chicken breast, cut into strips
- A splash olive oil
- 1 red onion, finely sliced
- 14 ounces tomatoes
- 1 tsp. chipotle, chopped
- 1/2 tsp. cumin

- A pinch sugar
- Lettuce as needed
- Fresh coriander leaves
- Jalapeno chilies, sliced
- Fresh tomato slices for garnish
- Lime wedges

Directions:
1. Take a non-stick frying pan and place it over medium heat
2. Add oil and heat it up
3. Add chicken and cook until brown
4. Keep the chicken on the side
5. Add tomatoes, sugar, chipotle, cumin to the same pan and simmer for 25 minutes until you have a nice sauce
6. Add chicken into the sauce and cook for 5 minutes
7. Transfer the mix to another place
8. Use lettuce wraps to take a portion of the mixture and serve with a squeeze of lemon
9. Enjoy!

Nutrition: Calories: 332; Fat: 15g; Carbohydrates: 13g; Protein: 34g

26. Stylish Chicken-Bacon Wrap

Preparation Time: 5 minutes
Cooking Time: 50 minutes
Servings: 3
Ingredients:
- 8 ounces lean chicken breast
- 6 bacon slices
- 3 ounces shredded cheese
- 4 slices ham

Directions:
1. Cut chicken breast into bite-sized portions
2. Transfer shredded cheese onto ham slices
3. Roll up chicken breast and ham slices in bacon slices
4. Take a skillet and place it over medium heat
5. Add olive oil and brown bacon for a while
6. Remove rolls and transfer to your oven
7. Bake for 45 minutes at 325°F
8. Serve and enjoy!

Nutrition: Calories: 275; Fat: 11g; Carbohydrates: .5g; Protein: 40g

27. Healthy Cottage Cheese Pancakes

Preparation Time: 10 minutes
Cooking Time: 15
Servings: 1
Ingredients:
- 1/2 cup Cottage cheese (low-fat)
- 1/3 cup (approx. 2 egg whites) Egg whites
- ¼ cup Oats
- 1 tsp. Vanilla extract
- Olive oil cooking spray
- 1 tbsp. Stevia (raw)
- Berries or sugar-free jam (optional)

Directions:
1. Begin by taking a food blender and adding in the egg whites and cottage cheese. Also add in the vanilla extract, a pinch of stevia, and oats. Palpitate until the consistency is well smooth.
2. Get a nonstick pan and oil it nicely with the cooking spray. Position the pan on low heat.
3. After it has been heated, scoop out half of the batter and pour it into the pan. Cook for about 2 1/2 minutes on each side.
4. Position the cooked pancakes on a serving plate and cover them with sugar-free jam or berries.

Nutrition: Calories: 205; Fat: 1.5 g; Protein: 24.5 g; Carbohydrates: 19 g

28. Avocado Lemon Toast

Preparation Time: 10 minutes
Cooking Time: 13 minutes
Servings: 2
Ingredients:
- 2 slices Whole-grain bread
- 2 tbsp. Fresh cilantro (chopped)
- ¼ tsp. Lemon zest
- 1 pinch Fine sea salt
- ½ Avocado
- 1/2 Fresh lemon juice
- 1 tsp. Cayenne pepper
- 1 pinch Chia seeds (¼ tsp.)

Directions:
1. Begin by getting a medium-sized mixing bowl and adding in the avocado. Make use of a fork to crush it properly.

2. Then, add in the cilantro, lemon zest, lemon juice, sea salt, and cayenne pepper. Mix well until combined.
3. Toast the bread slices in a toaster until golden brown. It should take about 3 minutes.
4. Top the toasted bread slices with the avocado mixture and finalize by drizzling with chia seeds.

Nutrition: Calories: 72; Protein: 3.6; Fat: 1.2 g; Carbohydrates: 11.6 g

29. <u>Healthy Baked Eggs</u>

Preparation Time: 10 minutes
Cooking Time: 1 hour
Servings: 3
Ingredients:
- 1 tbsp. Olive oil
- 2 Garlic cloves
- 8 large Eggs
- 1/2 tsp. Sea salt
- 3 cups Shredded mozzarella cheese (medium-fat)
- Olive oil spray
- 1 medium Onion (chopped)
- 8 ounces Spinach leaves
- 1 cup Half-and-half
- 1 tsp. Black pepper
- 1/2 cup Feta cheese

Directions:
1. Begin by heating the oven to 375°F.
2. Get a glass baking dish and grease it with olive oil spray. Arrange aside.
3. Now take a nonstick pan and pour in the olive oil. Position the pan on allows heat and allows it heat.
4. Immediately you are done, toss in the garlic, spinach, and onion. Prepare for about 5 minutes. Arrange aside.
5. You can now Get a large mixing bowl and add in half, eggs, pepper, and salt. Whisk thoroughly to combine.
6. Put in the feta cheese and chopped mozzarella cheese (reserve 1/2 cup of mozzarella cheese for later).
7. Put the egg mixture and prepared spinach into the prepared glass baking dish. Blend well to combine. Drizzle the reserved cheese over the top.
8. Bake the egg mix for about 45 minutes.

9. Extract the baking dish from the oven and allow it to stand for 10 minutes.
10. Dice and serve!

Nutrition: Calories: 323; Fat: 22.3 g; Protein: 22.6 g; Carbohydrates: 7.9 g

30. Quick Low-Carb Oatmeal

Preparation Time: 10 minutes
Cooking Time: 15 minutes
Servings: 2
Ingredients:
- 1/2 cup Almond flour
- 2 tbsp. Flax meal
- 1 tsp. Cinnamon (ground)
- 11/2 cups Almond milk (unsweetened)
- Salt, to taste
- 2 tbsp. Chia seeds
- 10–15 drops Liquid stevia
- 1 tsp. Vanilla extract

Directions:
1. Begin by taking a large mixing bowl and adding in the coconut flour, almond flour, ground cinnamon, flax seed powder, and chia seeds. Mix properly to combine.
2. Position a stockpot on low heat and add in the dry ingredients. Also add in the liquid stevia, vanilla extract, and almond milk. Mix well to combine.
3. Prepare the flour and almond milk for about 4 minutes. Add salt if needed.
4. Move the oatmeal to a serving bowl and top with nuts, seeds, and pure and neat berries.

Nutrition: Calories: Protein: 11.7 g; Fat: 24.3 g; Carbohydrates: 16.7 g

31. <u>Tofu and Vegetable Scramble</u>

Preparation Time: 10 minutes
Cooking Time: 15 minutes
Servings: 2
Ingredients:
- 16 ounces Firm tofu (drained)
- 1/2 tsp. Sea salt
- 1 tsp. Garlic powder
- Fresh coriander, for garnishing
- 1/2 medium Red onion

- 1 tsp. Cumin powder
- Lemon juice, for topping
- 1 medium Green bell pepper

Directions:
1. Begin by preparing the ingredients. For this, you are to extract the seeds of the tomato and green bell pepper. Shred the onion, bell pepper, and tomato into small cubes.
2. Get a small mixing bowl and position the fairly hard tofu inside it. Make use of your hands to break the fairly hard tofu. Arrange aside.
3. Get a nonstick pan and add in the onion, tomato, and bell pepper. Mix and cook for about 3 minutes.
4. Put the somewhat hard crumbled tofu into the pan and combine well.
5. Get a small bowl and put in the water, turmeric, garlic powder, cumin powder, and chili powder. Combine well and stream it over the tofu and vegetable mixture.
6. Allow the tofu and vegetable crumble to cook with seasoning for 5 minutes. Continuously stir so that the pan is not holding the ingredients.
7. Drizzle the tofu scramble with chili flakes and salt. Combine well.
8. Transfer the prepared scramble to a serving bowl and give it a proper spray of lemon juice.
9. Finalize by garnishing with pure and neat coriander. Serve while hot!

Nutrition: Calories: 238; Carbohydrates: 16.6 g; Fat: 4 g

2. Breakfast Smoothie Bowl with Fresh Berries

Preparation Time: 10 minutes
Cooking Time: 5 minutes
Servings: 2
Ingredients:
- 1/2 cup Almond milk (unsweetened)
- 1/2 tsp. Psyllium husk powder
- 2 ounces Strawberries (chopped)
- 1 tbsp. Coconut oil
- 3 cups Crushed ice
- 5 to 10 drops Liquid stevia
- 1/3 cup Pea protein powder

Directions:

1. Begin by taking a blender and adding in the mashed ice cubes. Allow them to rest for about 30 seconds.
2. Then put in the almond milk, shredded strawberries, pea protein powder, psyllium husk powder, coconut oil, and liquid stevia. Blend well until it turns into a smooth and creamy puree.
3. Vacant the prepared smoothie into 2 glasses.
4. Cover with coconut flakes and pure and neat strawberries.

Nutrition: Calories: 166; Fat: 9.2 g; Carbohydrates: 4.1 g; Protein: 17.6 g

33. Chia and Coconut Pudding

Preparation Time: 10 minutes
Cooking Time: 5 minutes
Servings: 2
Ingredients:
- 7 ounces Light coconut milk
- 3 to 4 drops Liquid stevia
- 1 Kiwi
- ¼ cup Chia seeds
- 1 Clementine
- Shredded coconut (unsweetened)

Directions:
1. Begin by getting a mixing bowl and putting in the light coconut milk. Set in the liquid stevia to sweeten the milk. Combine well.
2. Put the chia seeds into the milk and whisk until well-combined. Arrange aside.
3. Scrape the clementine and carefully extract the skin from the wedges. Leave aside.
4. Also, scrape the kiwi and dice it into small pieces.
5. Get a glass vessel and gather the pudding. For this, position the fruits at the bottom of the jar; then put a dollop of chia pudding. Then spray the fruits and then put another layer of chia pudding.
6. Finalize by garnishing with the rest of the fruits and chopped coconut.

Nutrition: Calories: 201; Protein: 5.4 g; Fat: 10 g; Carbohydrates: 22.8 g

34. Tomato and Zucchini Sauté

Preparation Time: 10 minutes
Cooking Time: 43 minutes
Servings: 3
Ingredients:

- 1 tbsp. Vegetable oil
- 2 Tomatoes (chopped)
- 1 Green bell pepper (chopped)
- Black pepper (freshly ground), to taste
- 1 Onion (sliced)
- 2 pounds Zucchini (peeled), cut into 1-inch-thick slices
- Salt, to taste
- ¼ cup uncooked white rice

Directions:

1. Begin by getting a nonstick pan and putting it over low heat. Stream in the oil and allow it to heat through.
Put in the onions and sauté for about 3 minutes.
2. Then pour in the zucchini and green peppers. Mix well and spice with black pepper and salt.
3. Reduce the heat and cover the pan with a lid. Allow the veggies to cook on low for 5 minutes.
4. While you're done, put in the water and rice. Place the lid back on and cook on low for 20 minutes.

Nutrition: Calories: 94; Fat: 2.8 g; Protein: 3.2 g; Carbohydrates: 16.1 g

35. Steamed Kale with Mediterranean Dressing

Preparation Time: 10 minutes
Cooking Time: 25 minutes
Servings: 3
Ingredients:

- 12 cups Kale (chopped)
- 1 tbsp. Olive oil
- 1 tsp. Soy sauce
- Pepper (freshly ground), to taste
- 2 tbsp. Lemon juice
- 1 tbsp. Garlic (minced)
- Salt, to taste

Directions:

1. Get a gas steamer or an electric steamer and fill the bottom pan with water. If making use of a gas steamer, position it on high heat. Making use of an electric steamer, place it on the highest setting.
2. Immediately the water comes to a boil, put in the shredded kale, and cover with a lid. Boil for about 8 minutes. The kale should be tender by now.
3. During the kale is boiling, take a big mixing bowl and put in the olive oil, lemon juice, soy sauce, garlic, pepper, and salt. Whisk well to mix.
4. Now toss in the steamed kale and carefully enclose it into the dressing. Be assured the kale is well-coated.
5. Serve while it's hot!

Nutrition: Calories: 91; Fat: 3.5 g; Protein: 4.6 g; Carbohydrates: 14.5 g

36. Healthy Carrot Muffins

Preparation Time: 10 minutes
Cooking Time: 40 minutes
Servings: 4
Ingredients:
Dry Ingredients:

- ¼ cup Tapioca starch
- 1 tsp. Baking soda
- 1 tbsp. Cinnamon
- ¼ tsp. Cloves

Wet Ingredients:

- 1 tsp. Vanilla extract
- 1 1/2 cups Water
- 1 1/2 cups Carrots (shredded)
- 1¾ cups Almond flour
- 1/2 cup Granulated sweetener of choice
- 1 tsp. Baking powder
- 1 tsp. Nutmeg
- 1 tsp. Salt
- 1/3 cup Coconut oil
- 4 tbsp. Flax meal
- 1 medium Banana (mashed)

Directions:

1. Begin by heating the oven to 350°F.
2. Get a muffin tray and position paper cups in all the molds. Arrange aside.

3. Get a small glass bowl and put half a cup of water and a flax meal. Allow this rest for about 5 minutes. Your flax egg is prepared.
4. Get a large mixing bowl and put in the almond flour, tapioca starch, granulated sugar, baking soda, baking powder, cinnamon, nutmeg, cloves, and salt. Mix well to combine.
5. Conform a well in the middle of the flour mixture and pour in the coconut oil, vanilla extract, and flax egg. Mix well to conform to a mushy dough.
6. Then put in the chopped carrots and mashed banana. Mix until well-combined.
7. Make use of a spoon to scoop out an equal amount of mixture into 8 muffin cups.
8. Position the muffin tray in the oven and allow it to bake for about 40 minutes.
9. Extract the tray from the microwave and allow the muffins to stand for about 10 minutes.
10. Extract the muffin cups from the tray and allow them to chill until they reach room degree of hotness and coldness.
11. Serve and enjoy!

Nutrition: Calories: 189; Fat: 13.9 g; Protein: 3.8 g; Carbohydrates: 17.3 g

37. Vegetable Noodles Stir-Fry

Preparation Time: 10 minutes
Cooking Time: 40 minutes
Servings: 4
Ingredients:

- 1 pound White sweet potato
- 8 ounces Zucchini
- 2 large Garlic cloves (finely chopped)
- 2 tbsp. Vegetable broth
- Salt, to taste
- 8 ounces Carrots
- 1 Shallot (finely chopped)
- 1 Red chili (finely chopped)
- 1 tbsp. Olive oil
- Pepper, to taste

Directions:
1. Begin by scrapping the carrots and sweet potato. Make Use a spiralizer to make noodles out of the sweet potato and carrots.
2. Rinse the zucchini thoroughly and spiralize it as well.
3. Get a large skillet and position it on a high flame. Stream in the vegetable broth and allow it to come to a boil.
4. Toss in the spiralized sweet potato and carrots. Then put in the chili, garlic, and shallots. Stir everything using tongs and cook for some minutes.
5. Transfer the vegetable noodles into a serving platter and generously spice with pepper and salt.
6. Finalize by sprinkling olive oil over the noodles. Serve while hot!

Nutrition: Calories: 169; Fat: 3.7 g; Protein: 3.6 g; Carbohydrates: 31.2 g

38. Cauliflower Rice with Chicken

Preparation Time: 15 Minutes
Cooking Time: 15 Minutes
Servings: 4
Ingredients:

- 1/2 large cauliflower
- 3/4 cup cooked meat
- 1/2 bell pepper
- 1 carrot
- 2 ribs celery
- 1 tbsp. stir fry sauce (low carb)
- 1 tbsp. extra virgin olive oil
- Salt and pepper to taste

Directions:

1. Chop cauliflower in a processor to "rice." Place in a bowl.
2. Properly chop all vegetables in a food processor into thin slices.
3. Add cauliflower and other plants to WOK with heated oil. Fry until all veggies are tender.
4. Add chopped meat and sauce to the wok and fry for 10 Minutes.
5. Serve.
6. This dish is very mouth-watering!

Nutrition: Calories: 200; Protein: 10 g; Fat: 12 g; Carbs: 10 g

39. Turkey with Fried Eggs

Preparation Time: 10 Minutes
Cooking Time: 20 Minutes
Servings: 4
Ingredients:

- 4 large potatoes
- 1 cooked turkey thigh
- 1 large onion (about 2 cups diced)
- Butter
- Chile flakes
- 4 eggs
- Salt to taste
- Pepper to taste

Directions:

1. Rub the cold boiled potatoes on the coarses holes of a box grater. Dice the turkey.
2. Cook the onion in as much unsalted butter a you feel comfortable with until it's just fragran and translucent.
3. Add the rubbed potatoes and a cup of dice cooked turkey, salt, and pepper to taste, an cook for 20 Minutes.
4. Top each with a fried egg. Yummy!

Nutrition: Calories: 170; Protein: 19 g; Fat: 7 g; Carb: 6 g

40. Sweet Potato, Kale, and White Bean Stew

Preparation Time: 15 minutes
Cooking Time: 25 minutes
Servings: 4
Ingredients:

- 1 (15-ounce) can low-sodium cannellini beans, rinsed and drained, divided
- 1 tbsp. olive oil
- 1 medium onion, chopped
- 2 garlic cloves, minced
- 2 celery stalks, chopped
- 3 medium carrots, chopped
- 2 cups low-sodium vegetable broth
- 1 tsp. apple cider vinegar
- 2 medium sweet potatoes (about 1¼ pounds)
- 2 cups chopped kale
- 1 cup shelled edamame
- ¼ cup quinoa
- 1 tsp. dried thyme
- 1/2 tsp. cayenne pepper
- 1/2 tsp. salt
- ¼ tsp. freshly ground black pepper

Directions:

1. Put half the beans into a blender and blend until smooth. Set aside.
2. In a large soup pot over medium heat, heat the oil. When the oil is shining, include the onion and garlic, and cook until the onion softens and the garlic is sweet, about 3 minutes. Add the celery and carrots, and continue cooking until the vegetables soften, about 5 minutes.
3. Add the broth, vinegar, sweet potatoes, unblended beans, kale, edamame, and quinoa, and bring the mixture to a boil. Reduce the heat and simmer until the vegetables soften, about 10 minutes.
4. Add the blended beans, thyme, cayenne, salt, and black pepper, increase the heat to medium-high, and bring the mixture to a boil. Reduce the heat and simmer, uncovered, until the flavors combine, about 5 minutes.
5. Into each of 4 containers, scoop 1¾ cup of stew.

Nutrition: Calories: 373; Total Fat: 7g; Saturated Fat: g; Protein: 15g; Total Carbs: 65g; Fiber: 15g; Sugar: 3g; Sodium: 540mg

41. Slow Cooker Two-Bean Sloppy Joes

Preparation Time: 10 minutes
Cooking Time: 6 hours
Servings: 4
Ingredients:

- 1 (15-ounce) can low-sodium black beans
- 1 (15-ounce) can low-sodium pinto beans
- 1 (15-ounce) can no-salt-added diced tomatoes
- 1 medium green bell pepper, cored, seeded, and chopped
- 1 medium yellow onion, chopped
- ¼ cup low-sodium vegetable broth
- 2 garlic cloves, minced
- 2 servings (¼ cup) meal prep barbecue sauce or bottled barbecue sauce
- ¼ tsp. salt
- ¼ tsp. freshly ground black pepper
- 4 whole-wheat buns

Directions:

1. In a slow cooker, combine the black beans, pinto beans, diced tomatoes, bell pepper, onion, broth, garlic, meal prep barbecue sauce, salt, and black pepper. Stir the ingredients, then cover and cook on low for 6 hours.
2. Into each of 4 containers, spoon 1¼ cups of sloppy joe mix. Serve with 1 whole-wheat bun.
3. Storage: place airtight containers in the refrigerator for up to 1 week. To freeze, place freezer-safe containers in the freezer for up to 2 months. To defrost, refrigerate overnight. To reheat individual portions, microwave uncovered on high for 2 to 21/2 minutes. Alternatively, reheat the entire dish in a saucepan on the stove top. Bring the sloppy joes to a boil, then reduce the heat and simmer until heated through, 10 to 15 minutes. Serve with a whole-wheat bun.

Nutrition: Calories: 392; Total Fat: 3g; Saturated Fat: 0g; Protein: 17g; Total Carbs: 79g; Fiber: 19g; Sugar: 15g; Sodium: 759mg

42. Lighter Eggplant Parmesan

Preparation Time: 15 minutes
Cooking Time: 35 minutes
Servings: 4
Ingredients:

- Nonstick cooking spray
- 3 eggs, beaten
- 1 tbsp. dried parsley
- 2 tsp. ground oregano
- 1/8 tsp. freshly ground black pepper

- 1 cup panko bread crumbs, preferably whole-wheat
- 1 large eggplant (about 2 pounds)
- 5 servings (2 1/2 cups) chunky tomato sauce or jarred low-sodium tomato sauce
- 1 cup part-skim mozzarella cheese
- ¼ cup grated parmesan cheese

Directions:
1. Preheat the oven to 450°F. Coat a baking sheet with cooking spray.
2. In a medium bowl, whisk together the eggs, parsley, oregano, and pepper.
3. Pour the panko into a separate medium bowl.
4. Slice the eggplant into ¼-inch-thick slices. Dip each slice of eggplant into the egg mixture, shaking off the excess. Then dredge both sides of the eggplant in the panko bread crumbs. Place the coated eggplant on the prepared baking sheet, leaving a 1/2-inch space between each slice.
5. Bake for about 15 minutes until soft and golden brown. Remove from the oven and set aside to slightly cool.
6. Pour 1/2 cup of chunky tomato sauce on the bottom of an 8-by-15-inch baking dish. Using a spatula or the back of a spoon spread the tomato sauce evenly. Place half the slices of cooked eggplant, slightly overlapping, in the dish, and top with 1 cup of chunky tomato sauce, 1/2 cup of mozzarella, and 2 tbsp. of grated parmesan. Repeat the layer, ending with the cheese.
7. Bake uncovered for 20 minutes until the cheese is bubbling and slightly browned.
8. Remove from the oven and allow cooling for 15 minutes before dividing the eggplant equally into 4 separate containers.

Nutrition: Calories: 333; Total Fat: 14g; Saturated Fat: 6g; Protein: 20g; Total Carbs: 35g; Fiber: 11g; Sugar: 15g; Sodium: 994mg

43. **Coconut-Lentil Curry**

Preparation Time: 15 minutes
Cooking Time: 35 minutes
Servings: 4
Ingredients:
- 1 tbsp. olive oil
- 1 medium yellow onion, chopped
- 1 garlic clove, minced

- 1 medium red bell pepper, diced
- 1 (15-ounce) can green or brown lentils, rinsed and drained
- 2 medium sweet potatoes, washed, peeled, and cut into bite-size chunks (about 1¼ pounds)
- 1 (15-ounce) can no-salt-added diced tomatoes
- 2 tbsp. tomato paste
- 4 tsp. curry powder
- 1/8 tsp. ground cloves
- 1 (15-ounce) can light coconut milk
- ¼ tsp. salt
- 2 pieces whole-wheat naan bread, halved, or 4 slices crusty bread

Directions:
1. In a large saucepan over medium heat, heat the olive oil. When the oil is shimmering, add both the onion and garlic and cook until the onion softens and the garlic is sweet, for about 3 minutes.
2. Add the bell pepper and continue cooking until it softens, about 5 minutes more. Add the lentils, sweet potatoes, tomatoes, tomato paste, curry powder, and cloves, and bring the mixture to a boil. Reduce the heat to medium low, cover, and simmer until the potatoes are softened, about 20 minutes.
3. Add the coconut milk and salt, and return to a boil. Reduce the heat and simmer until the flavors combine, about 5 minutes.
4. Into each of 4 containers, spoon 2 cups of curry.
5. Enjoy each serving with half of a piece of naan bread or 1 slice of crusty bread.

Nutrition: Calories: 559; Total Fat: 16g; Saturated Fat: 7g; Protein: 16g; Total Carbs: 86g; Fiber: 16g; Sugar: 18g; Sodium: 819mg

44. **Stuffed Portobello with Cheese**

Preparation Time: 15 minutes
Cooking Time: 25 minutes
Servings: 4
Ingredients:
- 4 Portobello mushroom caps
- 1 tbsp. olive oil
- 1/2 tsp. salt, divided
- ¼ tsp. freshly ground black pepper, divided
- 1 cup baby spinach, chopped

- 11/2 cups part-skim ricotta cheese
- 1/2 cup part-skim shredded mozzarella cheese
- ¼ cup grated parmesan cheese
- 1 garlic clove, minced
- 1 tbsp. dried parsley
- 2 tsp. dried oregano
- 4 tsp. unseasoned bread crumbs, divided
- 4 servings (4 cups) roasted broccoli with shallots

Directions:
1. Preheat the oven to 375°F. Line a baking sheet with aluminum foil.
2. Brush the mushroom caps with olive oil, and sprinkle with ¼ tsp. salt and 1/8 tsp. pepper. Put the mushroom caps on the prepared baking sheet and bake until soft, about 12 minutes.
3. In a medium bowl, mix together the spinach, ricotta, mozzarella, parmesan, garlic, parsley, oregano, and the remaining ¼ tsp. of salt and 1/8 tsp. of pepper.
4. Spoon 1/2 cup of cheese mixture into each mushroom cap, and sprinkle each with 1 tsp. of bread crumbs. Return the mushrooms to the oven for an additional 8 to 10 minutes until warmed through.
5. Remove from the oven and allow the mushrooms to cool for about 10 minutes before placing each in an individual container. Add 1 cup of roasted broccoli with shallots to each container.

Nutrition: Calories: 419; Total Fat: 30g; Saturated Fat: 10g; Protein: 23g; Total Carbs: 19g; Fiber: 2g; Sugar: 3g; Sodium: 790mg

45. <u>Lighter Shrimp Scampi</u>

Preparation Time: 15 minutes
Cooking Time: 15 minutes
Servings: 4
Ingredients:
- 11/2 pounds large peeled and deveined shrimp
- ¼ tsp. salt
- 1/8 tsp. freshly ground black pepper
- 2 tbsp. olive oil
- 1 shallot, chopped
- 2 garlic cloves, minced
- ¼ cup cooking white wine

- Juice of 1/2 lemon (1 tbsp.)
- 1/2 tsp. sriracha
- 2 tbsp. unsalted butter, at room temperature
- ¼ cup chopped fresh parsley
- 4 servings (6 cups) zucchini noodles with lemon vinaigrette

Directions:
1. Season the shrimp with salt and pepper.
2. In a medium saucepan over medium heat, heat the oil. Add the shallot and garlic, and cook until the shallot softens and the garlic is fragrant, about 3 minutes. Add the shrimp, cover, and cook until opaque, 2 to 3 minutes on each side. Using a slotted spoon, transfer the shrimp to a large plate.
3. Add the wine, lemon juice, and sriracha to the saucepan, and stir to combine. Bring the mixture to a boil, then reduce the heat and simmer until the liquid is reduced by about half, 3 minutes. Add the butter and stir until melted, about 3 minutes. Return the shrimp to the saucepan and toss to coat. Add the parsley and stir to combine.
4. Into each of 4 containers, place 11/2 cups of zucchini noodles with lemon vinaigrette, and top with ¾ cup of scampi.

Nutrition: Calories: 364; Total Fat: 21g; Saturated Fat: 6g; Protein: 37g; Total Carbs: 10g; Fiber: 2g; Sugar: 6g; Sodium: 557mg

46. <u>Maple-Mustard Salmon</u>

Preparation Time: 10 minutes, plus 30 minutes marinating time
Cooking Time: 20 minutes
Servings: 4
Ingredients:
- Nonstick cooking spray
- 1/2 cup 100% maple syrup
- 2 tbsp. Dijon mustard
- ¼ tsp. salt
- 4 (5-ounce) salmon fillets
- 4 servings (4 cups) roasted broccoli with shallots
- 4 servings (2 cups) parleyed whole-wheat couscous

Directions:
1. Preheat the oven to 400°F. Line a baking sheet with aluminum foil and coat with cooking spray.

2. In a medium bowl, whisk together the maple syrup, mustard, and salt until smooth.

3. Put the salmon fillets into the bowl and toss to coat. Cover and place in the refrigerator to marinate for at least 30 minutes and up to overnight.

4. Shake off excess marinade from the salmon fillets and place them on the prepared baking sheet, leaving a 1-inch space between each fillet. Discard the extra marinade.

5. Bake for about 20 minutes until the salmon is opaque and a thermometer inserted in the thickest part of a fillet reads 145°F.

6. Into each of 4 resealable containers, place 1 salmon fillet, 1 cup of roasted broccoli with shallots, and 1/2 cup of parleyed whole-wheat couscous.

Nutrition: Calories: 601; Total Fat: 29g; Saturated Fat: 4g; Protein: 36g; Total Carbs: 51g; Fiber: 3g; Sugar: 23g; Sodium: 610mg

47. <u>Chicken Salad with Grapes and Pecans</u>

Preparation Time: 15 Minutes
Cooking Time: 5 Minutes
Servings: 4
Ingredients:

- 1/3 cup unsalted pecans, chopped
- 10 ounces cooked skinless, boneless chicken breast or rotisserie chicken, finely chopped
- 1/2 medium yellow onion, finely chopped
- 1 celery stalk, finely chopped
- ¾ cup red or green seedless grapes, halved
- ¼ cup light mayonnaise
- ¼ cup nonfat plain Greek yogurt
- 1 tbsp. Dijon mustard
- 1 tbsp. dried parsley
- ¼ tsp. salt
- 1/8 tsp. freshly ground black pepper
- 1 cup shredded romaine lettuce
- 4 (8-inch) whole-wheat pitas

Directions:

1. Heat a small skillet over medium-low heat to toast the pecans. Cook the pecans until fragrant, about 3 minutes. Remove from the heat and set aside to cool.

2. In a medium bowl, mix the chicken, onion, celery, pecans, and grapes.

3. In a small bowl, whisk together the mayonnaise, yogurt, mustard, parsley, salt, and pepper. Spoon the sauce over the chicken mixture and stir until well combined.

4. Into each of 4 containers, place ¼ cup of lettuce and top with 1 cup of chicken salad. Store the pitas separately until ready to serve.

5. When ready to eat, stuff the serving of salad and lettuce into 1 pita.

Nutrition: Calories: 418; Total Fat: 14g; Saturated Fat: 2g; Protein: 31g; Total Carbs: 43g; Fiber: 6g;

48. <u>Roasted Vegetables</u>

Preparation Time: 14 minutes
Cooking Time: 17 minutes
Servings: 3
Ingredients:

- 4 tbsp. olive oil, reserve some for greasing
- 2 heads, large garlic, tops sliced off
- 2 large eggplants/aubergine, tops removed, cubed
- 2 large shallots, peeled, quartered
- 1 large carrot, peeled, cubed
- 1 large parsnips, peeled, cubed
- 1 small green bell pepper, deseeded, ribbed, cubed
- 1 small red bell pepper, deseeded, ribbed, cubed
- ½ pound Brussels sprouts, halved, do not remove cores
- 1 sprig, large thyme, leaves picked
- sea salt, coarse-grained

For garnish

- 1 large lemon, halved, ½ squeezed, ½ sliced into smaller wedges
- ⅛ cup fennel bulb, minced

Directions:

1. Preheat the oven to 425°F or 220°C for at least 5 minutes before using.

2. Line deep roasting pan with aluminum foil, lightly grease with oil. Tumble in bell pepper, Brussels sprouts, carrots, eggplants, garlic, parsnips, rosemary leaves, shallots, and thyme. Add a pinch of sea salt; drizzle in remaining oil and lemon juice. Toss well to combine.

3. Cover roasting pan with a sheet of aluminum foil. Place this on the middle rack of the oven. Bake for 20 to 30 minutes. Remove aluminum foil. Roast, for another 5 to 10 minutes, or until

some vegetables brown at the edges. Remove roasting pan from oven. Cool slightly before ladling equal portions into plates.

4. Garnish with fennel and a wedge of lemon. Squeeze lemon juice on top of the dish before eating.

Nutrition: Calories: 163; Total Fat: 4.2 g; Saturated Fat: 0.8 g; Cholesterol: 0 mg; Sodium: 861 mg; Total Carbs: 22.5 g; Fiber: 6.3 g; Sugar: 2.3 g; Protein: 9.2 g

49. Millet Pilaf

Preparation Time: 10 minutes
Cooking Time: 15 minutes
Servings: 4
Ingredients:

- 1 cup millet
- 2 tomatoes, rinsed, seeded, and chopped
- 1¾ cups filtered water
- 2 tbsp. extra-virgin olive oil
- ¼ cup chopped dried apricot
- Zest of 1 lemon
- Juice of 1 lemon
- ½ cup fresh parsley, rinsed and chopped
- Himalayan pink salt
- Freshly ground black pepper

Directions:

1. In an electric pressure cooker, combine the millet, tomatoes, and water. Lock the lid into place, select Manual and High Pressure, and cook for 7 minutes.
2. When the beep sounds, quickly release the pressure by pressing Cancel and twisting the steam valve to the Venting position. Carefully remove the lid.
3. Stir in the olive oil, apricot, lemon zest, lemon juice, and parsley. Taste, season with salt and pepper, and serve.

Nutrition: Calories: 270; Total Fat: 8g; Total Carbohydrates: 42g; Fiber: 5g; Sugar: 3g; Protein: 6g

50. Sweet and Sour Onions

Preparation Time: 10 minutes
Cooking Time: 11 minutes
Servings: 4
Ingredients:

- 4 large onions, halved
- 2 garlic cloves, crushed

- 3 cups vegetable stock
- 1 ½ tbsp. balsamic vinegar
- ½ tsp. Dijon mustard
- 1 tbsp. sugar

Directions:

1. Combine onions and garlic in a pan. Fry for 3 minutes, or till softened.
2. Pour stock, vinegar, Dijon mustard, and sugar. Bring to a boil.
3. Reduce heat. Cover and let the combination simmer for 10 minutes.
4. Remove from the heat. Continue stirring until the liquid is reduced and the onions are brown. Serve.

Nutrition: Calories: 203; Total Fat: 41.2 g; Saturated Fat: 0.8 g; Cholesterol: 0 mg; Sodium: 861 mg; Total Carbs: 29.5 g; Fiber: 16.3 g; Sugar: 29.3 g; Protein: 19.2 g

51. Sautéed Apples and Onions

Preparation Time: 14 minutes
Cooking Time: 16 minutes
Servings: 3
Ingredients:

- 2 cups dry cider
- 1 large onion, halved
- 2 cups vegetable stock
- 4 apples, sliced into wedges
- A pinch salt
- A pinch pepper

Directions:

1. Combine cider and onion in a saucepan. Bring to a boil until the onions are cooked and the liquid is almost gone.
2. Pour the stock and the apples. Season with salt and pepper. Stir occasionally. Cook for about 10 minutes or until the apples are tender but not mushy. Serve.

Nutrition: Calories: 343; Total Fat: 51.2 g; Saturated Fat: 0.8 g; Cholesterol: 0 mg; Sodium: 861 mg; Total Carbs: 22.5 g; Fiber: 6.3 g; Sugar: 2.3 g; Protein: 9.2 g

52. Zucchini Noodles with Portabella Mushrooms

Preparation Time: 14 minutes
Cooking Time: 16 minutes

Servings: 3
Ingredients:

- 1 zucchini, processed into spaghetti-like noodles
- 3 garlic cloves, minced
- 2 white onions, thinly sliced
- 1 thumb-sized ginger, julienned
- 1 lb. chicken thighs
- 1 lb. portabella mushrooms, sliced into thick slivers
- 2 cups chicken stock
- 3 cups water
- A pinch sea salt, add more if needed
- A pinch black pepper, add more if needed
- 2 tsp. sesame oil
- 4 tbsp. coconut oil, divided
- ¼ cup fresh chives, minced, for garnish

Directions:

1. Pour 2 tbsp. of coconut oil into a large saucepan. Fry mushroom slivers in batches for 5 minutes or until seared brown. Set aside. Transfer these to a plate.
2. Sauté the onion, garlic, and ginger for 3 minutes or until tender. Add in chicken thighs, cooked mushrooms, chicken stock, water, salt, and pepper stir mixture well. Bring to a boil.
3. Decrease gradually the heat and allow simmering for 20 minutes or until the chicken is forking tender. Tip in sesame oil.
4. Serve by placing an equal amount of zucchini noodles into bowls. Ladle soup and garnish with chives.

Nutrition: Calories: 163; Total Fat: 4.2 g; Saturated Fat: 0.8 g; Cholesterol: 0 mg; Sodium: 861 mg; Total Carbs: 22.5 g; Fiber: 6.3 g; Sugar: 2.3 g; Protein: 9.2 g

53. <u>Grilled Tempeh with Pineapple</u>

Preparation Time: 12 minutes
Cooking Time: 16 minutes
Servings: 3
Ingredients:

- 10 oz. tempeh, sliced
- 1 red bell pepper, quartered
- 1/4 pineapple, sliced into rings
- 6 oz. green beans
- 1 tbsp. coconut aminos

- 2 1/2 tbsp. orange juice, freshly squeeze
- 1 1/2 tbsp. lemon juice, freshly squeezed
- 1 tbsp. extra virgin olive oil
- 1/4 cup hoisin sauce

Directions:

1. Blend together the olive oil, orange and lemon juices, coconut aminos or soy sauce, and hoisin sauce in a bowl. Add the diced tempeh and set aside.
2. Heat up the grill or place a grill pan over medium-high flame. Once hot, lift the marinated tempeh from the bowl with a pair of tongs and transfer them to the grill or pan.
3. Grille for 2 to 3 minutes, or until browned all over.
4. Grill the sliced pineapples alongside the tempeh, then transfer them directly onto the serving platter.
5. Place the grilled tempeh beside the grilled pineapple and cover with aluminum foil to keep warm.
6. Meanwhile, place the green beans and bell peppers in a bowl and add just enough of the marinade to coat.
7. Prepare the grill pan and add the vegetables. Grill until fork tender and slightly charred.
8. Transfer the grilled vegetables to the serving platter and arrange artfully with the tempeh and pineapple. Serve at once.

Nutrition: Calories: 163; Total Fat: 4.2 g; Saturated Fat: 0.8 g; Cholesterol: 0 mg; Sodium: 861 mg; Total Carbs: 22.5 g; Fiber: 6.3 g; Sugar: 2.3 g; Protein: 9.2 g

54. <u>Courgettes in Cider Sauce</u>

Preparation Time: 13 minutes
Cooking Time: 17 minutes
Servings: 3
Ingredients:

- 2 cups baby courgettes
- 3 tbsp. vegetable stock
- 2 tbsp. apple cider vinegar
- 1 tbsp. light brown sugar
- 4 spring onions, finely sliced
- 1 piece fresh gingerroot, grated
- 1 tsp. corn flour
- 2 tsp. water

Directions:

1. Bring a pan with salted water to a boil. Add courgettes. Bring to a boil for 5 minutes.
2. Meanwhile, in a pan, combine vegetable stock, apple cider vinegar, brown sugar, onions, ginger root, lemon juice and rind, and orange juice and rind. Take to a boil. Lower the heat and allow simmering for 3 minutes.
3. Mix the cornflour with water. Stir well. Pour into the sauce. Continue stirring until the sauce thickens.
4. Drain courgettes. Transfer to the serving dish. Spoon over the sauce. Toss to coat courgettes. Serve.

Nutrition: Calories: 173; Total Fat: 9.2 g; Saturated Fat: 0.8 g; Cholesterol: 0 mg; Sodium: 861 mg; Total Carbs: 22.5 g; Fiber: 6.3 g; Sugar: 2.3 g; Protein: 9.2 g

55. <u>Baked Mixed Mushrooms</u>

Preparation Time: 8 minutes
Cooking Time: 20 minutes
Servings: 3
Ingredients:

- 2 cups mixed wild mushrooms
- 1 cup chestnut mushrooms
- 2 cups dried porcini
- 2 shallots
- 4 garlic cloves
- 3 cups raw pecans
- ½ bunch fresh thyme
- 1 bunch flat-leaf parsley
- 2 tbsp. olive oil
- 2 fresh bay leaves
- 1 ½ cups stale bread

Directions:

1. Remove skin and finely chop garlic and shallots. Roughly chop the wild mushrooms and chestnut mushrooms. Pick the leaves of the thyme and tear the bread into small pieces. Put inside the pressure cooker.
2. Place the pecans and roughly chop the nuts. Pick the parsley leaves and roughly chop.
3. Place the porcini in a bowl then add 300 ml of boiling water. Set aside until needed.
4. Heat oil in the pressure cooker. Add the garlic and shallots. Cook for 3 minutes while stirring occasionally.
5. Drain porcini and reserve the liquid. Add the porcini into the pressure cooker together with the wild mushrooms and chestnut mushrooms. Add the bay leaves and thyme.
6. Position the lid and lock it in place. Put to high heat and bring to high pressure. Adjust heat to stabilize. Cook for 10 minutes. Adjust taste if necessary.
7. Transfer the mushroom mixture into a bowl and set aside to cool completely.
8. Once the mushrooms are completely cool, add the bread, pecans, a pinch of black pepper and sea salt, and half of the reserved liquid into the bowl. Mix well. Add more reserved liquid if the mixture seems dry.
9. Add more than half of the parsley into the bowl and stir. Transfer the mixture into a 20cm x 25cm lightly greased baking dish and cover with tin foil.
10. Bake in the oven for 35 minutes. Then, get rid of the foil and cook for another 10 minutes. Once done, sprinkle the remaining parsley on top and serve with bread or crackers. Serve.

Nutrition: Calories: 343; Total Fat: 4.2 g; Saturated Fat: 0.8 g; Cholesterol: 0 mg; Sodium: 861 mg; Total Carbs: 22.5 g; Fiber: 6.3 g; Sugar: 2.3 g; Protein: 9.2 g

56. <u>Spiced Okra</u>

Preparation Time: 14 minutes
Cooking Time: 16 minutes
Servings: 3
Ingredients:

- 2 cups okra
- ¼ tsp. stevia
- 1 tsp. chili powder
- ½ tsp. ground turmeric
- 1 tbsp. ground coriander
- 2 tbsp. fresh coriander, chopped
- 1 tbsp. ground cumin
- ¼ tsp. salt
- 1 tbsp. desiccated coconut
- 3 tbsp. vegetable oil
- ½ tsp. black mustard seeds
- ½ tsp. cumin seeds
- Fresh tomatoes, to garnish

Directions:

1. Trim okra. Wash and dry.

2. Combine stevia, chili powder, turmeric, ground coriander, fresh coriander, cumin, salt, and desiccated coconut in a bowl.
3. Heat the oil in a pan. Cook mustard and cumin seeds for 3 minutes. Stir continuously. Add okra. Tip in the spice mixture. Cook on low heat for 8 minutes.
4. Transfer to a serving dish. Garnish with fresh tomatoes.

Nutrition: Calories: 163; Total Fat: 4.2 g; Saturated Fat: 0.8 g; Cholesterol: 0 mg; Sodium: 861 mg; Total Carbs: 22.5 g; Fiber: 6.3 g; Sugar: 2.3 g; Protein: 9.2 g

57. Lemony Salmon Burgers

Preparation Time: 10 Minutes
Cooking Time: 10 Minutes
Servings: 4
Ingredients:
- 2 (3-oz.) cans boneless, skinless pink salmon
- 1/4 cup panko breadcrumbs
- 4 tsp. lemon juice
- 1/4 cup red bell pepper
- 1/4 cup sugar-free yogurt
- 1 egg
- 2 (1.5-oz.) whole-wheat hamburger toasted buns

Directions:
1. Mix drained and flaked salmon, finely-chopped bell pepper, panko breadcrumbs.
2. Combine 2 tbsp. cup sugar-free yogurt, 3 tsp. fresh lemon juice, and egg in a bowl. Shape mixture into 2 (3-inch) patties, bake on the skillet over medium heat for 4 to 5 minutes per side.

3. Stir together 2 tbsp. sugar-free yogurt and 1 tsp. lemon juice; spread over bottom halves of buns.
4. Top each with 1 patty, and cover with bun tops.
5. This dish is very mouth-watering!

Nutrition: Calories: 131; Protein: 12; Fat: 1 g; Carbs: 19 g

58. Caprese Turkey Burgers

Preparation Time: 10 Minutes
Cooking Time: 10 Minutes
Servings: 4
Ingredients:
- 1/2 lb. 93% lean ground turkey
- 2 (1,5-oz.) whole-wheat hamburger bun (toasted)
- 1/4 cup shredded mozzarella cheese (part skim)
- 1 egg
- 1 big tomato
- 1 small garlic clove
- 4 large basil leaves
- 1/8 tsp. salt
- 1/8 tsp. pepper

Directions:
1. Combine turkey, white egg, Minced garlic, salt and pepper (mix until combined);
2. Shape into 2 cutlets. Put cutlets into a skillet cook 5 to 7 minutes per side.
3. Top cutlets properly with cheese and slice tomato at the end of cooking.
4. Put 1 cutlet on the bottom of each bun.
5. Top each patty with 2 basil leaves. Cover with bun tops.

ly guests enjoy this dish every time they visit my
ome.
Nutrition: Calories: 180; Protein: 7 g; Fat: 4 g; Carbs:
0 g

59. Pasta Salad

Preparation Time: 15 Minutes
Cooking Time: 15 Minutes
Servings: 4
Ingredients:
- 8 oz. whole-wheat pasta
- 2 tomatoes
- 1 (5-oz.) pkg spring mix
- 9 slices bacon
- 1/3 cup mayonnaise (reduced-fat)
- 1 tbsp. Dijon mustard
- 3 tbsp. apple cider vinegar
- 1/4 tsp. salt
- 1/2 tsp. pepper

Directions:
1. Cook pasta.
2. Chilled pasta, chopped tomatoes, and spring mix in a bowl.
3. Crumble-cooked bacon over pasta.
4. Combine mayonnaise, mustard, vinegar, salt, and pepper in a small bowl.
5. Pour dressing over pasta, stirring to coat.

Understanding diabetes is the first step in curing.
Nutrition: Calories: 200; Protein: 15 g; Fat: 3 g; Carbs: g

60. Chicken, Strawberry, And Avocado Salad

Preparation Time: 10 Minutes
Servings: 2
Cooking Time: 5 Minutes
Ingredients:
- 1,5 cups chicken (skin removed)
- 1/4 cup almonds
- 2 (5-oz.) pkg salad greens
- 1 (16-oz.) pkg strawberries
- 1 avocado
- 1/4 cup green onion
- 1/4 cup lime juice
- 3 tbsp. extra virgin olive oil
- 2 tbsp. honey
- 1/4 tsp. salt
- 1/4 tsp. pepper

Directions:
1. Toast almonds until golden and fragrant.
2. Mix lime juice, oil, honey, salt, and pepper.
3. Mix greens, sliced strawberries, chicken, diced avocado, and sliced green onion, and sliced almonds; drizzle with dressing. Toss to coat.
4. Yummy!

Nutrition: Calories: 150; Protein: 15 g; Fat: 10 g; Carbs: 5 g

61. <u>Lemon-Thyme Eggs</u>

Preparation Time: 10 Minutes
Cooking Time: 5 Minutes
Servings: 4
Ingredients:

- 7 large eggs
- 1/4 cup mayonnaise (reduced-fat)
- 2 tsp. lemon juice
- 1 tsp. Dijon mustard
- 1 tsp. chopped fresh thyme
- 1/8 tsp. cayenne pepper

Directions:

1. Bring eggs to a boil.
2. Peel and cut each egg in half lengthwise.
3. Remove yolks to a bowl. Add mayonnaise, lemon juice, mustard, thyme, and cayenne to egg yolks; mash to blend. Fill egg white halves with yolk mixture.
4. Chill until ready to serve.
5. Please your family with a delicious meal.

Nutrition: Calories: 40; Protein: 10 g; Fat: 6 g; Carbs: 2 g

62. <u>Spinach Salad with Bacon</u>

Preparation Time: 15 Minutes
Cooking Time: 0 Minutes

Servings:
Ingredients:

- 8 slices center-cut bacon
- 3 tbsp. extra virgin olive oil
- 1 (5-oz.) pkg baby spinach
- 1 tbsp. apple cider vinegar
- 1 tsp. Dijon mustard
- 1/2 tsp. honey
- 1/4 tsp. salt
- 1/2 tsp. pepper

Directions:

1. Mix vinegar, mustard, honey, salt, and pepper in a bowl.
2. Whisk in oil. Place spinach in a serving bowl drizzle with dressing, and toss to coat.
3. Sprinkle with cooked and crumbled bacon.

Nutrition: Calories: 110; Protein: 6 g; Fat: 2 g; Carbs 1 g

63. <u>Pea and Collards Soup</u>

Preparation Time: 10 Minutes
Cooking Time: 50 Minutes
Servings: 4
Ingredients:

- 1/2 (16-oz.) pkg black-eyed peas
- 1 onion
- 2 carrots
- 1,5 cups ham (low-sodium)
- 1 (1-lb.) bunch collard greens (trimmed)
- 1 tbsp. extra virgin olive oil
- 2 garlic cloves
- 1/2 tsp. black pepper
- Hot sauce

Directions:

1. Cook chopped onion and carrots for 1 Minutes.
2. Add peas, diced ham, collards, and Minced garlic. Cook 5 Minutes.

3. Add broth, 3 cups water, and pepper. Bring to a boil; simmer for 35 minutes, adding water if needed.
4. Serve with your favorite sauce.

Nutrition: Calories: 86; Protein: 15 g; Fat: 2 g; Carbs: g

4. **Spanish Stew**

Preparation Time: 10 Minutes
Cooking Time: 25 Minutes
Servings: 4
Ingredients:
- 1.1/2 (12-oz.) pkg smoked chicken sausage links
- 1 (5-oz.) pkg baby spinach
- 1 (15-oz.) can chickpeas
- 1 (14.5-oz.) can tomatoes with basil, garlic, and oregano
- 1/2 tsp. smoked paprika
- 1/2 tsp. cumin
- 3/4 cup onions
- 1 tbsp. extra virgin olive oil

Directions:
1. Cook sliced the sausage in hot oil until browned. Remove from pot.
2. Add chopped onions; cook until tender.
3. Add sausage, drained and rinsed chickpeas, diced tomatoes, paprika, and ground cumin. Cook 15 Minutes.
4. Add in spinach; cook for 1 to 2 Minutes.

This dish is ideal for every day and for a festive table.

Nutrition: Calories: 200; Protein: 10 g; Fat: 20 g; Carbs: 1 g

5. **Creamy Taco Soup**

Preparation Time: 10 Minutes
Cooking Time: 20 Minutes
Servings: 4

Ingredients:
- 3/4 lb. ground sirloin
- 1/2 (8-oz.) cream cheese
- 1/2 onion
- 1 garlic clove
- 1 (10-oz.) can tomatoes and green chiles
- 1 (14.5-oz.) can beef broth
- 1/4 cup heavy cream
- 1,5 tsp. cumin
- 1/2 tsp. chili powder

Directions:
1. Cook beef, chopped onion, and minced garlic until the meat is browned and crumbly; drain and return to pot.
2. Add ground cumin, chili powder, and cream cheese cut into small pieces and softened, stirring until cheese is melted.
3. Add diced tomatoes, broth, and cream; bring to a boil, and simmer for 10 Minutes. Season with pepper and salt to taste.

You've got to give someone the recipe for this soup dish!

Nutrition: Calories: 60; Protein: 3 g; Fat: 1 g; Carbs: 8 g

66. **Chicken with Caprese Salsa**

Preparation Time: 15 Minutes
Cooking Time: 5 Minutes
Servings: 4
Ingredients:
- 3/4 lb. boneless, skinless chicken breasts
- 2 big tomatoes
- 1/2 (8-oz.) ball fresh mozzarella cheese
- 1/4 cup red onion
- 2 tbsp. fresh basil
- 1 tbsp. balsamic vinegar

- 2 tbsp. extra virgin olive oil (divided)
- 1/2 tsp. salt (divided)
- 1/4 tsp. pepper (divided)

Directions:

1. Sprinkle cut in half lengthwise chicken with 1/4 tsp. salt and 1/8 tsp. pepper.
2. Heat 1 tbsp. olive oil, cook chicken for 5 Minutes.
3. Meanwhile, mix chopped tomatoes, diced cheese, finely chopped onion, chopped basil, vinegar, 1 tbsp. oil, and 1/4 tsp. salt and 1/8 tsp. pepper.
4. Spoon salsa over chicken.

Chicken with Caprese Salsa is a nutritious, simple, and very tasty dish that can be prepared in a few minutes.

Nutrition: Calories: 210; Protein: 28 g; Fat: 17 g; Carbs: 0, 1 g

67. Balsamic-Roasted Broccoli

Preparation Time: 10 Minutes
Cooking Time: 15 Minutes
Servings: 4
Ingredients:

- 1 lb. broccoli
- 1 tbsp. extra virgin olive oil
- 1 tbsp. balsamic vinegar
- 1 garlic clove
- 1/8 tsp. salt
- Pepper to taste

Directions:

1. Preheat oven to 450°F.
2. Combine broccoli, olive oil, vinegar, Minced garlic, salt, and pepper; toss.
3. Spread broccoli on a baking sheet.
4. Bake 12 to 15 Minutes.

Really good!
Nutrition: Calories: 27; Protein: 3 g; Fat: 0, 3 g; Carbs: 4 g

68. Hearty Beef and Vegetable Soup

Preparation Time: 10 Minutes
Cooking Time: 30 Minutes
Servings: 4
Ingredients:

- 1/2 lb. lean ground beef
- 2 cups beef broth
- 1,5 tbsp. vegetable oil (divided)
- 1 cup green bell pepper
- 1/2 cup red onion
- 1 cup green cabbage
- 1 cup frozen mixed vegetables
- 1/2 can tomatoes
- 1,5 tsp. Worcestershire sauce
- 1 small bay leaf
- 1,8 tsp. pepper
- 2 tbsp. ketchup

Directions:

1. Cook beef in 1/2 tbsp. hot oil 2 Minutes.
2. Stir in chopped bell pepper and chopped onion; cook for 4 Minutes.
3. Add chopped cabbage, mixed vegetables, stewed tomatoes, broth, Worcestershire sauce, bay leaf, and pepper; bring to a boil.
4. Reduce heat to medium; cover, and cook for 15 Minutes.
5. Stir in ketchup and 1 tbsp. oil, and remove from heat. Let stand 10 Minutes.

The right diet is an excellent diabetes remedy.
Nutrition: Calories: 170; Protein: 17 g; Fat: 8 g; Carbs 3 g

69. Cauliflower Muffin

Preparation Time: 15 Minutes
Cooking Time: 30 Minutes
Servings: 4
Ingredients:

- 2,5 cup cauliflower
- 2/3 cup ham
- 2,5 cups cheese
- 2/3 cup champignon
- 1,5 tbsp. flaxseed
- 3 eggs
- 1/4 tsp. salt
- 1/8 tsp. pepper

Directions:

1. Preheat the oven to 375°F.
2. Put muffin liners in a 12-muffin tin.
3. Combine diced cauliflower, ground flaxseed, beaten eggs, cup diced ham, grated cheese, and diced mushrooms, salt, pepper.
4. Divide mixture rightly between muffin liners.
5. Bake 30 Minutes.

This is a great lunch for the whole family.
Nutrition: Calories: 116; Protein: 10 g; Fat: 7 g; Carbs: g

70. Ham and Egg Cups

Preparation Time: 10 Minutes
Cooking Time: 15 Minutes
Servings: 4
Ingredients:

- 5 slices ham
- 4 tbsp. cheese
- 1,5 tbsp. cream
- 3 egg whites
- 1,5 tbsp. pepper (green)
- 1 tsp. salt
- pepper to taste

Directions:

1. Preheat oven to 350°F.
2. Arrange each slice of thinly sliced ham into 4 muffin tins.
3. Put 1/4 of grated cheese into the ham cup.
4. Mix eggs, cream, salt, and pepper and divide it into 2 tins.
5. Bake in oven 15 Minutes; after baking, sprinkle with green onions.

If you want to keep your current shape, also pay attention to this dish.
Nutrition: Calories: 180; Protein: 13 g; Fat: 13 g; Carbs: 2 g

71. Cauliflower Mac & Cheese

Preparation Time: 5 Minutes
Cooking Time: 25 Minutes
Effort: Easy
Servings: 4
Ingredients:

- 1 Cauliflower Head, torn into florets
- Salt & Black Pepper, as needed
- ¼ cup Almond Milk, unsweetened
- ¼ cup Heavy Cream
- 3 tbsp. Butter, preferably grass-fed
- 1 cup Cheddar Cheese, shredded

Directions:

1. Preheat the oven to 450°F.
2. Melt the butter in a small microwave-safe bowl and heat it for 30 seconds.
3. Pour the melted butter over the cauliflower florets along with salt and pepper. Toss them well.
4. Place the cauliflower florets in a parchment paper-covered large baking sheet.
5. Bake them for 15 minutes or until the cauliflower is crisp-tender.
6. Once baked, mix the heavy cream, cheddar cheese, almond milk, and the remaining butter in a large microwave-safe bowl and heat it on high heat for 2 minutes or until the cheese

mixture is smooth. Repeat the procedure until the cheese has melted.

7. Finally, stir in the cauliflower to the sauce mixture and coat well.

Nutrition: Calories: 294; Fat: 23g; Carbohydrates: 7g; Proteins: 11g

72. Easy Egg Salad

Preparation Time: 5 Minutes
Cooking Time: 15 to 20 Minutes
Effort: Easy
Servings: 4
Ingredients:

- 6 Eggs, preferably free-range
- ¼ tsp. Salt
- 2 tbsp. Mayonnaise
- 1 tsp. Lemon juice
- 1 tsp. Dijon mustard
- Pepper, to taste
- Lettuce leaves, to serve

Directions:

1. Keep the eggs in a saucepan of water and pour cold water until it covers the egg by another inch.
2. Bring to a boil and then remove the eggs from heat.
3. Peel the eggs under cold running water.
4. Transfer the cooked eggs into a food processor and pulse them until chopped.
5. Stir in the mayonnaise, lemon juice, salt, Dijon mustard, and pepper and mix them well.
6. Taste for seasoning and add more if required.
7. Serve in the lettuce leaves.

77. Pork Chop Diane

Preparation Time: 10 minutes
Cooking Time: 20 minutes
Servings: 4
Ingredients:

- ¼ cup low-sodium chicken broth
- 1 tbsp. freshly squeezed lemon juice
- 2 tsp. Worcestershire sauce
- 2 tsp. Dijon mustard
- 4 (5-ounce) boneless pork top loin chops
- 1 tsp. extra-virgin olive oil
- 1 tsp. lemon zest
- 1 tsp. butter
- 2 tsp. chopped fresh chives

Directions:

1. Blend together the chicken broth, lemon juice, Worcestershire sauce, and Dijon mustard and set it aside.
2. Season the pork chops lightly.
3. Situate a large skillet over medium-high heat and add the olive oil.
4. Cook the pork chops, turning once, until they are no longer pink, about 8 minutes per side.
5. Put aside the chops.
6. Pour the broth mixture into the skillet and cook until warmed through and thickened, about 2 minutes.
7. Blend lemon zest, butter, and chives.
8. Garnish with a generous spoonful of sauce.

Nutrition: Calories: 200; Fat: 8g; Carbohydrates: 1g

78. Autumn Pork Chops with Red Cabbage and Apples

Preparation Time: 15 minutes
Cooking Time: 30 minutes
Servings: 4
Ingredients:

- ¼ cup apple cider vinegar
- 2 tbsp. granulated sweetener
- 4 (4-ounce) pork chops, about 1 inch thick
- 1 tbsp. extra-virgin olive oil
- ½ red cabbage, finely shredded
- 1 sweet onion, thinly sliced
- 1 apple, peeled, cored, and sliced
- 1 tsp. chopped fresh thyme

Directions:

1. Scourge together the vinegar and sweetener. Set it aside.
2. Season the pork with salt and pepper.
3. Position a huge skillet over medium-high heat and add the olive oil.
4. Cook the pork chops until no longer pink, turning once, about 8 minutes per side.
5. Put chops aside.
6. Add the cabbage and onion to the skillet and sauté until the vegetables have softened, about 5 minutes.
7. Add the vinegar mixture and the apple slices to the skillet and bring the mixture to a boil.
8. Adjust heat to low and simmer, covered, for 5 additional minutes.
9. Return the pork chops to the skillet, along with any accumulated juices and thyme, cover, and cook for 5 more minutes.

Nutrition: Calories: 223; Carbohydrates: 12g; Fiber: 3g

79. Chipotle Chili Pork Chops

Preparation Time: 4 hours
Cooking Time: 20 minutes
Servings: 4
Ingredients:

- Juice and zest of 1 lime
- 1 tbsp. extra-virgin olive oil
- 1 tbsp. chipotle chili powder
- 2 tsp. minced garlic
- 1 tsp. ground cinnamon
- Pinch sea salt
- 4 (5-ounce) pork chops

Directions:

1. Combine the lime juice and zest, oil, chipotle chili powder, garlic, cinnamon, and salt in a resealable plastic bag. Add the pork chops. Remove as much air as possible and seal the bag.
2. Marinate the chops in the refrigerator for at least 4 hours, and up to 24 hours, turning them several times.
3. Ready the oven to 400°F and set a rack on a baking sheet. Let the chops rest at room temperature for 15 minutes, then arrange them on the rack and discard the remaining marinade.
4. Roast the chops until cooked through, turning once, about 10 minutes per side.
5. Serve with lime wedges.

Nutrition: Calories: 204; Carbohydrates: 1g; Sugar: 1g

80. Orange-Marinated Pork Tenderloin

Preparation Time: 2 hours
Cooking Time: 30 minutes
Servings: 4
Ingredients:

- ¼ cup freshly squeezed orange juice
- 2 tsp. orange zest
- 2 tsp. minced garlic
- 1 tsp. low-sodium soy sauce
- 1 tsp. grated fresh ginger
- 1 tsp. honey
- 1½ pounds pork tenderloin roast
- 1 tbsp. extra-virgin olive oil

Directions:

1. Blend together the orange juice, zest, garlic, soy sauce, ginger, and honey.
2. Pour the marinade into a resealable plastic bag and add the pork tenderloin.
3. Remove as much air as possible and seal the bag. Marinate the pork in the refrigerator, turning the bag a few times, for 2 hours.
4. Preheat the oven to 400°F.
5. Pull out the tenderloin from the marinade and discard the marinade.
6. Position big ovenproof skillet over medium-high heat and add the oil.
7. Sear the pork tenderloin on all sides, about 5 minutes in total.
8. Position the skillet in the oven and roast for 25 minutes.
9. Put aside for 10 minutes before serving.

Nutrition: Calories: 228; Carbohydrates: 4g; Sugar: 3g

81. Homestyle Herb Meatballs

Preparation Time: 10 minutes
Cooking Time: 15 minutes
Servings: 4
Ingredients:

- ½ pound lean ground pork
- ½ pound lean ground beef
- 1 sweet onion, finely chopped
- ¼ cup bread crumbs
- 2 tbsp. chopped fresh basil
- 2 tsp. minced garlic
- 1 egg

Directions:

1. Preheat the oven to 350°F.
2. Ready baking tray with parchment paper and set it aside.
3. In a large bowl, mix together the pork, beef, onion, bread crumbs, basil, garlic, egg, salt, and pepper until very well mixed.
4. Roll the meat mixture into 2-inch meatballs.
5. Transfer the meatballs to the baking sheet and bake until they are browned and cooked through, about 15 minutes.
6. Serve the meatballs with your favorite marinara sauce and some steamed green beans.

Nutrition: Calories: 332; Carbohydrates: 13g; Sugar: 3g

82. Lime-Parsley Lamb Cutlets

Preparation Time: 4 hours
Cooking Time: 10 minutes
Servings: 4
Ingredients:

- ¼ cup extra-virgin olive oil
- ¼ cup freshly squeezed lime juice
- 2 tbsp. lime zest
- 2 tbsp. chopped fresh parsley
- 12 lamb cutlets (about 1½ pounds total)

Directions:

1. Scourge the oil, lime juice, zest, parsley, salt and pepper.
2. Pour marinade into a resealable plastic bag.
3. Add the cutlets to the bag and remove as much air as possible before sealing.
4. Marinate the lamb in the refrigerator for about 4 hours, turning the bag several times.
5. Preheat the oven to broil.
6. Remove the chops from the bag and arrange them on an aluminum foil-lined baking sheet. Discard the marinade.
7. Broil the chops for 4 minutes per side for medium doneness.
8. Let the chops rest for 5 minutes before serving.

Nutrition: Calories: 413; Carbohydrates: 1g; Protein: 31g

83. Mediterranean Steak Sandwiches

Preparation Time: 1 hour
Cooking Time: 10 minutes
Servings: 4
Ingredients:

- 2 tbsp. extra-virgin olive oil
- 2 tbsp. balsamic vinegar
- 2 tsp. garlic
- 2 tsp. lemon juice
- 2 tsp. fresh oregano
- 1 tsp. fresh parsley
- 1-pound flank steak
- 4 whole-wheat pitas
- 2 cups shredded lettuce
- 1 red onion, thinly sliced
- 1 tomato, chopped
- 1 ounce low-sodium feta cheese

Directions:

1. Scourge olive oil, balsamic vinegar, garlic, lemon juice, oregano, and parsley.
2. Add the steak to the bowl, turning to coat it completely.
3. Marinate the steak for 1 hour in the refrigerator, turning it over several times.
4. Preheat the broiler. Line a baking sheet with aluminum foil.
5. Put steak out of the bowl and discard the marinade.
6. Situate steak on the baking sheet and broil for 5 minutes per side for medium.
7. Set aside for 10 minutes before slicing.
8. Stuff the pitas with the sliced steak, lettuce, onion, tomato, and feta.

Nutrition: Calories: 344; Carbohydrates: 22g; Fiber: 3g

84. Roasted Beef with Peppercorn Sauce

Preparation Time: 10 minutes
Cooking Time: 90 minutes
Servings: 4
Ingredients:

- 1½ pounds top rump beef roast
- 3 tsp. extra-virgin olive oil
- 3 shallots, minced
- 2 tsp. minced garlic
- 1 tbsp. green peppercorns
- 2 tbsp. dry sherry
- 2 tbsp. all-purpose flour
- 1 cup sodium-free beef broth

Directions:

1. Heat the oven to 300°F.
2. Season the roast with salt and pepper.
3. Position a huge skillet over medium-high heat and add 2 tsp. of olive oil.
4. Brown the beef on all sides, about 10 minutes in total, and transfer the roast to a baking dish.
5. Roast until desired doneness, about 1½ hours for medium. When the roast has been in the oven for 1 hour, start the sauce.
6. In a medium saucepan over medium-high heat, sauté the shallots in the remaining 1 tsp. of olive oil until translucent, about 4 minutes.
7. Stir in the garlic and peppercorns, and cook for another minute. Whisk in the sherry to deglaze the pan.
8. Whisk in the flour to form a thick paste, cooking for 1 minute and stirring constantly.
9. Fill in the beef broth and whisk for 4 minutes. Season the sauce.
10. Serve the beef with a generous spoonful of sauce.

Nutrition: Calories: 330; Carbohydrates: 4g; Protein: 36g

85. Coffee-And-Herb-Marinated Steak

Preparation Time: 2 hours
Cooking Time: 10 minutes
Servings: 3
Ingredients:

- ¼ cup whole coffee beans
- 2 tsp. garlic
- 2 tsp. rosemary
- 2 tsp. thyme
- 1 tsp. black pepper
- 2 tbsp. apple cider vinegar
- 2 tbsp. extra-virgin olive oil
- 1-pound flank steak, trimmed of visible fat

Directions:

1. Place the coffee beans, garlic, rosemary, thyme, and black pepper in a coffee grinder or food processor and pulse until coarsely ground.

2. Transfer the coffee mixture to a resealable plastic bag and add the vinegar and oil. Shake to combine.
3. Add the flank steak and squeeze the excess air out of the bag. Seal it. Marinate the steak in the refrigerator for at least 2 hours, occasionally turning the bag over.
4. Preheat the broiler. Line a baking sheet with aluminum foil.
5. Pull the steak out and discard the marinade.
6. Position steak on the baking sheet and broil until it is done to your liking.
7. Put aside for 10 minutes before cutting it.
8. Serve with your favorite side dish.

Nutrition: Calories: 313; Fat: 20g; Protein: 31g

86. **Traditional Beef Stroganoff**

Preparation Time: 10 minutes
Cooking Time: 30 minutes
Servings: 4
Ingredients:

- 1 tsp. extra-virgin olive oil
- 1-pound top sirloin, cut into thin strips
- 1 cup sliced button mushrooms
- ½ sweet onion, finely chopped
- 1 tsp. minced garlic
- 1 tbsp. whole-wheat flour
- ½ cup low-sodium beef broth
- ¼ cup dry sherry
- ½ cup fat-free sour cream
- 1 tbsp. chopped fresh parsley

Directions:

1. Position the skillet over medium-high heat and add the oil.
2. Sauté the beef until browned, about 10 minutes, then remove the beef with a slotted spoon to a plate and set it aside.
3. Add the mushrooms, onion, and garlic to the skillet and sauté until lightly browned, about 5 minutes.
4. Whisk in the flour and then whisk in the beef broth and sherry.
5. Return the sirloin to the skillet and bring the mixture to a boil.
6. Reduce the heat to low and simmer until the beef is tender, about 10 minutes.

7. Stir in the sour cream and parsley. Season with salt and pepper.

Nutrition: Calories: 257; Carbohydrates: 6g; Fiber: 1g

87. **Chicken and Roasted Vegetable Wraps**

Preparation Time: 10 minutes
Cooking Time: 20 minutes
Servings: 4
Ingredients:

- ½ small eggplant
- 1 red bell pepper
- 1 medium zucchini
- ½ small red onion, sliced
- 1 tbsp. extra-virgin olive oil
- 2 (8-ounce) cooked chicken breasts, sliced
- 4 whole-wheat tortilla wraps

Directions:

1. Preheat the oven to 400°F.
2. Wrap the baking sheet with foil and set it aside
3. In a large bowl, toss the eggplant, bell pepper zucchini, and red onion with olive oil.
4. Transfer the vegetables to the baking sheet and lightly season with salt and pepper.
5. Roast the vegetables until soft and slightly charred, about 20 minutes.
6. Divide the vegetables and chicken into four portions.
7. Wrap 1 tortilla around each portion of chicken and grilled vegetables, and serve.

Nutrition: Calories: 483; Carbohydrates: 45g; Fiber: 3

88. **Spicy Chicken Cacciatore**

Preparation Time: 20 minutes
Cooking Time: 1 hour
Servings: 6
Ingredients:

- 1 (2-pound) chicken
- ¼ cup all-purpose flour
- 2 tbsp. extra-virgin olive oil
- 3 slices bacon
- 1 sweet onion
- 2 tsp. minced garlic
- 4 ounces button mushrooms, halved
- 1 (28-ounce) can low-sodium stewed tomato
- ½ cup red wine

- 2 tsp. chopped fresh oregano

Directions:

1. Cut the chicken into pieces: 2 drumsticks, 2 thighs, 2 wings, and 4 breast pieces.
2. Dredge the chicken pieces in the flour and season each piece with salt and pepper.
3. Place a large skillet over medium-high heat and add the olive oil.
4. Brown the chicken pieces on all sides, about 20 minutes in total. Transfer the chicken to a plate.
5. Cook chopped bacon to the skillet for 5 minutes. With a slotted spoon, transfer the cooked bacon to the same plate as the chicken.
6. Pour off most of the oil from the skillet, leaving just a light coating. Sauté the onion, garlic, and mushrooms in the skillet until tender, about 4 minutes.
7. Stir in the tomatoes, wine, oregano, and red pepper flakes.
8. Bring the sauce to a boil. Return the chicken and bacon, plus any accumulated juices from the plate, to the skillet.
9. Reduce the heat to low and simmer until the chicken is tender, about 30 minutes.

Nutrition: Calories: 230; Carbohydrates: 14g; Fiber: 2g

89. Scallion Sandwich

Preparation Time: 10 minutes
Cooking Time: 10 minutes
Servings: 1
Ingredients:

- 2 slices wheat bread
- 2 tsp. butter, low fat
- 2 scallions, sliced thinly
- 1 tbsp. parmesan cheese, grated
- 3/4 cup of cheddar cheese, reduced-fat, grated

Directions:

1. Preheat the Air fryer to 356°F.
2. Spread butter on a slice of bread. Place inside the cooking basket with the butter side facing down.
3. Place cheese and scallions on top. Spread the rest of the butter on the other slice of bread Put it on top of the sandwich and sprinkle with parmesan cheese.
4. Cook for 10 minutes.

Nutrition: Calorie: 154; Carbohydrate: 9g; Fat: 2.5g; Protein: 8.6g; Fiber: 2.4g

90. Lean Lamb and Turkey Meatballs with Yogurt

Preparation Time: 10 minutes
Servings: 4
Cooking Time: 8 minutes
Ingredients:

- 1 egg white
- 4 ounces ground lean turkey
- 1 pound of ground lean lamb
- 1 tsp. each of cayenne pepper, ground coriander, red chili pastes, salt, and ground cumin
- 2 garlic cloves, minced
- 1 1/2 tbsp. parsley, chopped
- 1 tbsp. mint, chopped
- 1/4 cup of olive oil

For the yogurt

- 2 tbsp. of buttermilk
- 1 garlic clove, minced
- 1/4 cup mint, chopped
- 1/2 cup of Greek yogurt, non-fat
- Salt to taste

Directions:

1. Set the Air Fryer to 390°F.
2. Mix all the ingredients for the meatballs in a bowl. Roll and mold them into golf-size round pieces. Arrange in the cooking basket. Cook for 8 minutes.
3. While waiting, combine all the ingredients for the mint yogurt in a bowl. Mix well.
4. Serve the meatballs with mint yogurt. Top with olives and fresh mint.

Nutrition: Calorie: 154 Carbohydrate: 9g; Fat: 2.5g; Protein: 8.6g; Fiber: 2.4g

91. Air Fried Section and Tomato

Preparation Time: 10 minutes
Cooking Time: 5 minutes
Servings: 2
Ingredients:

- 1 aubergine, sliced thickly into 4 disks
- 1 tomato, sliced into 2 thick disks
- 2 tsp. feta cheese, reduced fat
- 2 fresh basil leaves, minced

- 2 balls, small buffalo mozzarella, reduced-fat, roughly torn
- A pinch salt
- A pinch black pepper

Directions:
1. Preheat Air Fryer to 330°F.
2. Spray a small amount of oil into the air fryer basket. Fry aubergine slices for 5 minutes or until golden brown on both sides. Transfer to a plate.
3. Fry tomato slices in batches for 5 minutes or until seared on both sides.
4. To serve, stack salad starting with an aborigine base, buffalo mozzarella, basil leaves, tomato slice, and 1/2-tsp. feta cheese.
5. Top of with another slice of aborigine and 1/2 tsp. feta cheese. Serve.

Nutrition: Calorie: 140.3; Carbohydrate: 26.6; Fat: 3.4g; Protein: 4.2g; Fiber: 7.3g

92. Cheesy Salmon Fillets

Preparation Time: 15 minutes
Cooking Time: 20 minutes
Servings: 2–3
Ingredients:
For the salmon fillets

- 2 pieces, 4 oz. each salmon fillets, choose even cuts
- 1/2 cup sour cream, reduced-fat
- ¼ cup cottage cheese, reduced-fat
- ¼ cup Parmigiano-Reggiano cheese, freshly grated

Garnish

- Spanish paprika
- 1/2 piece lemon, cut into wedges

Directions:
1. Preheat Air Fryer to 330°F.
2. To make the salmon fillets, mix sour cream, cottage cheese, and Parmigiano-Reggiano cheese in a bowl.
3. Layer salmon fillets in the Air fryer basket. Fry for 20 minutes or until cheese turns golden brown.
4. To assemble, place a salmon fillet and sprinkle paprika. Garnish with lemon wedges and squeeze lemon juice on top. Serve.

Nutrition: Calorie: 274; Carbohydrate: 1g; Fat: 19g; Protein: 24g; Fiber: 0.5g

93. Salmon with Asparagus

Preparation Time: 5 Minutes
Cooking Time: 10 Minutes
Servings: 3
Ingredients:

- 1 lb. Salmon, sliced into fillets
- 1 tbsp. Olive Oil
- Salt & Pepper, as needed
- 1 bunch Asparagus, trimmed
- 2 garlic cloves, minced
- Zest & Juice of 1/2 Lemon
- 1 tbsp. Butter, salted

Directions:
1. Spoon in the butter and olive oil into a lar pan and heat it over medium-high heat.
2. Once it becomes hot, place the salmon a season it with salt and pepper.
3. Cook for 4 minutes per side and then cook t other side.
4. Stir in the garlic and lemon zest to it.
5. Cook for further 2 minutes or until sligh browned.
6. Off the heat and squeeze the lemon juice ov it.
7. Serve it hot.

Nutrition: Calories: 409; Carbohydrates: 2.7 Proteins: 32.8g; Fat: 28.8g; Sodium: 497mg

94. <u>Shrimp in Garlic Butter</u>

Preparation Time: 5 Minutes
Cooking Time: 20 Minutes
Servings: 4
Ingredients:

- 1 lb. Shrimp, peeled & deveined
- ¼ tsp. Red Pepper Flakes
- 6 tbsp. Butter, divided
- 1/2 cup Chicken Stock
- Salt & Pepper, as needed
- 2 tbsp. Parsley, minced
- 5 garlic cloves, minced
- 2 tbsp. Lemon Juice

Directions:

1. Heat a large bottomed skillet over medium-high heat.
2. Spoon in two tbsp. of the butter and melt it. Add the shrimp.
3. Season it with salt and pepper. Sear for 4 minutes or until shrimp gets cooked.
4. Transfer the shrimp to a plate and stir in the garlic.
5. Sauté for 30 seconds or until aromatic.
6. Pour the chicken stock and whisk it well. Allow it to simmer for 5 to 10 minutes or until it has been reduced to half.
7. Spoon the remaining butter, red pepper, and lemon juice into the sauce. Mix.
8. Continue cooking for another 2 minutes.
9. Take off the pan from the heat and add the cooked shrimp to it.
10. Garnish with parsley and transfer to the serving bowl.
11. Enjoy.

Nutrition: Calories: 307; Carbohydrates: 3g; Proteins: 27g; Fat: 20g; Sodium: 522mg

95. <u>Cobb Salad</u>

Keto & Under 30 Minutes
Preparation Time: 5 Minutes
Cooking Time: 5 Minutes
Servings: 1
Ingredients:

- 4 Cherry Tomatoes, chopped
- ¼ cup Bacon, cooked & crumbled
- 1/2 Avocado, chopped
- 2 oz. Chicken Breast, shredded
- 1 Egg, hardboiled
- 2 cups Mixed Green salad
- 1 oz. Feta Cheese, crumbled

Directions:

1. Toss all the ingredients for the Cobb salad in a large mixing bowl and toss well.
2. Serve and enjoy it.

Nutrition: Calories: 307; Carbohydrates: 3g; Proteins: 27g; Fat: 20g; Sodium: 522mg

96. Seared Tuna Steak

Preparation Time: 10 Minutes
Cooking Time: 10 Minutes
Servings: 2
Ingredients:

- 1 tsp. Sesame Seeds
- 1 tbsp. Sesame Oil
- 2 tbsp. Soya Sauce
- Salt & Pepper, to taste
- 2 × 6 oz. Ahi Tuna Steaks

Directions:

1. Season the tuna steaks with salt and pepper. Keep it aside on a shallow bowl.
2. In another bowl, mix soya sauce and sesame oil.
3. Pour the sauce over the salmon and coat them generously with the sauce.
4. Keep it aside for 10 to 15 minutes and then heat a large skillet over medium heat.
5. Once hot, keep the tuna steaks and cook them for 3 minutes or until seared underneath.
6. Flip the fillets and cook them for a further 3 minutes.
7. Transfer the seared tuna steaks to the serving plate and slice them into 1/2 inch slices. Top with sesame seeds.

Nutrition: Calories: 255; Fat: 9g; Carbohydrates: 1g; Proteins: 40.5g; Sodium: 293mg

97. Beef Chili

Preparation Time: 10 Minutes
Cooking Time: 20 Minutes
Servings: 4
Ingredients:

- 1/2 tsp. Garlic Powder
- 1 tsp. Coriander, grounded
- 1 lb. Beef, grounded
- 1/2 tsp. Sea Salt
- 1/2 tsp. Cayenne Pepper
- 1 tsp. Cumin, grounded
- 1/2 tsp. Pepper, grounded
- 1/2 cup Salsa, low-carb & no-sugar

Directions:

1. Heat a large-sized pan over medium-high heat and cook the beef in it until browned.
2. Stir in all the spices and cook them for minutes or until everything is combined.
3. When the beef gets cooked, spoon in the salsa
4. Bring the mixture to a simmer and cook for another 8 minutes or until everything comes together.
5. Take it from heat and transfer it to a serving bowl.

Nutrition: Calories: 229; Fat: 10g; Carbohydrates: 2g; Proteins: 33g; Sodium: 675mg

98. Greek Broccoli Salad

Preparation Time: 10 Minutes
Cooking Time: 15 Minutes
Servings: 4
Ingredients:

- 1 ¼ lb. Broccoli, sliced into small bites
- ¼ cup Almonds, sliced

- 1/3 cup Sun-dried Tomatoes
- ¼ cup Feta Cheese, crumbled
- ¼ cup Red Onion, sliced

For the dressing
- 1/4 cup Olive Oil
- A dash Red Pepper Flakes
- 1 Garlic clove, minced
- ¼ tsp. Salt
- 2 tbsp. Lemon Juice
- 1/2 tsp. Dijon Mustard
- 1 tsp. Low Carb Sweetener Syrup
- 1/2 tsp. Oregano, dried

Directions:
1. Mix broccoli, onion, almonds, and sun-dried tomatoes in a large mixing bowl.
2. In another small-sized bowl, combine all the dressing ingredients until emulsified.
3. Spoon the dressing over the broccoli salad.
4. Allow the salad to rest for half an hour before serving.

Nutrition: Calories: 272; Carbohydrates: 11.9g; Proteins: 8g; Fat: 21.6g; Sodium: 321mg

99. Cheesy Cauliflower Gratin

Preparation Time: 5 Minutes
Cooking Time: 25 Minutes
Servings: 6
Ingredients:
- 6 deli slices Pepper Jack Cheese
- 4 cups Cauliflower florets
- Salt and Pepper, as needed
- 4 tbsp. Butter
- 1/3 cup Heavy Whipping Cream

Directions:
1. Mix the cauliflower, cream, butter, salt, and pepper in a safe microwave bowl and combine well.
2. Microwave the cauliflower mixture for 25 minutes on high until it becomes soft and tender.
3. Remove the ingredients from the bowl and mash with the help of a fork.
4. Taste for seasonings and spoon in salt and pepper as required.
5. Arrange the slices of pepper jack cheese on top of the cauliflower mixture and microwave for 3 minutes until the cheese starts melting.
6. Serve warm.

Nutrition: Calories: 421; Carbohydrates: 3g; Proteins: 19g; Fat: 37g; Sodium: 111mg

100. Strawberry Spinach Salad

Preparation Time: 5 Minutes
Cooking Time: 10 Minutes
Servings: 4
Ingredients:
- 4 oz. Feta Cheese, crumbled
- 8 Strawberries, sliced
- 2 oz. Almonds
- 6 Slices Bacon, thick-cut, crispy, and crumbled
- 10 oz. Spinach leaves, fresh
- 2 Roma Tomatoes, diced
- 2 oz. Red Onion, sliced thinly

Directions:
1. For making this healthy salad, mix all the ingredients needed to make the salad in a large-sized bowl and toss them well.

Nutrition: Calories: 255; Fat: 16g; Carbohydrates: 8g; Proteins: 14g; Sodium: 27mg

101.   Misto Quente

Preparation Time: 5 minutes
Cooking Time: 10 minutes
Servings: 4
Ingredients:

- 4 slices bread without shell
- 4 slices turkey breast
- 4 slices cheese
- 2 tbsp. cream cheese
- 2 spoons butter

Directions:

1. Preheat the air fryer. Set the timer of 5 minutes and the temperature to 200°C.
2. Pass the butter on one side of the slice of bread, and on the other side of the slice, the cream cheese.
3. Mount the sandwiches placing two slices of turkey breast and two slices of cheese between the breads, with the cream cheese inside and the side with butter.
4. Place the sandwiches in the basket of the air fryer. Set the timer of the air fryer for 5 minutes and press the power button.

Nutrition: Calories: 340; Fat: 15g; Carbohydrates: 32g; Protein: 15g; Sugar: 0g; Cholesterol: 0mg

102.   Garlic Bread

Preparation Time: 10 minutes
Cooking Time: 15 minutes
Servings: 4–5
Ingredients:

- 2 stale French rolls
- 4 tbsp. crushed or crumpled garlic
- 1 cup mayonnaise
- Powdered grated Parmesan
- 1 tbsp. olive oil

Directions:

1. Preheat the air fryer. Set the time of 5 minutes and the temperature to 200°C.
2. Mix mayonnaise with garlic and set aside.
3. Cut the baguettes into slices, but without separating them completely.
4. Fill the cavities of equals. Brush with olive oil and sprinkle with grated cheese.

5. Place in the basket of the air fryer. Set the timer to 10 minutes, adjust the temperature to 180°C, and press the power button.

Nutrition: Calories: 340; Fat: 15g; Carbohydrates: 32g; Protein: 15g; Sugar: 0g; Cholesterol: 0mg

103.   Bruschetta

Preparation Time: 5 minutes
Cooking Time: 10 minutes
Servings: 2
Ingredients:

- 4 slices Italian bread
- 1 cup chopped tomato tea
- 1 cup grated mozzarella tea
- Olive oil
- Oregano, salt, and pepper
- 4 fresh basil leaves

Directions:

1. Preheat the air fryer. Set the timer of 5 minutes and the temperature to 200°C.
2. Sprinkle the slices of Italian bread with olive oil. Divide the chopped tomatoes and mozzarella between the slices. Season with salt, pepper, and oregano.
3. Put oil in the filling. Place a basil leaf on top of each slice.
4. Put the bruschetta in the basket of the air fryer being careful not to spill the filling. Set the timer of 5 minutes, set the temperature to 180°C, and press the power button.
5. Transfer the bruschetta to a plate and serve.

Nutrition: Calories: 434; Fat: 14g; Carbohydrates: 63g; Protein: 11g; Sugar: 8g; Cholesterol: 0mg

104.   Cream Buns with Strawberries

Preparation Time: 10 minutes
Cooking Time: 12 minutes
Servings: 6
Ingredients:

- 240g all-purpose flour
- 50g granulated sugar
- 8g baking powder
- 1g salt
- 85g chopped cold butter
- 84g chopped fresh strawberries
- 120 ml whipping cream

- 2 large eggs
- 10 ml vanilla extract
- 5 ml water

Directions:

1. Sift flour, sugar, baking powder, and salt in a large bowl. Put the butter with the flour with the use of a blender or your hands until the mixture resembles thick crumbs.
2. Mix the strawberries in the flour mixture. Set aside for the mixture to stand. Beat the whipping cream, 1 egg, and the vanilla extract in a separate bowl.
3. Put the cream mixture in the flour mixture until they are homogeneous, and then spread the mixture to a thickness of 38 mm.
4. Use a round cookie cutter to cut the buns. Spread the buns with a combination of egg and water. Set aside
5. Preheat the air fryer, set it to 180°C.
6. Place baking paper in the preheated inner basket.
7. Place the buns on top of the baking paper and cook for 12 minutes at 180°C, until golden brown.

Nutrition: Calories: 150; Fat: 14g; Carbohydrates: 3g; Protein: 11g; Sugar: 8g; Cholesterol: 0mg

105.   Blueberry Buns

Preparation Time: 10 minutes
Cooking Time: 12 minutes
Servings: 6
Ingredients:

- 240g all-purpose flour
- 50g granulated sugar
- 8g baking powder
- 2g salt
- 85g chopped cold butter
- 85g fresh blueberries
- 3g grated fresh ginger
- 113 ml whipping cream
- 2 large eggs
- 4 ml vanilla extract
- 5 ml water

Directions:

1. Put sugar, flour, baking powder, and salt in a large bowl.

2. Put the butter with the flour using a blender or your hands until the mixture resembles thick crumbs.
3. Mix the blueberries and ginger in the flour mixture and set aside
4. Mix the whipping cream, 1 egg, and the vanilla extract in a different container.
5. Put the cream mixture with the flour mixture until combined.
6. Shape the dough until it reaches a thickness of approximately 38 mm and cut it into eighths.
7. Spread the buns with a combination of egg and water. Set aside Preheat the air fryer set it to 180°C.
8. Place baking paper in the preheated inner basket and place the buns on top of the paper. Cook for 12 minutes at 180°C, until golden brown

Nutrition: Calories: 105; Fat: 1.64g; Carbohydrates: 20.09g; Protein: 2.43g; Sugar: 2.1g; Cholesterol: 0mg

106.   Cauliflower Potato Mash

Preparation Time: 30 minutes
Cooking Time: 5 minutes
Servings: 4
Ingredients:

- 2 cups potatoes, peeled and cubed
- 2 tbsp. butter
- ¼ cup milk
- 10 oz. cauliflower florets
- ¾ tsp. salt

Directions:

1. Add water to the saucepan and bring to boil.
2. Reduce heat and simmer for 10 minutes.
3. Drain vegetables well. Transfer vegetables, butter, milk, and salt to a blender and blend until smooth.
4. Serve and enjoy.

Nutrition: Calories: 128; Fat: 6.2 g; Sugar: 3.3 g; Protein: 3.2 g; Cholesterol 17 mg

107.   French Toast In Sticks

Preparation Time: 5 minutes
Cooking Time: 10 minutes
Servings: 4
Ingredients:

- 4 slices white bread, 38 mm thick, preferably hard
- 2 eggs
- 60 ml milk
- 15 ml maple sauce
- 2 ml vanilla extract
- Nonstick Spray Oil
- 38g sugar
- 3g ground cinnamon
- Maple syrup, to serve
- Sugar to sprinkle

Directions:
1. Cut each slice of bread into thirds making 12 pieces. Place sideways
2. Beat the eggs, milk, maple syrup, and vanilla.
3. Preheat the air fryer, set it to 175°C.
4. Dip the sliced bread in the egg mixture and place it in the preheated air fryer. Sprinkle French toast generously with oil spray.
5. Cook French toast for 10 minutes at 175°C. Turn the toast halfway through cooking.
6. Mix the sugar and cinnamon in a bowl.
7. Cover the French toast with the sugar and cinnamon mixture when you have finished cooking.
8. Serve with Maple syrup and sprinkle with powdered sugar

Nutrition: Calories: 128; Fat: 6.2 g; Carbohydrates: 16.3 g; Sugar: 3.3 g; Protein: 3.2 g; Cholesterol 17 mg

108. Muffins Sandwich

Preparation Time: 2 minutes
Cooking Time: 10 minutes
Servings: 1
Ingredients:
- Nonstick Spray Oil
- 1 slice white cheddar cheese
- 1 slice Canadian bacon
- 1 English muffin, divided
- 15 ml hot water
- 1 large egg
- Salt and pepper to taste

Directions:
1. Spray the inside of an 85g mold with oil spray and place it in the air fryer.
2. Preheat the air fryer, set it to 160°C.
3. Add the Canadian cheese and bacon to the preheated air fryer.

4. Pour the hot water and the egg into the hot pan and season with salt and pepper.
5. Select Bread, set to 10 minutes.
6. Take out the English muffins after 7 minutes, leaving the egg for the full time.
7. Build your sandwich by placing the cooked egg on top of the English muffing and serve

Nutrition: Calories: 400; Fat 26g; Carbohydrates: 26g; Sugar: 15 g; Protein: 3 g; Cholesterol: 155 mg

109. Bacon BBQ

Preparation Time: 2 minutes
Cooking Time: 8 minutes
Servings: 2
Ingredients:
- 13g dark brown sugar
- 5g chili powder
- 1g ground cumin
- 1g cayenne pepper
- 4 slices bacon, cut in half

Directions:
1. Mix seasonings until well combined.
2. Dip the bacon in the dressing until it i completely covered. Leave aside.
3. Preheat the air fryer, set it to 160°C.
4. Place the bacon in the preheated air fryer
5. Select Bacon and press Start/Pause.

Nutrition: Calories: 1124; Fat: 72g; Carbohydrates 59g; Protein: 49g; Sugar: 11g; Cholesterol: 77mg

110. Stuffed French Toast

Preparation Time: 4 minutes
Cooking Time: 10 minutes
Servings: 1
Ingredients:
- 1 slice brioche bread,
- 64 mm thick, preferably rancid
- 113g cream cheese
- 2 eggs
- 15 ml milk
- 30 ml whipping cream
- 38g sugar
- 3g cinnamon
- 2 ml vanilla extract
- Nonstick Spray Oil
- Pistachios chopped to cover

- Maple syrup, to serve

Directions:

1. Preheat the air fryer, set it to 175°C.
2. Cut a slit in the middle of the muffin.
3. Fill the inside of the slit with cream cheese. Leave aside.
4. Mix the eggs, milk, whipping cream, sugar, cinnamon, and vanilla extract.
5. Moisten the stuffed French toast in the egg mixture for 10 seconds on each side.
6. Sprinkle each side of French toast with oil spray.
7. Place the French toast in the preheated air fryer and cook for 10 minutes at 175°C
8. Stir the French toast carefully with a spatula when you finish cooking.
9. Serve topped with chopped pistachios and acrid syrup.

Nutrition: Calories: 159; Fat: 7.5g; Carbohydrates: 25.2g; Protein: 14g; Sugar: 0g; Cholesterol: 90mg

111. Roasted Pork & Apples

Preparation Time: 15 minutes
Cooking Time: 30 minutes
Servings: 4
Ingredients:

- Salt and pepper to taste
- 1/2 tsp. dried, crushed
- 1 lb. pork tenderloin
- 1 tbsp. canola oil
- 1 onion, sliced into wedges
- 3 cooking apples, sliced into wedges
- 2/3 cup apple cider
- Sprigs fresh sage

Directions:

1. In a bowl, mix salt, pepper, and sage.
2. Season both sides of pork with this mixture.
3. Place a pan over medium heat.
4. Brown both sides.
5. Transfer to a roasting pan.
6. Add the onion on top and around the pork.
7. Drizzle oil on top of the pork and apples.
8. Roast in the oven at 425°F for 10 minutes.
9. Add the apples, roast for another 15 minutes.
10. In a pan, boil the apple cider and then simmer for 10 minutes.
11. Pour the apple cider sauce over the pork before serving.

Nutrition: Calories: 239; Total Fat: 6 g; Saturated Fat: 1 g; Cholesterol: 74 mg; Sodium: 209 mg; Total Carbohydrate: 22 g; Dietary Fiber: 3 g; Total Sugars: 16 g; Protein: 24 g; Potassium: 655 mg

112. Pork With Cranberry Relish

Preparation Time: 30 minutes
Cooking Time: 30 minutes
Servings: 4
Ingredients:

- 12 oz. pork tenderloin, fat trimmed and sliced crosswise
- Salt and pepper to taste
- ¼ cup all-purpose flour
- 2 tbsp. olive oil
- 1 onion, sliced thinly
- ¼ cup dried cranberries
- ¼ cup low-sodium chicken broth
- 1 tbsp. balsamic vinegar

Directions:

1. Flatten each slice of pork using a mallet.
2. In a dish, mix the salt, pepper, and flour.
3. Dip each pork slice into the flour mixture.
4. Add oil to a pan over medium-high heat.
5. Cook pork for 3 minutes per side or until golden crispy.
6. Transfer to a serving plate and cover with foil.
7. Cook the onion in the pan for 4 minutes.
8. Stir in the rest of the ingredients.
9. Simmer until the sauce has thickened.

Nutrition: Calories: 211; Total Fat: 9 g; Saturated Fat 2 g; Cholesterol: 53 mg; Sodium: 116 mg; Tota Carbohydrate: 15 g; Dietary Fiber: 1 g; Total Sugars: (g; Protein: 18 g; Potassium: 378 mg

113. Sesame Pork With Mustard Sauce

Preparation Time: 25 minutes
Cooking Time: 25 minutes
Servings: 4
Ingredients:

- 2 tbsp. low-sodium teriyaki sauce
- ¼ cup chili sauce
- 2 garlic cloves, minced
- 2 tsp. ginger, grated
- 2 pork tenderloins
- 2 tsp. sesame seeds
- ¼ cup low-fat sour cream
- 1 tsp. Dijon mustard
- Salt to taste
- 1 scallion, chopped

Directions:

1. Preheat your oven to 425°F.
2. Mix the teriyaki sauce, chili sauce, garlic, ar ginger.
3. Put the pork on a roasting pan.
4. Brush the sauce on both sides of the pork.
5. Bake in the oven for 15 minutes.
6. Brush with more sauce.

7. Top with sesame seeds.
8. Roast for 10 more minutes.
9. Mix the rest of the ingredients.
10. Serve the pork with mustard sauce.

Nutrition: Calories: 135; Total Fat: 3 g; Saturated Fat: 1 g; Cholesterol: 56 mg; Sodium: 302 mg; Total Carbohydrate: 7 g; Dietary Fiber: 1 g; Total Sugars: 15 g; Protein: 20 g; Potassium: 755 mg

114. Steak With Mushroom Sauce

Preparation Time: 20 minutes
Cooking Time: 5 minutes
Servings: 4
Ingredients:

- 12 oz. sirloin steak, sliced and trimmed
- 2 tsp. grilling seasoning
- 2 tsp. oil
- 6 oz. broccoli, trimmed
- 2 cups frozen peas
- 3 cups fresh mushrooms, sliced
- 1 cup beef broth (unsalted)
- 1 tbsp. mustard
- 2 tsp. cornstarch
- Salt to taste

Directions:

1. Preheat your oven to 350°F.
2. Season meat with grilling seasoning.
3. In a pan over medium-high heat, cook the meat and broccoli for 4 minutes.
4. Sprinkle the peas around the steak.
5. Put the pan inside the oven and bake for 8 minutes.
6. Remove both meat and vegetables from the pan.
7. Add the mushrooms to the pan.
8. Cook for 3 minutes.
9. Mix the broth, mustard, salt, and cornstarch.
10. Add to the mushrooms.
11. Cook for 1 minute.
12. Pour sauce over meat and vegetables before serving.

Nutrition: Calories: 226; Total Fat: 6 g; Saturated Fat: g; Cholesterol: 51 mg; Sodium: 356 mg; Total Carbohydrate: 16 g; Dietary Fiber: 5 g; Total Sugars: 6 g; Protein: 26 g; Potassium: 780 mg

115. Steak With Tomato & Herbs

Preparation Time: 30 minutes
Cooking Time: 30 minutes
Servings: 2
Ingredients:

- 8 oz. beef loin steak, sliced in half
- Salt and pepper to taste
- Cooking spray
- 1 tsp. fresh basil, snipped
- ¼ cup green onion, sliced
- 1/2 cup tomato, chopped

Directions:

1. Season the steak with salt and pepper.
2. Spray oil on your pan.
3. Put the pan over medium-high heat.
4. Once hot, add the steaks.
5. Reduce heat to medium.
6. Cook for 10 to 13 minutes for medium, turning once.
7. Add the basil and green onion.
8. Cook for 2 minutes.
9. Add the tomato.
10. Cook for 1 minute.
11. Let cool a little before slicing.

Nutrition: Calories: 170; Total Fat: 6 g; Saturated Fat: 2 g; Cholesterol: 66 mg; Sodium: 207 mg; Total Carbohydrate: 3 g; Dietary Fiber: 1 g; Total Sugars: 5 g; Protein: 25 g; Potassium: 477 mg

116. Barbecue Beef Brisket

Preparation Time: 25 minutes
Cooking Time: 10 hours
Servings: 10
Ingredients:

- 4 lb. beef brisket (boneless), trimmed and sliced
- 1 bay leaf
- 2 onions, sliced into rings
- 1/2 tsp. dried thyme, crushed
- ¼ cup chili sauce
- 1 garlic clove, minced
- Salt and pepper to taste
- 2 tbsp. light brown sugar
- 2 tbsp. cornstarch

- 2 tbsp. cold water

Directions:
1. Put the meat in a slow cooker.
2. Add the bay leaf and onion.
3. In a bowl, mix the thyme, chili sauce, salt, pepper, and sugar.
4. Pour the sauce over the meat.
5. Mix well.
6. Seal the pot and cook on low heat for 10 hours.
7. Discard the bay leaf.
8. Pour cooking liquid into a pan.
9. Add the mixed water and cornstarch.
10. Simmer until the sauce has thickened.
11. Pour the sauce over the meat.

Nutrition: Calories: 182; Total Fat: 6 g; Saturated Fat: 2 g; Cholesterol: 57 mg; Sodium: 217 mg; Total Sugars: 4 g; Protein: 20 g; Potassium: 383 mg

117.   Beef & Asparagus

Preparation Time: 15 minutes
Cooking Time: 10 minutes
Servings: 4
Ingredients:

- 2 tsp. olive oil
- 1 lb. lean beef sirloin, trimmed and sliced
- 1 carrot, shredded
- Salt and pepper to taste
- 12 oz. asparagus, trimmed and sliced
- 1 tsp. dried herbes de Provence, crushed
- 1/2 cup Marsala
- ¼ tsp. lemon zest

Directions:
1. Pour oil in a pan over medium heat.
2. Add the beef and carrot.
3. Season with salt and pepper.
4. Cook for 3 minutes.
5. Add the asparagus and herbs.
6. Cook for 2 minutes.
7. Add the Marsala and lemon zest.
8. Cook for 5 minutes, stirring frequently.

Nutrition: Calories: 327; Total Fat: 7 g; Saturated Fat: 2 g; Cholesterol: 69 mg; Sodium: 209 mg; Total Carbohydrate: 29 g; Dietary Fiber: 2 g; Total Sugars: 3 g; Protein: 28 g; Potassium: 576 mg

118.   Pork Chops With Grape Sauce

Preparation Time: 15 minutes

Cooking Time: 25 minutes
Servings: 4
Ingredients:

- Cooking spray
- 4 pork chops
- ¼ cup onion, sliced
- 1 garlic clove, minced
- 1/2 cup low-sodium chicken broth
- ¾ cup apple juice
- 1 tbsp. cornstarch
- 1 tbsp. balsamic vinegar
- 1 tsp. honey
- 1 cup seedless red grapes, sliced in half

Directions:
1. Spray oil on your pan.
2. Put it over medium heat.
3. Add the pork chops to the pan.
4. Cook for 5 minutes per side.
5. Remove and set aside.
6. Add onion and garlic.
7. Cook for 2 minutes.
8. Pour in the broth and apple juice.
9. Bring to a boil.
10. Reduce heat to simmer.
11. Put the pork chops back to the skillet.
12. Simmer for 4 minutes.
13. In a bowl, mix the cornstarch, vinegar, and honey.
14. Add to the pan.
15. Cook until the sauce has thickened.
16. Add the grapes.
17. Pour sauce over the pork chops before serving

Nutrition: Calories: 188; Total Fat: 4 g; Saturated Fat: 1 g; Cholesterol: 47 mg; Sodium: 117 mg; Total Carbohydrate: 18 g; Dietary Fiber: 1 g; Total Sugars: 1 g; Protein: 19 g; Potassium: 759 mg

119.   Italian Beef

Preparation Time: 20 minutes
Cooking Time: 1 hour and 20 minutes
Servings: 4
Ingredients:

- Cooking spray
- 1 lb. beef round steak, trimmed and sliced
- 1 cup onion, chopped
- 2 garlic cloves, minced
- 1 cup green bell pepper, chopped
- 1/2 cup celery, chopped

- 2 cups mushrooms, sliced
- 14 1/2 oz. canned diced tomatoes
- 1/2 tsp. dried basil
- ¼ tsp. dried oregano
- 1/8 tsp. crushed red pepper
- 2 tbsp. Parmesan cheese, grated

Directions:

1. Spray oil on the pan over medium heat.
2. Cook the meat until brown on both sides.
3. Transfer meat to a plate.
4. Add the onion, garlic, bell pepper, celery, and mushroom to the pan.
5. Cook until tender.
6. Add the tomatoes, herbs, and pepper.
7. Put the meat back into the pan.
8. Simmer while covered for 1 hour and 15 minutes.
9. Stir occasionally.
10. Sprinkle Parmesan cheese on top of the dish before serving.

Nutrition: Calories: 212; Total Fat: 4 g; Saturated Fat: g; Cholesterol: 51 mg; Sodium: 296 mg; Total Sugars: g; Protein: 30 g; Potassium: 876 mg

120. Lamb With Broccoli & Carrots

Preparation Time: 20 minutes
Cooking Time: 10 minutes
Servings: 4
Ingredients:

- 2 garlic cloves, minced
- 1 tbsp. fresh ginger, grated
- ¼ tsp. red pepper, crushed
- 2 tbsp. low-sodium soy sauce
- 1 tbsp. white vinegar
- 1 tbsp. cornstarch
- 12 oz. lamb meat, trimmed and sliced
- 2 tsp. cooking oil
- 1 lb. broccoli, sliced into florets
- 2 carrots, sliced into strips
- ¾ cup low-sodium beef broth
- 4 green onions, chopped
- 2 cups cooked spaghetti squash pasta

Directions:

1. Combine the garlic, ginger, red pepper, soy sauce, vinegar, and cornstarch in a bowl.
2. Add lamb to the marinade.

3. Marinate for 10 minutes.
4. Discard marinade.
5. In a pan over medium heat, add the oil.
6. Add the lamb and cook for 3 minutes.
7. Transfer lamb to a plate.
8. Add the broccoli and carrots.
9. Cook for 1 minute.
10. Pour in the beef broth.
11. Cook for 5 minutes.
12. Put the meat back into the pan.
13. Sprinkle with green onion and serve on top of spaghetti squash.

Nutrition: Calories: 205; Total Fat: 6 g; Saturated Fat: 1 g; Cholesterol: 40 mg; Sodium: 659 mg; Total Carbohydrate: 17 g

121. Rosemary Lamb

Preparation Time: 15 minutes
Cooking Time: 2 hours
Servings: 14
Ingredients:

- Salt and pepper to taste
- 2 tsp. fresh rosemary, snipped
- 5 lb. whole leg of lamb, trimmed and cut with slits on all sides
- 3 garlic cloves, slivered
- 1 cup water

Directions:

1. Preheat your oven to 375°F.
2. Mix salt, pepper, and rosemary in a bowl.
3. Sprinkle mixture all over the lamb.
4. Insert slivers of garlic into the slits.
5. Put the lamb on a roasting pan.
6. Add water to the pan.
7. Roast for 2 hours.

Nutrition: Calories: 136; Total Fat: 4 g; Saturated Fat: 1 g; Cholesterol: 71 mg; Sodium: 218 mg; Protein: 23 g; Potassium: 248 mg

122. Mediterranean Lamb Meatballs

Preparation Time: 10 minutes
Cooking Time: 20 minutes
Servings: 8
Ingredients:

- 12 oz. roasted red peppers
- 1 1/2 cups whole wheat breadcrumbs
- 2 eggs, beaten

- 1/3 cup tomato sauce
- 1/2 cup fresh basil
- ¼ cup parsley, snipped
- Salt and pepper to taste
- 2 lb. lean ground lamb

Directions:

1. Preheat your oven to 350°F.
2. In a bowl, mix all the ingredients and then form them into meatballs.
3. Put the meatballs on a baking pan.
4. Bake in the oven for 20 minutes.

Nutrition: Calories: 94; Total Fat: 3 g; Saturated Fat: 1 g; Cholesterol: 35 mg; Sodium: 170 mg; Total Carbohydrate: 2 g; Dietary Fiber: 1 g; Total Sugars: 0 g

123. Shrimp with Green Beans

Preparation Time: 10 minutes
Cooking Time: 2 Minutes
Servings: 4
Ingredients:

- ¾ pound fresh green beans, trimmed
- 1 pound medium frozen shrimp, peeled and deveined
- 2 tbsp. fresh lemon juice
- 2 tbsp. olive oil
- Salt and ground black pepper, as required

Directions:

1. Arrange a steamer trivet in the Instant Pot and pour a cup of water.
2. Arrange the green beans on top of the trivet in a single layer and top with shrimp.
3. Drizzle with oil and lemon juice.
4. Sprinkle with salt and black pepper.
5. Close the lid and place the pressure valve in the "Seal" position.
6. Press "Steam" and just use the default time of 2 minutes.
7. Press "Cancel" and allow a "Natural" release.
8. Open the lid and serve.

Nutrition: Calories: 223; Fat: 1g; Carbs: 7.9g; Sugar: .4g; Proteins: 27.4g; Sodium: 322mg

124. Crab Curry

Preparation Time: 10 minutes
Cooking Time: 20 Minutes
Servings: 2
Ingredients:

- 0.5 lb. chopped crab
- 1 thinly sliced red onion
- 0.5 cup chopped tomato
- 3 tbsp. curry paste
- 1 tbsp. oil or ghee

Directions:

1. Set the Instant Pot to sauté and add the onion, oil, and curry paste.
2. When the onion is soft, add the remaining ingredients and seal.
3. Cook on Stew for 20 minutes.

4. Release the pressure naturally.

Nutrition: Calories: 2; Carbs: 11g; Sugar: 4g; Fat: 10g; Protein: 24g; GL: 9

125. Mixed Chowder

Preparation Time: 10 minutes
Cooking Time: 35 Minutes
Servings: 2
Ingredients:

- 1 lb. fish stew mix
- 2 cups white sauce
- 3 tbsp. old bay seasoning

Directions:

1. Mix all the ingredients in your Instant Pot.
2. Cook on Stew for 35 minutes.
3. Release the pressure naturally.

Nutrition: Calories: 320; Carbs: 9g; Sugar: 2g; Fat: 16g; Protein: GL: 4

126. Mussels In Tomato Sauce

Preparation Time: 10 minutes
Cooking Time: 3 Minutes
Servings: 4
Ingredients:

- 2 tomatoes, seeded and chopped finely
- 2 pounds mussels, scrubbed and de-bearded
- 1 cup low-sodium chicken broth
- 1 tbsp. fresh lemon juice
- 2 garlic cloves, minced

Directions:

1. In the pot of Instant Pot, place tomatoes, garlic, wine, and bay leaf and stir to combine.
2. Arrange the mussels on top.
3. Close the lid and place the pressure valve in the "Seal" position.
4. Press "Manual" and cook under "High Pressure" for about 3 minutes.
5. Press "Cancel" and carefully allow a "Quick" release.
6. Open the lid and serve hot.

Nutrition: Calories: 213; Fat: 25.2g; Carbs: 11g; Sugar: 1g; Proteins: 28.2g; Sodium: 670mg

127.   Citrus Salmon

Preparation Time: 10 minutes
Cooking Time: 7 Minutes
Servings: 4
Ingredients:

- 4 (4-ounce) salmon fillets
- 1 cup low-sodium chicken broth
- 1 tsp. fresh ginger, minced
- 2 tsp. fresh orange zest, grated finely
- 3 tbsp. fresh orange juice
- 1 tbsp. olive oil
- Ground black pepper, as required

Directions:

1. In Instant Pot, add all ingredients and mix.
2. Close the lid and place the pressure valve in the "Seal" position.
3. Press "Manual" and cook under "High Pressure" for about 7 minutes.
4. Press "Cancel" and allow a "Natural" release.
5. Open the lid and serve the salmon fillets with the topping of cooking sauce.

Nutrition: Calories: 190; Fat: 10.5g; Carbs: 1.8g; Sugar: 1g; Proteins: 22g; Sodium: 68mg

128.   Herbed Salmon

Preparation Time: 10 minutes
Cooking Time: 3 Minutes
Servings: 4
Ingredients:

- 4 (4-ounce) salmon fillets
- ¼ cup olive oil
- 2 tbsp. fresh lemon juice
- 1 garlic clove, minced
- ¼ tsp. dried oregano
- Salt and ground black pepper, as required
- 4 fresh rosemary sprigs
- 4 lemon slices

Directions:

1. For the dressing: in a large bowl, add oil, lemon juice, garlic, oregano, salt, and black pepper and beat until well co combined.
2. Arrange a steamer trivet in the Instant Pot and pour 1 1/2 cups of water in Instant Pot.
3. Place the salmon fillets on top of the trivet in a single layer and top with dressing.
4. Arrange 1 rosemary sprig and 1 lemon slice over each fillet.

5. Close the lid and place the pressure valve in the "Seal" position.
6. Press "Steam" and just use the default time of 3 minutes.
7. Press "Cancel" and carefully allow a "Quick" release.
8. Open the lid and serve hot.

Nutrition: Calories: 262; Fat: 17g; Carbs: 0.7g; Sugar: 0.2g; Proteins: 22.1g; Sodium: 91mg

129.   Salmon In Green Sauce

Preparation Time: 10 minutes
Cooking Time: 12 Minutes
Servings: 4
Ingredients:

- 4 (6-ounce) salmon fillets
- 1 avocado, peeled, pitted, and chopped
- 1/2 cup fresh basil, chopped
- 3 garlic cloves, chopped
- 1 tbsp. fresh lemon zest, grated finely

Directions:

1. Grease a large piece of foil.
2. In a large bowl, add all ingredients except salmon and water, and with a fork, mash completely.
3. Place fillets in the center of foil and top with the avocado mixture evenly.
4. Fold the foil around fillets to seal them.
5. Arrange a steamer trivet in the Instant Pot and pour 1/2 cup of water.
6. Place the foil packet on top of the trivet.
7. Close the lid and place the pressure valve in the "Seal" position.
8. Press "Manual" and cook under "High Pressure" for about minutes.
9. Meanwhile, preheat the oven to broil.
10. Press "Cancel" and allow a "Natural" release
11. Open the lid and transfer the salmon fille onto a broiler pan.
12. Broil for about 3–4 minutes.
13. Serve warm.

Nutrition: Calories: 333; Fat: 20.3g; Carbs: 5.5 Sugar: 0.4g; Proteins: 34.2g; Sodium: 79mg

130.   Braised Shrimp

Preparation Time: 10 minutes
Cooking Time: 4 Minutes
Servings: 4

Ingredients:

- 1 pound frozen large shrimp, peeled and deveined
- 2 shallots, chopped
- ¾ cup low-sodium chicken broth
- 2 tbsp. fresh lemon juice
- 2 tbsp. olive oil
- 1 tbsp. garlic, crushed
- Ground black pepper, as required

Directions:

1. In the Instant Pot, place oil and press "Sauté." Now add the shallots and cook for about 2 minutes.
2. Add the garlic and cook for about 1 minute.
3. Press "Cancel" and stir in the shrimp, broth, lemon juice, and black pepper.
4. Close the lid and place the pressure valve in the "Seal" position.
5. Press "Manual" and cook under "High Pressure" for about 1 minute.
6. Press "Cancel" and carefully allow a "Quick" release.
7. Open the lid and serve hot.

Nutrition: Calories: 209; Fat: 9g; Carbs: 4.3g; Sugar: 0.2g; Proteins: 26.6g; Sodium: 293mg

131. Shrimp Coconut Curry

Preparation Time: 10 minutes
Cooking Time: 20 Minutes
Servings: 2
Ingredients:

- 0.5 lb. cooked shrimp
- 1 thinly sliced onion
- 1 cup coconut yogurt
- 3 tbsp. curry paste
- 1 tbsp. oil or ghee

Directions:

1. Set the Instant Pot to sauté and add the onion, oil, and curry paste.
2. When the onion is soft, add the remaining ingredients and seal.
3. Cook on Stew for 20 minutes.
4. Release the pressure naturally.

Nutrition: Calories: 380; Carbs: 13g; Sugar: 4g; Fat: 2g; Protein: 40g; GL: 14

132. Trout Bake

Preparation Time: 10 minutes
Cooking Time: 35 Minutes
Servings: 2
Ingredients:

- 1 lb. trout fillets, boneless
- 1 lb. chopped winter vegetables
- 1 cup low sodium fish broth
- 1 tbsp. mixed herbs
- Sea salt as desired

Directions:

1. Mix all the ingredients except the broth in a foil pouch.
2. Place the pouch in the steamer basket in your Instant Pot.
3. Pour the broth into the Instant Pot.
4. Cook on Steam for 35 minutes.
5. Release the pressure naturally.

Nutrition: Calories: 310; Carbs: 14g; Sugar: 2g; Fat: 12g; Protein: 40g; GL: 5

133. Sardine Curry

Preparation Time: 10 minutes
Cooking Time: 35 Minutes
Servings: 2
Ingredients:

- 5 tins sardines in tomato
- 1 lb. chopped vegetables
- 1 cup low sodium fish broth
- 3 tbsp. curry paste

Directions:

1. Mix all the ingredients in your Instant Pot.
2. Cook on Stew for 35 minutes.
3. Release the pressure naturally.

Nutrition: Calories: 320; Carbs: 8; Sugar: 2; Fat: 16; Protein: GL: 3

134. Swordfish Steak

Preparation Time: 10 minutes
Cooking Time: 35 Minutes
Servings: 2
Ingredients:

- 1 lb. swordfish steak, whole
- 1 lb. chopped Mediterranean vegetables
- 1 cup low sodium fish broth
- 2 tbsp. soy sauce

Directions:

1. Mix all the ingredients except the broth in a foil pouch.
2. Place the pouch in the steamer basket for your Instant Pot.
3. Pour the broth into the Instant Pot. Lower the steamer basket into the Instant Pot.
4. Cook on Steam for 35 minutes.
5. Release the pressure naturally.

Nutrition: Calories: 270; Carbs: 5g; Sugar: 1g; Fat: 10g; Protein: 48g; GL: 1

135.   Lemon Sole

Preparation Time: 10 minutes
Cooking Time: 5 Minutes
Servings: 2
Ingredients:

- 1 lb. sole fillets, boned and skinned
- 1 cup low sodium fish broth
- 2 shredded sweet onions
- juice of half a lemon
- 2 tbsp. dried cilantro

Directions:

1. Mix all the ingredients in your Instant Pot.
2. Cook on Stew for 5 minutes.
3. Release the pressure naturally.

Nutrition: Calories: 230; Sugar: 1g; Fat: 6; Protein: 46g; GL: 1

136.   Lemony Salmon

Preparation Time: 10 minutes
Cooking Time: 3 Minutes
Servings: 3
Ingredients:

- 1 pound salmon fillet, cut into 3 pieces
- 3 tsp. fresh dill, chopped
- 5 tbsp. fresh lemon juice, divided
- Salt and ground black pepper, as required

Directions:

1. Arrange a steamer trivet in Instant Pot and pour ¼ cup of lemon juice.
2. Season the salmon with salt and black pepper evenly.
3. Place the salmon pieces on top of the trivet, skin side down, and drizzle with remaining lemon juice.
4. Now, sprinkle the salmon pieces with dill evenly.
5. Close the lid and place the pressure valve in the "Seal" position.

6. Press "Steam" and use the default time of 3 minutes.
7. Press "Cancel" and allow a "Natural" release.
8. Open the lid and serve hot.

Nutrition: Calories: 20; Fats: 9.6g; Carbs: 1.1g; Sugar: 0.5g; Proteins: 29.7g; Sodium: 74mg

137.   Tuna Sweet Corn Casserole

Preparation Time: 10 minutes
Cooking Time: 35 Minutes
Servings: 2
Ingredients:

- 3 small tins tuna
- 0.5 lb. sweet corn kernels
- 1 lb. chopped vegetables
- 1 cup low sodium vegetable broth
- 2 tbsp. spicy seasoning

Directions:

1. Mix all the ingredients in your Instant Pot.
2. Cook on Stew for 35 minutes.
3. Release the pressure naturally.

Nutrition: Calories: 300; Carbs: 6; Sugar: 1; Fat: 9; GL: 2

138.   Lemon Pepper Salmon

Preparation Time: 10 minutes
Cooking Time: 10 Minutes
Servings: 4
Ingredients:

- 3 tbsp. ghee or avocado oil
- 1 lb. skin-on salmon filet
- 1 julienned red bell pepper
- 1 julienned green zucchini
- 1 julienned carrot
- ¾ cup water
- A few sprigs parsley, tarragon, dill, basil, or combination
- 1/2 sliced lemon
- 1/2 tsp. black pepper
- ¼ tsp. sea salt

Directions:

1. Add the water and the herbs into the bottom of the Instant Pot and put in a wire steam rack making sure the handles extend upward

2. Place the salmon filet onto the wire rack, with the skin side facing down.
3. Drizzle the salmon with ghee, season with black pepper and salt, and top with the lemon slices.
4. Close and seal the Instant Pot, making sure the vent is turned to "Sealing."
5. Select the "Steam" setting and cook for 3 minutes.
6. While the salmon cooks, julienne the vegetables, and set them aside.
7. Once done, quickly release the pressure, and then press the "Keep Warm/Cancel" button.
8. Uncover and wear oven mitts to carefully remove the steamer rack with the salmon.
9. Remove the herbs and discard them.
10. Add the vegetables to the pot and put the lid back on.
11. Select the "Sauté" function and cook for 1–2 minutes.
12. Serve the vegetables with salmon and add the remaining fat to the pot.
13. Pour a little of the sauce over the fish and vegetables if desired.

Nutrition: Calories: 296; Carbs: 8g; Fat: 15 g; Protein: 31 g; Potassium (K): 1084 mg; Sodium (Na): 284 mg

139. Baked Salmon With Garlic Parmesan Topping

Preparation Time: 5 minutes,
Cooking Time: 20 minutes,
Servings: 4
Ingredients:

- 1 lb. wild-caught salmon filets
- 2 tbsp. margarine

What you'll need from the store cupboard:

- ¼ cup reduced-fat parmesan cheese, grated
- ¼ cup light mayonnaise
- 2–3 garlic cloves, diced
- 2 tbsp. parsley
- Salt and pepper

Directions:

1. Heat oven to 350°F and line a baking pan with parchment paper.
2. Place salmon on pan and season with salt and pepper.

3. In a medium skillet, over medium heat, melt butter. Add garlic and cook, stirring 1 minute.
4. Reduce heat to low and add remaining ingredients. Stir until everything is melted and combined.
5. Spread evenly over salmon and bake 15 minutes for thawed fish or 20 for frozen. Salmon is done when it flakes easily with a fork. Serve.

Nutrition: Calories: 408; Total Carbs: 4g; Protein: 41g; Fat: 24g; Sugar: 1g; Fiber: 0g

140. Blackened Shrimp

Preparation Time: 5 minutes
Cooking Time: 5 minutes
Servings: 4
Ingredients:

- 1 1/2 lb. shrimp, peel & devein
- 4 lime wedges
- 4 tbsp. cilantro, chopped

What you'll need from the store cupboard:

- 4 garlic cloves, diced
- 1 tbsp. chili powder
- 1 tbsp. paprika
- 1 tbsp. olive oil
- 2 tsp. Splenda brown sugar
- 1 tsp. cumin
- 1 tsp. oregano
- 1 tsp. garlic powder
- 1 tsp. salt
- 1/2 tsp. pepper

Directions:

1. In a small bowl combine seasonings and Splenda brown sugar.
2. Heat oil in a skillet over med-high heat. Add shrimp, in a single layer, and cook 1–2 minutes per side.
3. Add seasonings, and cook, stirring, 30 seconds. Serve garnished with cilantro and a lime wedge.

Nutrition: Calories: 252; Total Carbs: 7g; Net Carbs: 6g; Protein: 39g; Fat: 7g; Sugar: 2g; Fiber: 1g

141. Cajun Catfish

Preparation Time: 5 minutes
Cooking Time: 15 minutes
Servings: 4
Ingredients:

- 4 (8 oz.) catfish fillets

What you'll need from the store cupboard:
- 2 tbsp. olive oil
- 2 tsp. garlic salt
- 2 tsp. thyme
- 2 tsp. paprika
- 1/2 tsp. cayenne pepper
- 1/2 tsp. red hot sauce
- ¼ tsp. black pepper
- Nonstick cooking spray

Directions:
1. Heat oven to 450°F. Spray a 9x13-inch baking dish with cooking spray.
2. In a small bowl whisk together everything but catfish. Brush both sides of fillets, using all the spice mix.
3. Bake 10–13 minutes or until fish flakes easily with a fork. Serve.

Nutrition: Calories: 366; Total Carbs: 0g; Protein: 35g; Fat: 24g; Sugar: 0g; Fiber: 0g

142. Cajun Flounder & Tomatoes

Preparation Time: 10 minutes
Cooking Time: 15 minutes
Servings: 4
Ingredients:
- 4 flounder fillets
- 2 1/2 cups tomatoes, diced
- ¾ cup onion, diced
- ¾ cup green bell pepper, diced

What you'll need from the store cupboard:
- 2 garlic cloves, diced fine
- 1 tbsp. Cajun seasoning
- 1 tsp. olive oil

Directions:
1. Heat oil in a large skillet over med-high heat. Add onion and garlic and cook 2 minutes, or until soft. Add tomatoes, peppers, and spices, and cook 2–3 minutes until tomatoes soften.
2. Lay fish over top. Cover, reduce heat to medium, and cook, 5–8 minutes, or until fish flakes easily with a fork. Transfer fish to serving plates and top with sauce.

Nutrition: Calories: 194; Total Carbs: 8g; Net Carbs: 6g; Protein: 32g; Fat: 3g; Sugar: 5g; Fiber: 2g

143. Cajun Shrimp & Roasted Vegetables

Preparation Time: 5 minutes
Cooking Time: 15 minutes
Servings: 4
Ingredients:
- 1 lb. large shrimp, peeled and deveined
- 2 zucchinis, sliced
- 2 yellow squash, sliced
- 1/2 bunch asparagus, cut into thirds
- 2 red bell pepper, cut into chunks

What you'll need from the store cupboard:
- 2 tbsp. olive oil
- 2 tbsp. Cajun Seasoning
- Salt & pepper, to taste

Directions:
1. Heat oven to 400°F.
2. Combine shrimp and vegetables in a large bowl. Add oil and seasoning and toss to coat.
3. Spread evenly in a large baking sheet and bake 15–20 minutes, or until vegetables are tender. Serve.

Nutrition: Calories: 251; Total Carbs: 13g; Net Carbs 9g; Protein: 30g; Fat: 9g; Sugar: 6g; Fiber: 4g

144. Cilantro Lime Grilled Shrimp

Preparation Time: 5 minutes,
Cooking Time: 5 minutes,
Servings: 6
Ingredients:
- 1 1/2 lb. large shrimp raw, peeled, deveine with tails on
- Juice and zest of 1 lime
- 2 tbsp. fresh cilantro chopped

What you'll need from the store cupboard:
- ¼ cup olive oil
- 2 garlic cloves, diced fine
- 1 tsp. smoked paprika
- ¼ tsp. cumin
- 1/2 tsp. salt
- ¼ tsp. cayenne pepper

Directions:
1. Place the shrimp in a large Ziploc bag.

2. Mix remaining ingredients in a small bowl and pour over shrimp. Let marinate for 20–30 minutes.
3. Heat up the grill. Skewer the shrimp and cook 2–3 minutes, per side, just until they turn pink. Be careful not to overcook them. Serve garnished with cilantro.

Nutrition: Calories: 317; Total Carbs: 4g; Protein: 39g; Fat: 15g; Sugar: 0g; Fiber: 0g

145.   Crab Frittata

Preparation Time: 10 minutes
Cooking Time: 50 minutes
Servings: 4
Ingredients:

- 4 eggs
- 2 cups lump crabmeat
- 1 cup half-n-half
- 1 cup green onions, diced

What you'll need from the store cupboard:

- 1 cup reduced-fat parmesan cheese, grated
- 1 tsp. salt
- 1 tsp. pepper
- 1 tsp. smoked paprika
- 1 tsp. Italian seasoning
- Nonstick cooking spray

Directions:

1. Heat oven to 350°F. Spray an 8-inch springform pan, or pie plate with cooking spray.
2. In a large bowl, whisk together the eggs and half-n-half. Add seasonings and parmesan cheese, stir to mix.
3. Stir in the onions and crab meat. Pour into prepared pan and bake for 35–40 minutes, or until eggs are set and the top is lightly browned.
4. Let cool for 10 minutes, then slice and serve warm or at room temperature.

Nutrition: Calories: 276; Total Carbs: 5g; Net Carbs: g; Protein: 25g; Fat: 17g; Sugar: 1g; Fiber: 1g

146.   Crunchy Lemon Shrimp

Preparation Time: 5 minutes
Cooking Time: 10 minutes
Servings: 4
Ingredients:

- 1 lb. raw shrimp, peeled and deveined

- 2 tbsp. Italian parsley, roughly chopped
- 2 tbsp. lemon juice, divided

What you'll need from the store cupboard:

- 2/3 cup panko bread crumbs
- 2 1/2 tbsp. olive oil, divided
- Salt and pepper, to taste

Directions:

1. Heat oven to 400°F.
2. Place the shrimp evenly in a baking dish and sprinkle with salt and pepper. Drizzle on 1 tbsp. lemon juice and 1 tbsp. of olive oil. Set aside.
3. In a medium bowl, combine parsley, remaining lemon juice, bread crumbs, remaining olive oil, and ¼ tsp. each of salt and pepper. Layer the panko mixture evenly on top of the shrimp.
4. Bake 8–10 minutes or until shrimp are cooked through and the panko is golden brown.

Nutrition: Calories: 283; Total Carbs: 15g; Net Carbs: 14g; Protein: 28g; Fat: 12g; Sugar: 1g; Fiber: 1g

147.   Grilled Tuna Steaks

Preparation Time: 5 minutes
Cooking Time: 10 minutes
Servings: 6
Ingredients:

- 6 6 oz. tuna steaks
- 3 tbsp. fresh basil, diced

What you'll need from the store cupboard:

- 4 1/2 tsp. olive oil
- ¾ tsp. salt
- ¼ tsp. pepper
- Nonstick cooking spray

Directions:

1. Heat grill to medium heat. Spray rack with cooking spray.
2. Drizzle both sides of the tuna with oil. Sprinkle with basil, salt, and pepper.
3. Place on grill and cook 5 minutes per side, tuna should be slightly pink in the center. Serve.

Nutrition: Calories: 343; Total Carbs: 0g; Protein: 51g; Fat: 14g; Sugar: 0g; Fiber: 0g

148.   Red Clam Sauce & Pasta

Preparation Time: 10 minutes

Cooking Time: 3 hours
Servings: 4
Ingredients:

- 1 onion, diced
- ¼ cup fresh parsley, diced

What you'll need from the store cupboard:

- 2 6 1/2 oz. cans clams, chopped, undrained
- 14 1/2 oz. tomatoes, diced, undrained
- 6 oz. tomato paste
- 2 garlic cloves, diced
- 1 bay leaf
- 1 tbsp. sunflower oil
- 1 tsp. Splenda
- 1 tsp. basil
- 1/2 tsp. thyme
- 1/2 Homemade Pasta, cook & drain

Directions:

1. Heat oil in a small skillet over med-high heat. Add onion and cook until tender, add garlic and cook 1 minute more. Transfer to the crockpot.
2. Add remaining ingredients, except pasta, cover, and cook on low for 3–4 hours.
3. Discard bay leaf and serve over cooked pasta.

Nutrition: Calories: 223; Total Carbs: 32g; Net Carbs: 27g; Protein: 12g; Fat: 6g; Sugar: 15g; Fiber: 5g

149. Salmon Milano

Preparation Time: 10 minutes
Cooking Time: 20 minutes
Servings: 6
Ingredients:

- 2 1/2 lb. salmon filet
- 2 tomatoes, sliced
- 1/2 cup margarine

What you'll need from the store cupboard:

- 1/2 cup basil pesto

Directions:

1. Heat the oven to 400°F. Line a 9x15-inch baking sheet with foil, making sure it covers the sides. Place another large piece of foil onto the baking sheet and place the salmon filet on top of it.
2. Place the pesto and margarine in a blender or food processor and pulse until smooth. Spread evenly over salmon. Place tomato slices on top.

3. Wrap the foil around the salmon, tenting around the top to prevent foil from touching the salmon as much as possible. Bake 15–25 minutes, or salmon flakes easily with a fork. Serve.

Nutrition: Calories: 444; Total Carbs: 2g; Protein: 55g; Fat: 24g; Sugar: 1g; Fiber: 0g

150. Shrimp & Artichoke Skillet

Preparation Time: 5 minutes
Cooking Time: 10 minutes
Servings: 4
Ingredients:

- 1 1/2 cups shrimp, peel & devein
- 2 shallots, diced
- 1 tbsp. margarine

What you'll need from the store cupboard

- 2 12 oz. jars artichoke hearts, drain & rinse
- 2 cups white wine
- 2 garlic cloves, diced fine

Directions:

1. Melt margarine in a large skillet over med-high heat. Add shallot and garlic and cook until the start to brown, stirring frequently.
2. Add artichokes and cook for 5 minutes. Reduce heat and add wine. Cook 3 minutes stirring occasionally.
3. Add the shrimp and cook just until they turn pink. Serve.

Nutrition: Calories: 487; Total Carbs: 26g; Net Carbs: 17g; Protein: 64g; Fat: 5g; Sugar: 3g; Fiber: 9g

151. Tuna Carbonara

Preparation Time: 5 minutes
Cooking Time: 25 minutes
Servings: 4
Ingredients:

- 1/2 lb. tuna fillet, cut into pieces
- 2 eggs
- 4 tbsp. fresh parsley, diced

What you'll need from the store cupboard:

- 1/2 Homemade Pasta, cook & drain,
- 1/2 cup reduced-fat parmesan cheese
- 2 garlic cloves, peeled
- 2 tbsp. extra virgin olive oil
- Salt & pepper, to taste

Directions:

1. In a small bowl, beat the eggs, parmesan, and a dash of pepper.
2. Heat the oil in a large skillet over med-high heat. Add garlic and cook until browned. Add the tuna and cook 2–3 minutes, or until the tuna is almost cooked through. Discard the garlic.
3. Add the pasta and reduce heat. Stir in egg mixture and cook, stirring constantly, 2 minutes. If the sauce is too thick, thin with water, a little bit at a time, until it has a creamy texture.
4. Salt and pepper to taste and serve garnished with parsley.

Nutrition: Calories: 409; Total Carbs: 7g; Net Carbs: 6g; Protein: 25g; Fat: 30g; Sugar: 3g; Fiber: 1g

152. Mediterranean Fish Fillets

Preparation Time: 10 minutes
Cooking Time: 3 minutes
Servings: 4
Ingredients:

- 4 cod fillets
- 1 lb. grape tomatoes, halved
- 1 cup olives, pitted and sliced
- 2 tbsp. capers
- 1 tsp. dried thyme
- 2 tbsp. olive oil
- 1 tsp. garlic, minced
- Pepper
- Salt

Directions:

1. Pour 1 cup of water into the instant pot then place the steamer rack in the pot.
2. Spray heat-safe baking dish with cooking spray.
3. Add half grape tomatoes into the dish and season with pepper and salt.
4. Arrange fish fillets on top of cherry tomatoes. Drizzle with oil and season with garlic, thyme, capers, pepper, and salt.
5. Spread olives and remaining grape tomatoes on top of fish fillets.
6. Place dish on top of steamer rack in the pot.
7. Seal pot with a lid and select manual and cook on high for 3 minutes.
8. Once done, release pressure using quick release. Remove lid.
9. Serve and enjoy.

Nutrition: Calories: 212; Fat: 11.9 g; Carbohydrates: 7.1 g; Sugar: 3 g; Protein: 21.4 g; Cholesterol: 55 mg

153.   Thai Quinoa Salad

Preparation Time: 10 minutes
Cooking Time: 0 minutes
Servings: 1–2
Ingredients:
For the dressing:

- 1 tbsp. Sesame seed
- 1 tsp. Chopped garlic
- 1 tsp. Lemon, fresh juice
- 3 tsp. Apple Cider Vinegar
- 2 tsp. Tamari, gluten-free.
- 1/4 cup tahini (sesame butter)
- 1 pitted date
- 1/2 tsp. Salt
- 1/2 tsp. toasted Sesame oil

For the salad:

- 1 cup quinoa, steamed
- 1 big handful arugula
- 1 tomato cut into pieces
- 1/4 red onion, diced

Directions:

1. Add the following to a small blender: 1/4 cup + 2 tbsp.
2. Filtered water, the rest of the ingredients. Blend, man. Steam 1 cup of quinoa in a steamer or a rice pan, then set aside.
3. Combine the quinoa, the arugula, the tomatoes sliced, the red onion diced on a serving plate or bowl, add the Thai dressing and serve with a spoon.

Nutrition: Calories: 100; Carbohydrates: 12 g

154.   Green Goddess Bowl And Avocado Cumin Dressing

Preparation Time: 10 minutes
Cooking Time: 0 minutes
Servings: 1–2
Ingredients:
For the avocado cumin dressing:

- 1 Avocado
- 1 tbsp. Cumin Powder

- 2 limes, freshly squeezed
- 1 cup of filtered water
- 1/4 seconds. sea salt
- 1 tbsp. Olive extra virgin olive oil
- Cayenne pepper dash
- Optional: 1/4 tsp. Smoked pepper

Tahini Lemon Dressing:

- 1/4 cup tahini (sesame butter)
- 1/2 cup filtered water (more if you want thinner, less thick)
- 1/2 lemon, freshly squeezed
- 1 garlic clove, minced
- 3/4 tsp. Sea salt (Celtic Gray, Himalayan Redmond Real Salt)
- 1 tbsp. Olive extra virgin olive oil
- black pepper taste

Salad:

- 3 cups kale, chopped
- 1/2 cup broccoli flowers, chopped
- 1/2 zucchini (make spiral noodles)
- 1/2 cup kelp noodles, soaked and drained
- 1/3 cup cherry tomatoes, halved.
- 2 tsp. hemp seeds

Directions:

1. Gently steam the kale and the broccoli (flash the steam for 4 minutes), set aside.
2. Mix the zucchini noodles and kelp noodles an toss with a generous portion of the smoke avocado cumin dressing. Add the cherr tomatoes and stir again.
3. Place the steamed kale and broccoli and drizzl with the lemon tahini dressing. Top the kal and the broccoli with the noodles an tomatoes and sprinkle the whole dish with th hemp seeds.

Nutrition: Calories: 89; Carbohydrates: 11g; Fat: 1.2 Protein: 4g

155.   7 Sweet And Savory Salad

Preparation Time: 10 minutes
Cooking Time: 0 minutes
Servings: 1–2
Ingredients:

- 1 big head butter lettuce

- 1/2 cucumber, sliced
- 1 pomegranate, seed, or 1/3 cup seed
- 1 avocado, 1 cubed
- 1/4 cup shelled pistachio, chopped

Ingredients: for dressing:
- 1/4 cup apple cider vinegar
- 1/2 cup olive oil
- 1 garlic clove, minced

Directions:
1. Put the butter lettuce in a salad bowl.
2. Add the remaining ingredients and toss with the salad dressing.

Nutrition: Calories: 68; Carbohydrates: 8g; Fat: 1.2g; Protein: 2g

156. Kale Pesto's Pasta

Preparation Time: 10 minutes
Cooking Time: 0 minutes
Servings: 1–2
Ingredients:
- 1 bunch kale
- 2 cups fresh basil
- 1/4 cup extra virgin olive oil
- 1/2 cup walnuts
- 2 limes, freshly squeezed
- Sea salt and chili pepper
- 1 zucchini, noodle (spiralizer)
- Optional: garnish with chopped asparagus, spinach leaves, and tomato.

Directions:
1. The night before, soak the walnuts to improve absorption.
2. Put all the recipe ingredients in a blender and blend until the consistency of the cream is reached.
3. Add the zucchini noodles and enjoy.

Nutrition: Calories: 55; Carbohydrates: 9 g; Fat: 1.2g

157. Beet Salad With Basil Dressing

Preparation Time: 10 minutes
Cooking Time: 0 minutes
Servings: 4
Ingredients:
for the dressing
- ¼ cup blackberries
- ¼ cup extra-virgin olive oil

- Juice of 1 lemon
- 2 tbsp. minced fresh basil
- 1 tsp. poppy seeds
- A pinch sea salt

For the salad
- 2 celery stalks, chopped
- 4 cooked beets, peeled and chopped
- 1 cup blackberries
- 4 cups spring mix

Directions:
1. To make the dressing, mash the blackberries in a bowl. Whisk in the oil, lemon juice, basil, poppy seeds, and sea salt.
2. To make the salad: Add the celery, beets, blackberries, and spring mix to the bowl with the dressing.
3. Combine and serve.

Nutrition: Calories: 192; Fat: 15g; Carbohydrates: 15g; Protein: 2g

158. Basic Salad with Olive Oil Dressing

Preparation Time: 10 minutes
Cooking Time: 0 minute
Servings: 4
Ingredients:
- 1 cup coarsely chopped iceberg lettuce
- 1 cup coarsely chopped romaine lettuce
- 1 cup fresh baby spinach
- 1 large tomato, hulled and coarsely chopped
- 1 cup diced cucumber
- 2 tbsp. extra-virgin olive oil
- ¼ tsp. of sea salt

Directions:
1. In a bowl, combine the spinach and lettuces. Add the tomato and cucumber.
2. Drizzle with oil and sprinkle with sea salt.
3. Mix and serve.

Nutrition: Calories: 77; Fat: 4g; Carbohydrates: 3g; Protein: 1g

159. Spinach & Orange Salad with Oil Drizzle

Preparation Time: 10 minutes
Cooking Time: 0 minute
Servings: 4
Ingredients:

- 4 cups fresh baby spinach
- 1 blood orange, coarsely chopped
- ½ red onion, thinly sliced
- ½ shallot, finely chopped
- 2 tbsp. minced fennel fronds
- Juice of 1 lemon
- 1 tbsp. extra-virgin olive oil
- Pinch sea salt

Directions:
1. In a bowl, toss together the spinach, orange, red onion, shallot, and fennel fronds.
2. Add the lemon juice, oil, and sea salt.
3. Mix and serve.

Nutrition: Calories: 79; Fat: 2g; Carbohydrates: 8g; Protein: 1g

160. Fruit Salad With Coconut-Lime Dressing

Preparation Time: 5 minutes
Cooking Time: 0 minutes
Servings: 4
Ingredients:
For the dressing
- ¼ cup full-fat canned coconut milk
- 1 tbsp. raw honey
- Juice of ½ lime
- Pinch sea salt

For the salad
- 2 bananas, thinly sliced
- 2 mandarin oranges, segmented
- ½ cup strawberries, thinly sliced
- ½ cup raspberries
- ½ cup blueberries

Directions:
1. To make the dressing: whisk all the dressing ingredients in a bowl.
2. To make the salad: Add the salad ingredients to a bowl and mix.
3. Drizzle with the dressing and serve.

Nutrition: Calories: 141; Fat: 3g; Carbohydrates: 30g; Protein: 2g

161. Cranberry and Brussels Sprouts with Dressing

Preparation Time: 10 minutes

Cooking Time: 0 minute
Servings: 4
Ingredients:
For the dressing
- ⅓ cup extra-virgin olive oil
- 2 tbsp. apple cider vinegar
- 1 tbsp. pure maple syrup
- Juice of 1 orange
- ½ tbsp. dried rosemary
- 1 tbsp. scallion, whites only
- Pinch sea salt

For the salad
- 1 bunch scallions, greens only, finely chopped
- 1 cup Brussels sprouts, stemmed, halved, and thinly sliced
- ½ cup fresh cranberries
- 4 cups fresh baby spinach

Directions:
1. To make the dressing: In a bowl, whisk the dressing ingredients.
2. To make the salad: Add the scallions, Brussel sprouts, cranberries, and spinach to the bowl with the dressing.
3. Combine and serve.

Nutrition: Calories: 267; Fat: 18g; Carbohydrates: 26g Protein: 2g

162. Parsnip, Carrot, and Kale Salad with Dressing

Preparation Time: 10 minutes
Cooking Time: 0 minutes
Servings: 4
Ingredients:
For the dressing
- ⅓ cup extra-virgin olive oil
- Juice of 1 lime
- 2 tbsp. minced fresh mint leaves
- 1 tsp. pure maple syrup
- Pinch sea salt

For the salad
- 1 bunch kale, chopped
- ½ parsnip, grated
- ½ carrot, grated
- 2 tbsp. sesame seeds

Directions:

1. To make the dressing, mix all the dressing ingredients in a bowl.
2. To make the salad, add the kale to the dressing and massage the dressing into the kale for 1 minute.
3. Add the parsnip, carrot, and sesame seeds.
4. Combine and serve.

Nutrition: Calories: 214; Fat: 2g; Carbohydrates: 12g; Protein: 2g

163.   Tomato Toasts

Preparation Time: 5 minutes
Cooking Time: 5 minutes
Servings: 4
Ingredients:

- 4 slices sprouted bread toasts
- 2 tomatoes, sliced
- 1 avocado, mashed
- 1 tsp. olive oil
- 1 pinch salt
- ¾ tsp. ground black pepper

Directions:

1. Blend together the olive oil, mashed avocado, salt, and ground black pepper.
2. When the mixture is homogenous—spread it over the sprouted bread.
3. Then place the sliced tomatoes over the toasts.
4. Enjoy!

Nutrition: Calories: 125; Fat: 11.1g; Carbohydrates: ?.0g; Protein: 1.5g

164.   Everyday Salad

Preparation Time: 10 minutes
Cooking Time: 40 minutes
Servings: 6
Ingredients:

- 5 halved mushrooms
- 6 halved Cherry (Plum) Tomatoes
- 6 rinsed Lettuce Leaves
- 10 olives
- ½ chopped cucumber
- Juice from ½ Key Lime
- 1 tsp. olive oil
- Pure Sea Salt

Directions:

1. Tear rinsed lettuce leaves into medium pieces and put them in a medium salad bowl.

2. Add mushrooms halves, chopped cucumber, olives, and cherry tomato halves into the bowl. Mix well. Pour olive and Key Lime juice over the salad.
3. Add pure sea salt to taste. Mix it all till it is well combined.

Nutrition: Calories: 88; Carbohydrates: 11g; Fat: .5g; Protein: .8g

165.   Super-Seedy Salad With Tahini Dressing

Preparation Time: 10 minutes
Cooking Time: 0 minutes
Servings: 1–2
Ingredients:

- 1 slice stale sourdough, torn into chunks
- 50g mixed seeds
- 1 tsp. cumin seeds
- 1 tsp. coriander seeds
- 50g baby kale
- 75g long-stemmed broccoli, blanched for a few minutes then roughly chopped
- ½ red onion, thinly sliced
- 100g cherry tomatoes, halved
- ½ a small bunch flat-leaf parsley, torn

Dressing

- 100ml natural yogurt
- 1 tbsp. tahini
- 1 lemon, juiced

Directions:

1. Heat the oven to 200°C/fan 180°C/gas.
2. Put the bread into a food processor and pulse into very rough breadcrumbs. Put into a bowl with the mixed seeds and spices, season, and spray well with oil.
3. Tip onto a non-stick baking tray and roast for 15–20 minutes, stirring and tossing regularly, until deep golden brown.
4. Whisk together the dressing ingredients, some seasoning, and a splash of water in a large bowl. Tip the baby kale, broccoli, red onion, cherry tomatoes, and flat-leaf parsley into the dressing, and mix well. Divide between 2 plates and top with the crispy breadcrumbs and seeds.

Nutrition: Calories: 78; Carbohydrates: 6 g; Fat: 2g; Protein: 1.5g

166.   Vegetable Salad

Preparation Time: 10 minutes
Cooking Time: 0 minutes
Servings: 1–2
Ingredients:

- 4 cups each raw spinach and romaine lettuce
- 2 cups each cherry tomatoes, sliced cucumber, chopped baby carrots, and chopped red, orange, and yellow bell pepper
- 1 cup each chopped broccoli, sliced yellow squash, zucchini, and cauliflower.

Directions:

1. Wash all these vegetables.
2. Mix in a large mixing bowl and top off with a non-fat or low-fat dressing of your choice.

Nutrition: Calories: 48; Carbohydrates: 11g; Protein: 3g

167.   Greek Salad

Preparation Time: 10 minutes
Cooking Time: 0 minutes
Servings: 1–2
Ingredients:

- 1 Romaine head, torn in bits
- 1 cucumber sliced
- 1 pint cherry tomatoes, halved
- 1 green pepper, thinly sliced
- 1 onion sliced into rings
- 1 cup kalamata olives
- 1 ½ cups feta cheese, crumbled

For dressing, combine:

- 1 cup olive oil
- 1/4 cup lemon juice
- 2 tsp. oregano
- Salt and pepper

Directions:

1. Lay ingredients on a plate.
2. Drizzle dressing over salad

Nutrition: Calories: 107; Carbohydrates: 18g; Fat: 1.2 g; Protein: 1g

168.   Alkaline Spring Salad

Preparation Time: 10 minutes
Cooking Time: 0 minutes
Servings: 1–2

Eating seasonal fruits and vegetables is a fabulous way of taking care of yourself and the environment at the same time. This alkaline-electric salad is delicious and nutritious.

Ingredients:

- 4 cups seasonal approved greens of your choice
- 1 cup cherry tomatoes
- 1/4 cup walnuts
- 1/4 cup approved herbs of your choice

For the dressing:

- 3–4 key limes
- 1 tbsp. homemade raw sesame "tahini" butter
- Sea salt and cayenne pepper

Directions:

1. First, get the juice of the key limes. In a small bowl, whisk together the key lime juice with the homemade raw sesame "tahini" butter. Add sea salt and cayenne pepper, to taste.
2. Cut the cherry tomatoes in half.
3. In a large bowl, combine the greens, cherry tomatoes, and herbs. Pour the dressing on top and "massage" with your hands.
4. Let the greens soak up the dressing. Add more sea salt, cayenne pepper, and herbs on top if you wish. Enjoy!

Nutrition: Calories: 77; Carbohydrates: 11g

169.   Tuna Salad

Preparation Time: 10 minutes
Cooking Time: none
Servings: 3
Ingredients:

- 1 can tuna (6 oz.)
- 1/3 cup fresh cucumber, chopped
- 1/3 cup fresh tomato, chopped
- 1/3 cup avocado, chopped
- 1/3 cup celery, chopped
- 2 garlic cloves, minced
- 4 tsp. olive oil
- 2 tbsp. lime juice
- A pinch black pepper

Directions:

1. Prepare the dressing by combining olive oil, lime juice, minced garlic, and black pepper.
2. Mix the salad ingredients in a salad bowl and drizzle with the dressing.

Nutrition: Carbohydrates: 4.8 g; Protein: 14.3 g; Total sugars: 1.1 g; Calories: 212 g

170. Roasted Portobello Salad

Preparation Time: 10 minutes
Cooking Time: none
Servings: 4
Ingredients:

- 11/2 lb. Portobello mushrooms, stems trimmed
- 3 heads Belgian endive, sliced
- 1 small red onion, sliced
- 4 oz. blue cheese
- 8 oz. mixed salad greens

Dressing:

- 3 tbsp. red wine vinegar
- 1 tbsp. Dijon mustard
- 2/3 cup olive oil
- Salt and pepper to taste

Directions:

1. Preheat the oven to 450°F.
2. Prepare the dressing by whisking together vinegar, mustard, salt, and pepper. Slowly add olive oil while whisking.
3. Cut the mushrooms and arrange them on a baking sheet, stem-side up. Coat the mushrooms with some dressing and bake for 15 minutes.
4. In a salad bowl toss the salad greens with onion, endive, and cheese. Sprinkle with the dressing.
5. Add mushrooms to the salad bowl.

Nutrition: Carbohydrates: 22.3 g; Protein: 14.9 g; Total sugars: 2.1 g; Calories: 501

171. Shredded Chicken Salad

Preparation Time: 5 minutes
Cooking Time: 10 minutes
Servings: 6
Ingredients:

- 2 chicken breasts, boneless, skinless
- 1 head iceberg lettuce, cut into strips
- 2 bell peppers, cut into strips
- 1 fresh cucumber, quartered, sliced
- 3 scallions, sliced
- 2 tbsp. chopped peanuts
- 1 tbsp. peanut vinaigrette
- Salt to taste
- 1 cup water

Directions:

1. In a skillet simmer one cup of salted water.
2. Add the chicken breasts, cover, and cook on low for 5 minutes. Remove the cover. Then remove the chicken from the skillet and shred with a fork.
3. In a salad bowl mix the vegetables with the cooled chicken, season with salt and sprinkle with peanut vinaigrette and chopped peanuts.

Nutrition: Carbohydrates: 9 g; Protein: 11.6 g; Total sugars: 4.2 g; Calories: 117

172. Broccoli Salad

Preparation Time: 10 minutes
Cooking Time: none
Servings: 6
Ingredients:

- 1 medium head broccoli, raw, florets only
- 1/2 cup red onion, chopped
- 12 oz. turkey bacon, chopped, fried until crisp
- 1/2 cup cherry tomatoes, halved
- ¼ cup sunflower kernels
- ¾ cup raisins
- ¾ cup mayonnaise
- 2 tbsp. white vinegar

Directions:

1. In a salad bowl combine the broccoli, tomatoes, and onion.
2. Mix mayo with vinegar and sprinkle over the broccoli.
3. Add the sunflower kernels, raisins, and bacon, and toss well.

Nutrition: Carbohydrates: 17.3 g; Protein: 11 g; Total sugars: 10 g; Calories: 220

173. Cherry Tomato Salad

Preparation Time: 10 minutes
Cooking Time: none
Servings: 6
Ingredients:

- 40 cherry tomatoes, halved
- 1 cup mozzarella balls, halved
- 1 cup green olives, sliced
- 1 can (6 oz.) black olives, sliced

- 2 green onions, chopped
- 3 oz. roasted pine nuts

Dressing:
- 1/2 cup olive oil
- 2 tbsp. red wine vinegar
- 1 tsp. dried oregano
- Salt and pepper to taste

Directions:
1. In a salad bowl, combine the tomatoes, olives, and onions.
2. Prepare the dressing by combining olive oil with red wine vinegar, dried oregano, salt, and pepper.
3. Sprinkle with the dressing and add the nuts.
4. Let marinate in the fridge for 1 hour.

Nutrition: Carbohydrates: 10.7 g; Protein: 2.4 g; Total sugars: 3.6 g

174. Ground Turkey Salad

Preparation Time: 10 minutes
Cooking Time: 35 minutes
Servings: 6
Ingredients:
- 1 lb. lean ground turkey
- 1/2 inch ginger, minced
- 2 garlic cloves, minced
- 1 onion, chopped
- 1 tbsp. olive oil
- 1 bag lettuce leaves (for serving)
- ¼ cup fresh cilantro, chopped
- 2 tsp. coriander powder
- 1 tsp. red chili powder
- 1 tsp. turmeric powder
- Salt to taste
- 4 cups water

Dressing:
- 2 tbsp. fat-free yogurt
- 1 tbsp. sour cream, non-fat
- 1 tbsp. low-fat mayonnaise
- 1 lemon, juiced
- 1 tsp. red chili flakes
- Salt and pepper to taste

Directions:
1. In a skillet sauté the garlic and ginger in olive oil for 1 minute. Add onion and season with salt. Cook for 10 minutes over medium heat.

2. Add the ground turkey and sauté for 3 more minutes. Add the spices (turmeric, red chili powder, and coriander powder).
3. Add 4 cups water and cook for 30 minutes, covered.
4. Prepare the dressing by combining yogurt, sour cream, mayo, lemon juice, chili flakes, salt, and pepper.
5. To serve arrange the salad leaves on serving plates and place the cooked ground turkey on them. Top with the dressing.

Nutrition: Carbohydrates: 9.1 g; Protein: 17.8 g; Total sugars: 2.5 g; Calories: 176

175. Asian Cucumber Salad

Preparation Time: 10 minutes
Cooking Time: none
Servings: 6
Ingredients:
- 1 lb. cucumbers, sliced
- 2 scallions, sliced
- 2 tbsp. sliced pickled ginger, chopped
- ¼ cup cilantro
- 1/2 red jalapeño, chopped
- 3 tbsp. rice wine vinegar
- 1 tbsp. sesame oil
- 1 tbsp. sesame seeds

Directions:
1. In a salad bowl combine all ingredients an toss together.

Nutrition: Carbohydrates: 5.7 g; Protein: 1 g; Tot sugars: 3.1 g; Calories: 52

176. Cauliflower Tofu Salad

Preparation Time: 10 minutes
Cooking Time: 15 minutes
Servings: 4
Ingredients:
- 2 cups cauliflower florets, blended
- 1 fresh cucumber, diced
- 1/2 cup green olives, diced
- 1/3 cup red onion, diced
- 2 tbsp. toasted pine nuts
- 2 tbsp. raisins
- 1/3 cup feta, crumbled

- 1/2 cup pomegranate seeds
- 2 lemons (juiced, zest grated)
- 8 oz. tofu
- 2 tsp. oregano
- 2 garlic cloves, minced
- 1/2 tsp. red chili flakes
- 3 tbsp. olive oil
- Salt and pepper to taste

Directions:
1. Season the processed cauliflower with salt and transfer it to a strainer to drain.
2. Prepare the marinade for the tofu by combining 2 tbsp. lemon juice, 1.5 tbsp. olive oil, minced garlic, chili flakes, oregano, salt, and pepper. Coat tofu in the marinade and set aside.
3. Preheat the oven to 450°F.
4. Bake tofu on a baking sheet for 12 minutes.
5. In a salad bowl mix the remaining marinade with onions, cucumber, cauliflower, olives, and raisins. Add in the remaining olive oil and grated lemon zest.
6. Top with tofu, pine nuts, and feta, and pomegranate seeds.

Nutrition: Carbohydrates: 34.1 g; Protein: 11.1 g; Total sugars: 11.5 g; Calories: 328

177. Scallop Caesar Salad

Preparation Time: 5 minutes
Cooking Time: 2 minutes
Servings: 2
Ingredients:
- 8 sea scallops
- 4 cups romaine lettuce
- 2 tsp. olive oil
- 3 tbsp. Caesar Salad Dressing
- 1 tsp. lemon juice
- Salt and pepper to taste

Directions:
1. In a frying pan heat olive oil and cook the scallops in one layer no longer than 2 minutes on both sides. Season with salt and pepper to taste.
2. Arrange lettuce on plates and place scallops on top.
3. Pour over the Caesar dressing and lemon juice.

Nutrition: Carbohydrates: 14 g; Protein: 30.7 g; Total sugars: 2.2 g; Calories: 340 g

178. Chicken Avocado Salad

Preparation Time: 30 minutes
Cooking Time: 15 minutes
Servings: 4
Ingredients:
- 1 lb. chicken breast, cooked, shredded
- 1 avocado, pitted, peeled, sliced
- 2 tomatoes, diced
- 1 cucumber, peeled, sliced
- 1 head lettuce, chopped
- 3 tbsp. olive oil
- 2 tbsp. lime juice
- 1 tbsp. cilantro, chopped
- Salt and pepper to taste

Directions:
1. In a bowl whisk together oil, lime juice, cilantro, salt, and a pinch of pepper.
2. Combine lettuce, tomatoes, cucumber in a salad bowl and toss with half of the dressing.
3. Toss chicken with the remaining dressing and combine with vegetable mixture.
4. Top with avocado.

Nutrition: Carbohydrates: 10 g; Protein: 38 g; Total sugars: 11.5 g; Calories: 380

179. California Wraps

Preparation Time: 5 minutes
Cooking Time: 15 minutes
Servings: 4
Ingredients:
- 4 slices turkey breast, cooked
- 4 slices ham, cooked
- 4 lettuce leaves
- 4 slices tomato
- 4 slices avocado
- 1 tsp. lime juice
- A handful watercress leaves
- 4 tbsp. Ranch dressing, sugar-free

Directions:
1. Top a lettuce leaf with a turkey slice, ham slice, and tomato.

2. In a bowl combine avocado and lime juice and place on top of tomatoes. Top with water cress and dressing.
3. Repeat with the remaining ingredients for 4. Topping each lettuce leaf with a turkey slice, ham slice, tomato, and dressing.

Nutrition: Carbohydrates: 4 g; Protein: 9 g; Total sugars: 0.5 g; Calories: 140

180. Chicken Salad In Cucumber Cups

Preparation Time: 5 minutes
Cooking Time: 15 minutes
Servings: 4
Ingredients:

- 1/2 chicken breast, skinless, boiled, and shredded
- 2 long cucumbers, cut into 8 thick rounds each, scooped out (won't use in a).
- 1 tsp. ginger, minced
- 1 tsp. lime zest, grated
- 4 tsp. olive oil
- 1 tsp. sesame oil
- 1 tsp. lime juice
- Salt and pepper to taste

Directions:

1. In a bowl combine lime zest, juice, olive and sesame oils, ginger, and season with salt.
2. Toss the chicken with the dressing and fill the cucumber cups with the salad.

Nutrition: Carbohydrates: 4 g; Protein: 12 g; Total sugars: 0.5 g; Calories: 116 g

181. Sunflower Seeds and Arugula Garden Salad

Preparation Time: 5 minutes
Cooking Time: 10 minutes
Servings: 6
Ingredients:

- ¼ tsp. black pepper
- ¼ tsp. salt
- 1 tsp. fresh thyme, chopped
- 2 tbsp. sunflower seeds, toasted
- 2 cups red grapes, halved
- 7 cups baby arugula, loosely packed

- 1 tbsp. coconut oil
- 2 tsp. honey
- 3 tbsp. red wine vinegar
- 1/2 tsp. stone-ground mustard

Directions:

1. In a small bowl, whisk together mustard, honey, and vinegar. Slowly pour oil as you whisk.
2. In a large salad bowl, mix thyme, seeds, grapes, and arugula.
3. Drizzle with dressing and serve.

Nutrition: Calories: 86.7g; Protein: 1.6g; Carbs: 13.1g; Fat: 3.1g.

182. Supreme Caesar Salad

Preparation Time: 5 minutes
Cooking Time: 10 minutes
Servings: 4
Ingredients:

- ¼ cup olive oil
- ¾ cup mayonnaise
- 1 head romaine lettuce, torn into bite-sized pieces
- 1 tbsp. lemon juice
- 1 tsp. Dijon mustard
- 1 tsp. Worcestershire sauce
- 3 garlic cloves, peeled and minced
- 3 garlic cloves, peeled and quartered
- 4 cups day-old bread, cubed
- 5 anchovy filets, minced
- 6 tbsp. grated parmesan cheese, divided
- Ground black pepper to taste
- Salt to taste

Directions:

1. In a small bowl, whisk well lemon juice, mustard, Worcestershire sauce, 2 tbsp. parmesan cheese, anchovies, mayonnaise, and minced garlic. Season with pepper and salt to taste. Set aside in the ref.
2. On medium fire, place a large nonstick saucepan and heat oil.
3. Sauté quartered garlic until browned around, minute or two. Remove and discard.
4. Add bread cubes in the same pan, sauté until lightly browned. Season with pepper and salt. Transfer to a plate.

5. In a large bowl, place lettuce and pour in the dressing. Toss well to coat. Top with remaining parmesan cheese.
6. Garnish with bread cubes, serve, and enjoy.

Nutrition: Calories: 443.3g; Fat: 32.1g; Protein: 11.6g; Carbs: 27g

183. Tabbouleh— Arabian Salad

Preparation Time: 5 minutes
Cooking Time: 10 minutes
Servings: 6
Ingredients:

- ¼ cup chopped fresh mint
- 1 2/3 cups boiling water
- 1 cucumber, peeled, seeded, and chopped
- 1 cup bulgur
- 1 cup chopped fresh parsley
- 1 cup chopped green onions
- 1 tsp. salt
- 1/3 cup lemon juice
- 1/3 cup olive oil
- 3 tomatoes, chopped
- Ground black pepper to taste

Directions:

1. In a large bowl, mix together boiling water and bulgur. Let soak and set aside for an hour while covered.
2. After one hour, toss in cucumber, tomatoes, mint, parsley, onions, lemon juice, and oil. Then season with black pepper and salt to taste. Toss well and refrigerate for another hour while covered before serving.

Nutrition: Calories: 185.5g; Fat: 13.1g; Protein: 4.1g; Carbs: 12.8g

184. Creamy Avocado-Broccoli Soup

Preparation Time: 10 minutes
Cooking Time: 15 minutes
Servings: 1–2
Ingredients:

- 2–3 flowers broccoli
- 1 small avocado
- 1 yellow onion
- 1 green or red pepper
- 1 celery stalk
- 2 cups vegetable broth (yeast-free)
- Celtic Sea Salt to taste

Directions:

1. Warmth vegetable stock (don't bubble). Include hacked onion and broccoli, and warm for a few minutes. At that point put it in a blender, including the avocado, pepper, and celery, and blend until the soup is smooth (include some more water whenever wanted).
2. Flavor and serve warm. Delicious!!

Nutrition: Calories: 60g; Carbohydrates: 11g; Fat: 2 g; Protein: 2g

185. Fresh Garden Vegetable Soup

Preparation Time: 7 minutes
Cooking Time: 20 minutes
Servings: 1–2
Ingredients:

- 2 huge carrots
- 1 little zucchini
- 1 celery stem
- 1 cup broccoli
- 3 stalks of asparagus
- 1 yellow onion
- 1 quart (antacid) water
- 4–5 tsp. sans yeast vegetable stock
- 1 tsp. new basil
- 2 tsp. Sea salt to taste

Directions:

1. Put water in a pot, include the vegetable stock just as the onion, and bring it to a bubble.
2. In the meantime, leave the zucchini, the broccoli, and the asparagus, and shred the carrots and the celery stem in a food processor.
3. When the water is bubbling, it would be ideal if you turn off the oven as we would prefer not to heat up the vegetables. Simply put them all in the high temp water and hold up until the vegetables arrive at the wanted delicacy.
4. Permit to cool somewhat, at that point put all fixings into a blender and blend until you get a thick, smooth consistency.

Nutrition: Calories: 43; Carbohydrates: 7g; Fat: 1 g

186. Raw Some Gazpacho Soup

Preparation Time: 7 minutes
Cooking Time: 3 hours
Servings: 3–4
Ingredients:

- 500g tomatoes
- 1 small cucumber
- 1 red pepper
- 1 onion
- 2 garlic cloves
- 1 small chili
- 1 quart of water (preferably alkaline water)
- 4 tbsp. cold-pressed olive oil
- Juice of one fresh lemon
- 1 dash cayenne pepper
- Sea salt to taste

Directions:

1. Remove the skin of the cucumber and cut a vegetables into large pieces.
2. Put all ingredients except the olive oil in blender and mix until smooth.
3. Add the olive oil and mix again until the oil emulsified.
4. Put the soup in the fridge and chill for at lea 2 hours (soup should be served ice cold).
5. Add some salt and pepper to taste, mix, pla the soup in bowls, garnish with chopp scallions, cucumbers, tomatoes, and peppe and enjoy!

Nutrition: Calories: 39; Carbohydrates: 8g; Fat: 0.5 g; Protein: 0.2g

187.   Alkaline Carrot Soup With Fresh Mushrooms

Preparation Time: 10 minutes
Cooking Time: 20 minutes
Servings: 1–2
Ingredients:

- 4 mid-sized carrots
- 4 mid-sized potatoes
- 10 enormous new mushrooms (champignons or chanterelles)
- 1/2 white onion
- 2 tbsp. olive oil (cold squeezed, additional virgin)
- 3 cups vegetable stock
- 2 tbsp. parsley, new and cleaved
- Salt and new white pepper

Directions:

1. Wash and strip carrots and potatoes and dice them.
2. Warm-up vegetable stock in a pot on medium heat. Cook carrots and potatoes for around 15 minutes. Meanwhile finely shape onion and braise them in a container with olive oil for around 3 minutes.
3. Wash mushrooms, slice them to the wanted size, and add to the container, cooking approx. an additional 5 minutes, blending at times. Blend carrots, vegetable stock, and potatoes, and put the substance of the skillet into the pot.
4. When nearly done, season with parsley, salt, and pepper and serve hot. Appreciate this alkalizing soup!

Nutrition: Calories: 75 Carbohydrates: 13g; Fat: 1.8g; Protein: 1 g

88.   Swiss Cauliflower-Omental-Soup

Preparation Time: 10 minutes
Cooking Time: 15 minutes
Servings: 3–4
Ingredients:

- 2 cups cauliflower pieces
- 1 cup potatoes, cubed
- 2 cups vegetables stock (without yeast)
- 3 tbsp. Swiss Omental cheddar, cubed
- 2 tbsp. new chives
- 1 tbsp. pumpkin seeds
- 1 touch of nutmeg and cayenne pepper

Directions:

1. Cook cauliflower and potato in vegetable stock until delicate and Blend with a blender.
2. Season the soup with nutmeg and cayenne, and possibly somewhat salt and pepper.
3. Include emmenthal cheddar and chives and mix a couple of moments until the soup is smooth and prepared to serve. Enhance it with pumpkin seeds.

Nutrition: Calories: 65 Carbohydrates: 13g; Fat: 2g; Protein: 1g

189.   Chilled Parsley-Gazpacho with Lime & Cucumber

Preparation Time: 10 minutes
Cooking Time: 2 hours
Servings: 1
Ingredients:

- 4–5 middle-sized tomatoes
- 2 tbsp. olive oil, extra virgin, and cold-pressed
- 2 large cups fresh parsley
- 2 ripe avocados
- 2 garlic cloves, diced
- 2 limes, juiced
- 4 cups vegetable broth
- 1 middle-sized cucumber
- 2 small red onions, diced
- 1 tsp. dried oregano
- 1½ tsp. paprika powder
- ½ tsp. cayenne pepper
- Sea salt and freshly ground pepper to taste

Directions:

1. In a pan, heat up olive oil and sauté onions and garlic until translucent. Set aside to cool down.
2. Use a large blender and blend parsley, avocado, tomatoes, cucumber, vegetable broth, lime juice, and onion-garlic mix until smooth. Add some water if desired, and season with cayenne pepper, paprika powder, oregano, salt, and pepper. Blend again and put in the fridge for at least 1, 5 hours.

3. Tip: Add chives or dill to the gazpacho. Enjoy this great alkaline (cold) soup!

Nutrition: Calories: 48; Carbohydrates: 12 g; Fat: 0.8g

190. Chilled Avocado Tomato Soup

Preparation Time: 7 minutes
Cooking Time: 20 minutes
Servings: 1–2
Ingredients:

- 2 small avocados
- 2 large tomatoes
- 1 stalk celery
- 1 small onion
- 1 garlic clove
- Juice of 1 fresh lemon
- 1 cup water (best: alkaline water)
- A handful fresh lavage
- Parsley and sea salt to taste

Directions:

1. Scoop the avocados and cut all veggies into little pieces.
2. Spot all fixings in a blender and blend until smooth.
3. Serve chilled and appreciate this nutritious and sound-soluble soup formula!

Nutrition: Calories: 68 Carbohydrates: 15g; Fat: 2g; Protein: .8g

191. Dill Celery Soup

Preparation Time: 10 minutes
Cooking Time: 30 minutes
Servings: 4
Ingredients:

- 6 cups celery stalk, chopped
- 2 cups filtered alkaline water
- 1 medium onion, chopped
- 1/2 tsp. dill
- 1 cup coconut milk
- 1/4 tsp. sea salt

Directions:

1. Combine all elements into the direct pot and mix fine.
2. Cover pot with lid and select soup mode it takes 30 minutes.
3. Release pressure using the quick release directions then open the lid carefully.

4. Blend the soup utilizing a submersion blender until smooth.
5. Stir well and serve.

Nutrition: Calories: 193; Fat: 15.3 g; Carbohydrates 10.9 g; Protein: 5.2 g; Sugar: 5.6 g; Cholesterol: 0 mg

192. Pumpkin and White Bean Soup with Sage

Preparation Time: 10 minutes
Cooking Time: 40 minutes
Servings: 3–4
Ingredients:

- 1 ½ pound pumpkin
- ½ pound yams
- ½ pound white beans
- 1 onion
- 2 garlic cloves
- 1 tbsp. cold squeezed additional virgin olive oil
- 1 tbsp. spices (your top picks)
- 1 tbsp. sage
- 1 ½ quart water (best: antacid water)
- A spot sea salt and pepper

Directions:

1. Cut the pumpkin and potatoes in shapes, cut the onion, and cut the garlic, the spices, and the sage into fine pieces.
2. Sauté the onion and also the garlic in olive oil for around two or three minutes.
3. Include the potatoes, pumpkin, spices, and sage and fry for an additional 5 minutes.
4. At that point include the water and cook for around 30 minutes (spread the pot with a top until vegetables are delicate.
5. At long last include the beans and some salt and pepper. Cook for an additional 5 minutes and serve right away. Prepared!! Appreciate this antacid soup. Alkalizing tasty!

Nutrition: Calories: 78; Carbohydrates: 12g

193. Alkaline Carrot Soup With Millet

Preparation Time: 7 minutes
Cooking Time: 40 minutes
Servings: 3–4
Ingredients:

- 2 cups cauliflower pieces

- 1 cup potatoes, cubed
- 2 cups vegetables stock (without yeast)
- 3 tbsp. Swiss Emmenthal cheddar, cubed
- 2 tbsp. new chives
- 1 tbsp. pumpkin seeds
- Drizzle nutmeg and cayenne pepper

Directions:
1. Cook cauliflower and potato in vegetable stock until delicate and Blend with a blender.
2. Season the soup with nutmeg and cayenne, and possibly somewhat salt and pepper.
3. Include emmenthal cheddar and chives and mix a couple of moments until the soup is smooth and ready to serve. Can enhance with pumpkin seeds.

Nutrition: Calories: 65; Carbohydrates: 15g; Fat: 1g; Protein: 2g

194. Alkaline Pumpkin Tomato Soup

Preparation Time: 15 minutes
Cooking Time: 30 minutes
Servings: 3–4
Ingredients:

- 1 quart water (if accessible: soluble water)
- 400g new tomatoes, stripped and diced
- 1 medium-sized sweet pumpkin
- 5 yellow onions
- 1 tbsp. Cold squeezed additional virgin olive oil
- 2 tsp. sea salt or natural salt
- Drizzle Cayenne pepper
- Your preferred spices (discretionary)
- Bunch new parsley

Directions:
1. Cut onions in little pieces and sauté with some oil in a significant pot.
2. Cut the pumpkin down the middle, at that point remove the stem and scoop out the seeds.
3. At long last scoop out the fragile living creature and put it in the pot.
4. Include likewise the tomatoes and the water and cook for around 20 minutes.
5. At that point empty the soup into a food processor and blend well for a couple of moments. Sprinkle with salt pepper and other spices.

6. Fill bowls and trim new parsley. Make the most of your alkalizing soup!

Nutrition: Calories: 78; Carbohydrates: 20; Fat: 0.5g; Protein: 1.5g

195. Alkaline Pumpkin Coconut Soup

Preparation Time: 10 minutes
Cooking Time: 15 minutes
Servings: 3–4
Ingredients:

- 2 lb. pumpkin
- 6 cups water (best: soluble water delivered with a water ionizer)
- 1 cup low fat coconut milk
- 5 ounces potatoes
- 2 major onions
- 3 ounces leek
- 1 bunch new parsley
- 1 touch nutmeg
- 1 touch cayenne pepper
- 1 tsp. sea salt or natural salt
- 4 tbsp. cold squeezed additional virgin olive oil

Directions:
1. As a matter of first significance: cut the onions, the pumpkin, and the potatoes just as the hole into little pieces.
2. At this point, heat the olive oil in a significant pot and sauté the onions for a couple of moments.
3. Then, include the water and heat up the pumpkin, potatoes, and the leek until delicate.
4. Include the coconut milk.
5. Presently utilize a hand blender and puree for around 1 moment. The soup should turn out to be extremely velvety.
6. Season with salt, pepper, and nutmeg lastly include the parsley.
7. Appreciate this alkalizing pumpkin soup hot or cold!

Nutrition: Calories: 88; Carbohydrates: 23g; Fat: 2.5 g; Protein: 1.8g

196. Cold Cauliflower-Coconut Soup

Preparation Time: 7 minutes
Cooking Time: 20 minutes

Servings: 3–4

Ingredients:

- 1 pound (450g) new cauliflower
- 1 ¼ cup (300ml) unsweetened coconut milk
- 1 cup water (best: antacid water)
- 2 tbsp. new lime juice
- 1/3 cup cold squeezed additional virgin olive oil
- 1 cup new coriander leaves, slashed
- A pinch salt and cayenne pepper
- 1 bunch unsweetened coconut chips

Directions:

1. Steam cauliflower for around 10 minutes.
2. At that point, set up the cauliflower with coconut milk and water in a food processor and procedure until extremely smooth.
3. Include a new lime squeeze, salt and pepper, a large portion of the cleaved coriander, and the oil and blend for an additional couple of moments.
4. Pour in soup bowls and embellishment with coriander and coconut chips. Appreciate!

Nutrition: Calories: 65 Carbohydrates: 11g; Fat: 0.3g; Protein: 1.5g

197. Raw Avocado-Broccoli Soup With Cashew Nuts

Preparation Time: 10 minutes
Cooking Time: 30 minutes
Servings: 1–2

Ingredients:

- ½ cup water (if available: alkaline water)
- ½ avocado
- 1 cup chopped broccoli
- ½ cup cashew nuts
- ½ cup alfalfa sprouts
- 1 garlic clove
- 1 tbsp. cold-pressed extra virgin olive oil
- 1 pinch sea salt and pepper
- Some parsley to garnish

Directions:

1. Put the cashew nuts in a blender or food processor, include some water and puree for a couple of moments.

2. Include the various fixings (except for the avocado) individually and puree each an ideal opportunity for a couple of moments.
3. Dispense the soup in a container and warm it up to normal room temperature. Enhance with salt and pepper. In the interim dice the avocado and slash the parsley.
4. Dispense the soup in a container or plate; include the avocado dices and embellishment with parsley.
5. That's it! Enjoy this excellent healthy soup!

Nutrition: Calories: 48 Carbohydrates: 18g; Fat: 3g; Protein: 1.4g

198. White Bean Soup

Preparation Time: 10 minutes
Cooking Time: 40 minutes
Servings: 6

Ingredients:

- 2 cups white beans, rinsed
- ¼ tsp. cayenne pepper
- 1 tsp. dried oregano
- ½ tsp. fresh rosemary, chopped
- 3 cups filtered alkaline water
- 3 cups unsweetened almond milk
- 3 garlic cloves, minced
- 2 celery stalks, diced
- 1 onion, chopped
- 1 tbsp. olive oil
- ½ tsp. sea salt

Directions:

1. Add oil into the instant pot and set the pot o sauté mode.
2. Add carrots, celery, and onion in oil and saut until softened, about 5 minutes.
3. Add garlic and sauté for a minute.
4. Add beans, seasonings, water, and almond mil and stir to combine.
5. Cover pot with lid and cook on high pressu for 35 minutes.
6. When finished, allow to release pressu naturally then open the lid.
7. Stir well and serve.

Nutrition: Calories: 276; Fat: 4.8 g; Carbohydrate 44.2 g; Sugar: 2.3 g; Protein: 16.6 g; Cholesterol: 0 m

199. Kale Cauliflower Soup

Preparation Time: 10 minutes
Cooking Time: 25 minutes
Servings: 4
Ingredients:

- 2 cups baby kale
- ½ cup unsweetened coconut milk
- 4 cups water
- 1 large cauliflower head, chopped
- 3 garlic cloves, peeled
- 2 carrots, peeled and chopped
- 2 onion, chopped
- 3 tbsp. olive oil
- Pepper
- Salt

Directions:

1. Add oil into the instant pot and set the pot on sauté mode.
2. Add carrot, garlic, and onion to the pot and sauté for 5–7 minutes.
3. Add water and cauliflower and stir well.
4. Cover pot with lid and cook on high pressure for 20 minutes.
5. When finished, release pressure using the quick release directions then open the lid.
6. Add kale and coconut milk and stir well.
7. Blend the soup utilizing a submersion blender until smooth.
8. Season with pepper and salt.

Nutrition: Calories: 261; Fat: 18.1 g; Carbohydrates: 3.9 g; Sugar: 9.9 g; Protein: 6.6 g; Cholesterol: 0 mg

200. Healthy Broccoli Asparagus Soup

Preparation Time: 10 minutes
Cooking Time: 20 minutes
Servings: 6
Ingredients:

- 2 cups broccoli florets, chopped
- 15 asparagus spears, ends trimmed and chopped
- 1 tsp. dried oregano
- 1 tbsp. fresh thyme leaves
- ½ cup unsweetened almond milk
- 3 ½ cups filtered alkaline water
- 2 cups cauliflower florets, chopped
- 2 tsp. garlic, chopped
- 1 cup onion, chopped
- 2 tbsp. olive oil
- Pepper
- Salt

Directions:

1. Add oil to the instant pot and set the pot on sauté mode.
2. Add onion to the olive oil and sauté until onion is softened.
3. Add garlic and sauté for 30 seconds.
4. Add all vegetables and water and stir well.
5. Cover pot with lid and cook on manual mode for 3 minutes.
6. When finished, allow to release pressure naturally then open the lid.
7. Blend the soup utilizing a submersion blender until smooth.
8. Stir in almond milk, herbs, pepper, and salt.
9. Serve and enjoy.

Nutrition: Calories: 85; Fat: 5.2 g; Carbohydrates: 8.8 g; Sugar: 3.3 g; Protein: 3.3 g; Cholesterol: 0 mg

201. Creamy Asparagus Soup

Preparation Time: 10 minutes
Cooking Time: 30 minutes
Servings: 6
Ingredients:

- 2 lb. fresh asparagus cut off woody stems
- ¼ tsp. lime zest
- 2 tbsp. lime juice
- 14 oz. coconut milk
- 1 tsp. dried thyme
- ½ tsp. oregano
- ½ tsp. sage
- 1 ½ cups filtered alkaline water
- 1 cauliflower head, cut into florets
- 1 tbsp. garlic, minced
- 1 leek, sliced
- 3 tbsp. coconut oil
- A pinch Himalayan salt

Directions:

1. Preheat the oven to 400°F/200°C.
2. Line baking tray with parchment paper and set aside.

3. Arrange asparagus spears on a baking tray. Drizzle with 2 tbsp. of coconut oil and sprinkle with salt, thyme, oregano, and sage.
4. Bake in preheated oven for 20–25 minutes.
5. Add remaining oil to the instant pot and set the pot on sauté mode.
6. Put some garlic and leek to the pot and sauté for 2–3 minutes.
7. Add cauliflower florets and water in the pot and stir well.
8. Cover pot with lid and select steam mode and set timer for 4 minutes.
9. When finished, release pressure using the quick release directions.
10. Add roasted asparagus, lime zest, lime juice, and coconut milk and stir well.
11. Blend the soup utilizing a submersion blender until smooth.
12. Serve and enjoy.

Nutrition: Calories: 265; Fat: 22.9 g; Carbohydrates: 14.7 g; Sugar: 6.7 g; Protein: 6.1 g; Cholesterol: 0 mg

202. Quick Broccoli Soup

Preparation Time: 5 minutes
Cooking Time: 10 minutes
Servings: 6
Ingredients:

- 1 lb. broccoli, chopped
- 6 cups filtered alkaline water
- 1 onion, diced
- 2 tbsp. olive oil
- Pepper
- Salt

Directions:

1. Add oil into the instant pot and set the pot on sauté mode.
2. Add the onion in olive oil and sauté until softened.
3. Add broccoli and water and stir well.
4. Cover pot with top and cook on manual high pressure for 3 minutes.
5. When finished, release pressure using the quick release directions then open the lid.
6. Blend the soup utilizing a submersion blender until smooth.
7. Season soup with pepper and salt.
8. Serve and enjoy.

Nutrition: Calories: 73; Fat: 4.9 g; Carbohydrates: 6.7 g; Protein: 2.3 g; Sugar: 2.1 g; Cholesterol: 0 mg

203. Green Lentil Soup

Preparation Time: 10 minutes
Cooking Time: 30 minutes
Servings: 4
Ingredients:

- 1 ½ cups green lentils, rinsed
- 4 cups baby spinach
- 4 cups filtered alkaline water
- 1 tsp. Italian seasoning
- 2 tsp. fresh thyme
- 14 oz. tomatoes, diced
- 3 garlic cloves, minced
- 2 celery stalks, chopped
- 1 carrot, chopped
- 1 onion, chopped
- Pepper
- Sea salt

Directions:

1. Add all ingredients except spinach into the direct pot and mix fine.
2. Cover pot with top and cook on manual high pressure for 18 minutes.
3. When finished, release pressure using the quick release directions then open the lid.
4. Add spinach and stir well.
5. Serve and enjoy.

Nutrition: Calories: 306; Fat: 1.5 g; Carbohydrate: 53.7 g; Sugar: 6.4 g; Protein: 21 g; Cholesterol: 1 mg

204. Squash Soup

Preparation Time: 10 minutes
Cooking Time: 40 minutes
Servings: 4
Ingredients:

- 3 lb. butternut squash, peeled and cubed
- 1 tbsp. curry powder
- 1/2 cup unsweetened coconut milk
- 3 cups filtered alkaline water
- 2 garlic cloves, minced
- 1 large onion, minced
- 1 tsp. olive oil

Directions:

1. Add olive oil to the instant pot and set the pot on sauté mode.

2. Add onion and cook until tender, about 8 minutes.
3. Add curry powder and garlic and sauté for a minute.
4. Add butternut squash, water, and salt and stir well.
5. Cover pot with lid and cook on soup mode for 30 minutes.
6. When finished, allow to release pressure naturally for 10 minutes then release using quick-release Directions: then open the lid.
7. Blend the soup utilizing a submersion blender until smooth.
8. Add coconut milk and stir well.
9. Serve warm and enjoy.

Nutrition: Calories: 254; Fat: 8.9 g; Carbohydrates: 46.4 g; Sugar: 10.1 g; Protein: 4.8 g; Cholesterol: 0 mg

205. Tomato Soup

Preparation Time: 5 minutes
Cooking Time: 20 minutes
Servings: 4
Ingredients:

- 6 tomatoes, chopped
- 1 onion, diced
- 14 oz. coconut milk
- 1 tsp. turmeric
- 1 tsp. garlic, minced
- 1/4 cup cilantro, chopped
- 1/2 tsp. cayenne pepper
- 1 tsp. ginger, minced
- 1/2 tsp. sea salt

Directions:

1. Add all ingredients to the direct pot and mix fine.
2. Cover the instant pot with lid and cook on manual high pressure for 5 minutes.
3. When finished, allow to release pressure naturally for 10 minutes then release using the quick release directions.
4. Blend the soup utilizing a submersion blender until smooth.
5. Stir well and serve.

Nutrition: Calories: 81; Fat: 3.5 g; Carbohydrates: 11.6 Sugar: 6.1 g; Protein: 2.5 g; Cholesterol: 0 mg

206. Basil Zucchini Soup

Preparation Time: 10 minutes
Cooking Time: 20 minutes
Servings: 4
Ingredients:

- 3 medium zucchinis, peeled and chopped
- 1/4 cup basil, chopped
- 1 large leek, chopped
- 3 cups filtered alkaline water
- 1 tbsp. lemon juice
- 3 tbsp. olive oil
- 2 tsp. sea salt

Directions:

1. Add 2 tbsp. oil into the pot and set the pot on sauté mode.
2. Add zucchini and sauté for 5 minutes.
3. Add basil and leeks and sauté for 2–3 minutes.
4. Add lemon juice, water, and salt. Stir well.
5. Cover pot with lid and cook on high pressure for 8 minutes.
6. When finished, allow to release pressure naturally then open the lid.
7. Blend the soup utilizing a submersion blender until smooth.
8. Top with remaining olive oil and serve.

Nutrition: Calories: 157; Fat: 11.9 g; Carbohydrates: 8.9 g; Protein: 5.8 g; Sugar: 4 g; Cholesterol: 0 mg

207. Summer Vegetable Soup

Preparation Time: 5 minutes
Cooking Time: 20 minutes
Servings: 10
Ingredients:

- 1/2 cup basil, chopped
- 2 bell peppers, seeded and sliced
- 1/ cup green beans, trimmed and cut into pieces
- 8 cups filtered alkaline water
- 1 medium summer squash, sliced
- 1 medium zucchini, sliced
- 2 large tomatoes, sliced
- 1 small eggplant, sliced
- 6 garlic cloves, smashed
- 1 medium onion, diced

- Pepper
- Salt

Directions:

1. Combine all elements into the direct pot and mix fine.
2. Cover pot with lid and cook on soup mode for 10 minutes.
3. Release pressure using the quick release directions then open the lid.
4. Blend the soup utilizing a submersion blender until smooth.
5. Serve and enjoy.

Nutrition: Calories: 84; Fat: 1.6 g; Carbohydrates: 12.8 g; Protein: 6.1 g; Sugar: 6.1 g; Cholesterol: 0 mg

208. Almond-Red Bell Pepper Dip

Preparation Time: 14 minutes
Cooking Time: 16 minutes
Servings: 3
Ingredients:

- 2–3 garlic cloves
- 1 pinch sea salt
- 1 pinch cayenne pepper
- 1 tbsp. Extra virgin olive oil (cold-pressed)
- 60g Almonds
- 280g Red bell pepper

Directions:

1. First of all, cook garlic and pepper until they are soft.
2. Add all ingredients to a mixer and blend until the mix becomes smooth and creamy.
3. Finally, add pepper and salt to taste.
4. Serve.

Nutrition: Calories: 51; Carbohydrates: 10g; Fat: 1g; Protein: 2g

209. Spicy Carrot Soup

Preparation Time: 10 minutes
Cooking Time: 20 minutes
Servings: 6
Ingredients:

- 8 large carrots, peeled and chopped
- 1 1/2 cups filtered alkaline water
- 14 oz. coconut milk
- 3 garlic cloves, peeled
- 1 tbsp. red curry paste

- 1/4 cup olive oil
- 1 onion, chopped
- Salt

Directions:

1. Combine all elements into the direct pot and mix fine.
2. Cover pot with lid and select manual and set timer for 15 minutes.
3. Allow to release pressure naturally then open the lid.
4. Blend the soup utilizing a submersion blender until smooth.
5. Serve and enjoy.

Nutrition: Calories: 267; Fat: 22 g; Carbohydrates: 1 g; Protein: 4 g; Sugar: 5 g; Cholesterol: 20 mg

210. Zucchini Soup

Preparation Time: 10 minutes
Cooking Time: 30 minutes
Servings: 10
Ingredients:

- 10 cups zucchini, chopped
- 32 oz. filtered alkaline water
- 13.5 oz. coconut milk
- 1 tbsp. Thai curry paste

Directions:

1. Combine all elements into the direct pot and mix fine.
2. Cover pot with lid and cook on manual high pressure for 10 minutes.
3. Release pressure using the quick-release directions then open the lid.
4. Using a blender, blend the soup until smooth.
5. Serve and enjoy.

Nutrition: Calories: 122; Fat: 9.8 g; Carbohydrates: 6 g; Protein: 4.1 g; Sugar: 3.6 g; Cholesterol: 0 mg

211. Kidney Bean Stew

Preparation Time: 15 minutes
Cooking Time: 15 minutes
Servings: 2
Ingredients:

- 1 lb. cooked kidney beans
- 1 cup tomato passata
- 1 cup low sodium beef broth
- 3 tbsp. Italian herbs

Directions:

1. Mix all the ingredients in your Instant Pot.

2. Cook on Stew for 15 minutes.
3. Release the pressure naturally.

Nutrition: Calories: 270; Carbs: 16; Sugar: 3; Fat: 10 Protein: 23; GL: 8

212. Cabbage Soup

Preparation Time: 15 minutes
Cooking Time: 35 minutes
Servings: 2
Ingredients:

- 1 lb. shredded cabbage
- 1 cup low sodium vegetable broth
- 1 shredded onion
- 2 tbsp. mixed herbs
- 1 tbsp. black pepper

Directions:

1. Mix all the ingredients in your Instant Pot.
2. Cook on Stew for 35 minutes.
3. Release the pressure naturally.

Nutrition: Calories: 60; Carbs: 2; Sugar: 0; Fat: 2; Protein: 4 GL: 1

213. Pumpkin Spice Soup

Preparation Time: 10 minutes
Cooking Time: 35 minutes
Servings: 2
Ingredients:

- 1 lb. cubed pumpkin
- 1 cup low sodium vegetable broth
- 2 tbsp. mixed spice

Directions:

1. Mix all the ingredients in your Instant Pot.
2. Cook on Stew for 35 minutes.
3. Release the pressure naturally.
4. Blend the soup.

Nutrition: Calories: 100; Carbs: 7; Sugar: 1; Fat: 2; Protein: 3 GL: 1

214. Cream Of Tomato Soup

Preparation Time: 15 minutes
Cooking Time: 15 minutes
Servings: 2
Ingredients:

- 1 lb. fresh tomatoes, chopped
- 1.5 cups low sodium tomato puree

- 1 tbsp. black pepper

Directions:

1. Mix all the ingredients in your Instant Pot.
2. Cook on Stew for 15 minutes.
3. Release the pressure naturally.
4. Blend.

Nutrition: Calories: 20; Carbs: 2; Sugar: 1; Fat: 0; Protein: 3; GL: 1

215. Shiitake Soup

Preparation Time: 15 minutes
Cooking Time: 35 minutes
Servings: 2
Ingredients:

- 1 cup shiitake mushrooms
- 1 cup diced vegetables
- 1 cup low sodium vegetable broth
- 2 tbsp. 5 spice seasoning

Directions:

1. Mix all the ingredients in your Instant Pot.
2. Cook on Stew for 35 minutes.
3. Release the pressure naturally.

Nutrition: Calories: 70; Carbs: 5; Sugar: 1; Fat: 2 Protein: 2; GL: 1

216. Spicy Pepper Soup

Preparation Time: 15 minutes
Cooking Time: 15 minutes
Servings: 2
Ingredients:

- 1 lb. chopped mixed sweet peppers
- 1 cup low sodium vegetable broth
- 3 tbsp. chopped chili peppers
- 1 tbsp. black pepper

Directions:

1. Mix all the ingredients in your Instant Pot.
2. Cook on Stew for 15 minutes.
3. Release the pressure naturally. Blend.

Nutrition: Calories: 100; Carbs: 11; Sugar: 4; Fat: 2 Protein: 3; GL: 6

217. Zoodle Won-Ton Soup

Preparation Time: 15 minutes
Cooking Time: 5 minutes
Servings: 2
Ingredients:

- 1 lb. spiralized zucchini
- 1 pack unfried won-tons
- 1 cup low sodium beef broth
- 2 tbsp. soy sauce

Directions:
1. Mix all the ingredients in your Instant Pot.
2. Cook on Stew for 5 minutes.
3. Release the pressure naturally.

Nutrition: Calories: 300; Carbs: 6; Sugar: 1; Fat: 9; Protein: 43; GL: 2

218.   Broccoli Stilton Soup

Preparation Time: 15 minutes
Cooking Time: 35 minutes
Servings: 2
Ingredients:
- 1 lb. chopped broccoli
- 0.5 lb. chopped vegetables
- 1 cup low sodium vegetable broth
- 1 cup Stilton

Directions:
1. Mix all the ingredients in your Instant Pot.
2. Cook on Stew for 35 minutes.
3. Release the pressure naturally.
4. Blend the soup.

Nutrition: Calories: 280; Carbs: 9; Sugar: 2; Fat: 22; Protein: 13; GL: 4

219.   Lamb Stew

Preparation Time: 15 minutes
Cooking Time: 35 minutes
Servings: 2
Ingredients:
- 1 lb. diced lamb shoulder
- 1 lb. chopped winter vegetables
- 1 cup low sodium vegetable broth
- 1 tbsp. yeast extract
- 1 tbsp. star anise spice mix

Directions:
1. Mix all the ingredients in your Instant Pot.
2. Cook on Stew for 35 minutes.
3. Release the pressure naturally.

Nutrition: Calories: 320; Carbs: 10; Sugar: 2; Fat: 8; Protein: 42; GL: 3

220.   Irish Stew

Preparation Time: 15 minutes
Cooking Time: 35 minutes
Servings: 2
Ingredients:
- 1.5 lb. diced lamb shoulder
- 1 lb. chopped vegetables
- 1 cup low sodium beef broth
- 3 minced onions
- 1 tbsp. ghee

Directions:
1. Mix all the ingredients in your Instant Pot.
2. Cook on Stew for 35 minutes.
3. Release the pressure naturally.

Nutrition: Calories: 330 Carbs: 9 Sugar: 2; Fat: 12 Protein: 49 GL: 3

221.   Sweet and Sour Soup

Preparation time: 15 minutes
Cooking time: 35 minutes
Servings: 2
Ingredients:
- 1 lb. cubed chicken breast
- 1 lb. chopped vegetables
- 1 cup low carb sweet and sour sauce
- 0.5 cup diabetic marmalade

Directions:
1. Mix all the ingredients in your Instant Pot.
2. Cook on Stew for 35 minutes.
3. Release the pressure naturally.

Nutrition: Calories: 275 Carbs: 7; Sugar: 4; Fat: 1 Protein: 38; GL: 3

222.   ½Meatball Stew

Preparation time: 15 minutes
Cooking time: 25 minutes
Servings: 2
Ingredients:
- 1 lb. sausage meat
- 2 cups chopped tomato
- 1 cup chopped vegetables
- 2tbsp. Italian seasonings
- 1tbsp. vegetable oil

Directions:
1. Roll the sausage into meatballs.

2. Put the Instant Pot on Sauté and fry the meatballs in the oil until brown.
3. Mix all the ingredients in your Instant Pot.
4. Cook on Stew for 25 minutes.
5. Release the pressure naturally.

Nutrition: Calories: 300; Carbs: 4g; Sugar: 1g; Fat: 12g; Protein: 40g; GL: 2

223.   Kebab Stew

Preparation time: 15 minutes
Cooking time: 35 minutes
Servings: 2
Ingredients:

- 1 lb. cubed, seasoned kebab meat
- 1 lb. cooked chickpeas
- 1 cup low sodium vegetable broth
- 1tbsp. black pepper

Directions:

1. Mix all the ingredients in your Instant Pot.
2. Cook on Stew for 35 minutes.
3. Release the pressure naturally.

Nutrition: Calories: 290; Carbs: 22g; Sugar: 4g; Fat: 0g; Protein: 34g; GL: 6

224.   French Onion Soup

Preparation time: 35 minutes
Cooking time: 35 minutes
Servings: 2
Ingredients:

- 6 onions, chopped finely
- 2 cups vegetable broth
- 2tbsp. oil
- 2tbsp. Gruyere

Directions:

1. Place the oil in your Instant Pot and cook the onions on Sauté until soft and brown.
2. Mix all the ingredients in your Instant Pot.
3. Cook on Stew for 35 minutes.
4. Release the pressure naturally.

Nutrition: Calories: 110; Carbs: 8g; Sugar: 3g; Fat: 10g; Protein: 3g; GL: 4

225.   Meatless Ball Soup

Preparation time: 15 minutes
Cooking time: 15 minutes
Servings: 2

Ingredients:

- 1 lb. minced tofu
- 0.5lb chopped vegetables
- 2 cups low sodium vegetable broth
- 1tbsp. almond flour
- salt and pepper

Directions:

1. Mix the tofu, flour, salt, and pepper.
2. Form the meatballs.
3. Place all the ingredients in your Instant Pot.
4. Cook on Stew for 15 minutes.
5. Release the pressure naturally.

Nutrition: Calories: 240; Carbs: 9g; Sugar: 3g; Fat: 10g; Protein: 35g; GL: 5

226.   Fake-On Stew

Preparation time: 15 minutes
Cooking time: 25 minutes
Servings: 2
Ingredients:

- 0.5lb soy bacon
- 1 lb. chopped vegetables
- 1 cup low sodium vegetable broth
- 1tbsp. nutritional yeast

Directions:

1. Mix all the ingredients in your Instant Pot.
2. Cook on Stew for 25 minutes.
3. Release the pressure naturally.

Nutrition: Calories: 200; Carbs: 12g; Sugar: 3g; Fat: 7g; Protein: 41g; GL: 5

227.   Chickpea Soup

Preparation time: 15 minutes
Cooking time: 35 minutes
Servings: 2
Ingredients:

- 1 lb. cooked chickpeas
- 1 lb. chopped vegetables
- 1 cup low sodium vegetable broth
- 2tbsp. mixed herbs

Directions:

1. Mix all the ingredients in your Instant Pot.
2. Cook on Stew for 35 minutes.
3. Release the pressure naturally.

Nutrition: Calories: 310; Carbs: 20g; Sugar: 3g; Fat: 5g; Protein: 27g; GL: 5

228. Chicken Zoodle Soup

Preparation time: 15 minutes
Cooking time: 35 minutes
Servings: 2
Ingredients:

- 1 lb. chopped cooked chicken
- 1 lb. spiralized zucchini
- 1 cup low sodium chicken soup
- 1 cup diced vegetables

Directions:

1. Mix all the ingredients except the zucchini in your Instant Pot.
2. Cook on Stew for 35 minutes.
3. Release the pressure naturally.
4. Stir in the zucchini and allow to heat thoroughly.

Nutrition: Calories: 250; Carbs: 5g; Sugar: 0g; Fat: 10g; Protein: 40g; GL: 1

229. Lemon-Tarragon Soup

Preparation time: 10 minutes
Cooking time: 10 minutes
Servings: 1–2

Cashews and coconut milk replace heavy cream in this healthy version of the lemon-tarragon soup, balanced by tart freshly squeezed lemon juice and fragrant tarragon. It's a light, airy soup that you won't want to miss.

Ingredients:

- 1 tbsp. avocado oil
- ½ cup diced onion
- 3 garlic cloves, crushed
- ¼ plus ⅛ tsp. sea salt
- ¼ plus ⅛ tsp. freshly ground black pepper
- 1 (13.5-ounce) can full-fat coconut milk
- 1 tbsp. freshly squeezed lemon juice
- ½ cup raw cashews
- 1 celery stalk
- 2 tbsp. chopped fresh tarragon

Directions:

1. In a medium skillet over medium-high warmth, heat the avocado oil. Add the onion, garlic, salt, and pepper, and sauté for 3 to 5 minutes or until the onion is soft.

2. In a high-speed blender, blend together the coconut milk, lemon juice, cashews, celery, and tarragon with the onion mixture until smooth. Adjust seasonings, if necessary.
3. Fill 1 huge or 2 little dishes and enjoy immediately, or transfer to a medium saucepan and warm on low heat for 3 to 5 minutes before serving.

Nutrition: Calories: 60; Carbohydrates: 13g; Protein: 0.8g

230. Chilled Cucumber and Lime Soup

Preparation time: 5 minutes
Cooking time: 20 minutes
Servings: 1–2
Ingredients:

- 1 cucumber, peeled
- ½ zucchini, peeled
- 1 tbsp. freshly squeezed lime juice
- 1 tbsp. fresh cilantro leaves
- 1 garlic clove, crushed
- ¼ tsp. sea salt

Directions:

1. In a blender, blend together the cucumber, zucchini, lime juice, cilantro, garlic, and salt until well combined. Add more salt, if necessary.
2. Fill 1 huge or 2 little dishes and enjoy immediately, or refrigerate for 15 to 20 minutes to chill before serving.

Nutrition: Calories: 48; Carbohydrates: 8g; Fat: 1g; Protein: .5g

231. Coconut, Cilantro, And Jalapeño Soup

Preparation time: 5 minutes
Cooking time: 5 minutes
Servings: 1–2

This soup is a nutrient dream. Cilantro is a natural anti-inflammatory and is also excellent for detoxification. And one single jalapeño has an entire day's worth of vitamin C!

Ingredients:

- 2 tbsp. avocado oil
- ½ cup diced onions
- 3 garlic cloves, crushed

- ¼ tsp. sea salt
- 1 (13.5-ounce) can full-fat coconut milk
- 1 tbsp. freshly squeezed lime juice
- ½ to 1 jalapeño
- 2 tbsp. fresh cilantro leaves

Directions:
1. In a medium skillet over medium-high warmth, heat the avocado oil. Include the garlic, onion salt, and pepper, and sauté for 3 to 5 minutes, or until the onions are soft.
2. In a blender, blend together the coconut milk, lime juice, jalapeño, and cilantro with the onion mixture until creamy.
3. Fill 1 huge or 2 little dishes and enjoy.

Nutrition: Calories: 75; Carbohydrates: 13g; Fat: 2g; Protein: 4g

232. Spicy Watermelon Gazpacho

Preparation time: 5 minutes
Cooking time: 5 minutes
Servings: 1–2

At first taste, this soup may have you wondering if you're lunching on a hot and spicy salsa. It has the heat and seasonings of traditional tomato-based salsa, but it also has a faint sweetness from the cool watermelon. The soup is really hot with a whole jalapeño, so if you don't like food too hot, just use half a jalapeño.

Ingredients:
- 2 cups cubed watermelon
- ¼ cup diced onion
- ¼ cup packed cilantro leaves
- ½ to 1 jalapeño
- 2 tbsp. freshly squeezed lime juice

Directions:
1. In a blender or food processor, pulse to combine the watermelon, onion, cilantro, jalapeño, and lime juice only long enough to break down the ingredients, leaving them very finely diced and taking care to not over process.
2. Pour into 1 large or 2 small bowls and enjoy.

Nutrition: Calories: 35; Carbohydrates: 12g; Fat: .4g

233. Roasted Carrot and Leek Soup

Preparation time: 4 minutes

Cooking time: 30 minutes
Servings: 3–4

The carrot, a root vegetable, is an excellent source of antioxidants (1 cup has 113 percent of your daily value of vitamin A) and Fiber: (1 cup has 14 percent of your daily value). This bright and colorful soup freezes well to enjoy later when you're short on time.

Ingredients:
- 6 carrots
- 1 cup chopped onion
- 1 fennel bulb, cubed
- 2 garlic cloves, crushed
- 2 tbsp. avocado oil
- 1 tsp. sea salt
- 1 tsp. freshly ground black pepper
- 2 cups almond milk, plus more if desired

Directions:
1. Preheat the oven to 400°F. Line a baking sheet with parchment paper.
2. Cut the carrots into thirds, and then cut each third in half. Transfer to a medium bowl.
3. Add the onion, fennel, garlic, and avocado oil, and toss to coat. Season with salt and pepper, and toss again.
4. Transfer the vegetables to the prepared baking sheet, and roast for 30 minutes.
5. Remove from the oven and allow the vegetables to cool.
6. In a high-speed blender, blend together the almond milk and roasted vegetables until creamy and smooth. Adjust the seasonings, if necessary, and add additional milk if you prefer a thinner consistency.
7. Pour into 2 large or 4 small bowls and enjoy.

Nutrition: Calories: 55; Carbohydrates: 12g; Fat: 1.5g; Protein: 1.8g

234. Creamy Lentil and Potato Stew

Preparation time: 10 minutes
Cooking time: 30 minutes
Servings: 4

This is a hearty stew that is sure to be a favorite. It's a one-pot meal that is the perfect comfort food. With fresh vegetables and herbs along with protein-rich lentils, it's both healthy and filling. Any lentil variety would work, even a mixed, sprouted lentil blend. Another bonus of this recipe: It's freezer-friendly.

Ingredients:

- 2 tbsp. avocado oil
- ½ cup diced onion
- 2 garlic cloves, crushed
- 1 to 1½ tsp. sea salt
- 1 tsp. freshly ground black pepper
- 1 cup dry lentils
- 2 carrots, sliced
- 1 cup peeled and cubed potato
- 1 celery stalk, diced
- 2 fresh oregano sprigs, chopped
- 2 fresh tarragon sprigs, chopped
- 5 cups vegetable broth, divided
- 1 (13.5-ounce) can full-fat coconut milk

Directions:

1. In a great soup pot over average-high hotness, heat the avocado oil. Include the garlic, onion, salt, and pepper, and sauté for 3 to 5 minutes, or until the onion is soft.
2. Add the lentils, carrots, potato, celery, oregano, tarragon, and 2½ cups of vegetable broth, and stir.
3. Get to a boil, decrease the heat to medium-low, and cook, stirring frequently and adding additional vegetable broth a half cup at a time to make sure there is enough liquid for the lentils and potatoes to cook, for 20 to 25 minutes, or until the potatoes and lentils are soft.
4. Take away from the heat, and stir in the coconut milk. Pour into 4 soup bowls and enjoy.

Nutrition: Calories: 85; Carbohydrates: 20g; Fat: 3g; Protein: 3g

235. Roasted Garlic and Cauliflower Soup

Preparation time: 10 minutes
Cooking time: 35 minutes
Servings: 1–2

Roasted garlic is always a treat, and paired with cauliflower in this wonderful soup, what you get is a deeply satisfying soup with savory, rustic flavors. Blended, the result is a smooth, thick, and creamy soup, but if you prefer a thinner consistency, just adds a little more vegetable broth to thin it out. Cauliflower is anti-inflammatory, high in antioxidants, and a good source of vitamin C (1 cup has 86 percent of your daily value).

Ingredients:

- 4 cups bite-size cauliflower florets
- 5 garlic cloves
- 1½ tbsp. avocado oil
- ¾ tsp. sea salt
- ½ tsp. freshly ground black pepper
- 1 cup almond milk
- 1 cup vegetable broth, plus more if desired

Directions:

1. Preheat the oven to 450°F. Line a baking sheet with parchment paper.
2. In a medium bowl, toss the cauliflower and garlic with the avocado oil to coat. Season with salt and pepper, and toss again.
3. Transfer to the prepared baking sheet and roast for 30 minutes. Cool before adding to the blender.
4. In a high-speed blender, blend together the cooled vegetables, almond milk, and vegetable broth until creamy and smooth. Adjust the salt and pepper, if necessary, and add additional vegetable broth if you prefer a thinner consistency.
5. Transfer to a medium saucepan, and lightly warm on medium-low heat for 3 to 5 minutes.
6. Ladle into 1 large or 2 small bowls and enjoy.

Nutrition: Calories: 48; Carbohydrates: 11g; Protein 1.5g

236. Beefless "Beef" Stew

Preparation time: 10 minutes
Cooking time: 0 minutes
Servings: 4

The potatoes, carrots, aromatics, and herbs in this soup meld so well together, you'll forget there's typical beef in this stew. Hearty and flavorful, this one-pot comfort food is perfect for a fall or winter dinner.

Ingredients:

- 1 tbsp. avocado oil
- 1 cup onion, diced
- 2 garlic cloves, crushed
- 1 tsp. sea salt
- 1 tsp. freshly ground black pepper
- 3 cups vegetable broth, plus more if desired
- 2 cups water, plus more if desired
- 3 cups sliced carrot
- 1 large potato, cubed

- 2 celery stalks, diced
- 1 tsp. dried oregano
- 1 dried bay leaf

Directions:
1. In a medium soup pot over medium heat, heat the avocado oil. Include the onion, garlic, salt, and pepper, and sauté for 2 to 3 minutes, or until the onion is soft.
2. Add the vegetable broth, water, carrot, potato, celery, oregano, and bay leaf, and stir. Get to a boil, decrease the heat to medium-low, and cook for 30 to 45 minutes, or until the potatoes and carrots are soft.
3. Adjust the seasonings, if necessary, and add additional water or vegetable broth, if a soupier consistency is preferred, in half-cup increments.
4. Ladle into 4 soup bowls and enjoy.

Nutrition: Calories: 59; Carbohydrates: 12g

237. Creamy Mushroom Soup

Preparation time: 5 minutes
Cooking time: 20 minutes
Servings: 4

This savory, earthy soup is a must-try if you love mushrooms. Shiitake and baby Portobello (cremini) mushrooms are used here, but you can substitute them with your favorite mushroom varieties. Full-fat coconut milk gives it that close-your-eyes-and-savor-it creaminess that pushes the soup into the comfort food realm—perfect for those cold evenings when you need a warm soup to heat up your insides.

Ingredients:
- 1 tbsp. avocado oil
- 1 cup sliced shiitake mushrooms
- 1 cup sliced cremini mushrooms
- 1 cup diced onion
- 1 garlic clove, crushed
- ¾ tsp. sea salt
- ½ tsp. freshly ground black pepper
- 1 cup vegetable broth
- 1 (13.5-ounce) can full-fat coconut milk
- ½ tsp. dried thyme
- 1 tbsp. coconut aminos

Directions:
1. In a great soup pot over average-high hotness, heat the avocado oil. Add the mushrooms,

onion, garlic, salt, and pepper, and sauté for 2 to 3 minutes, or until the onion is soft.
2. Add the vegetable broth, coconut milk, thyme, and coconut aminos. Reduce the heat to medium-low, and simmer for about 15 minutes, stirring occasionally.
3. Adjust seasonings, if necessary, ladle into 2 large or 4 small bowls, and enjoy.

Nutrition: Calories: 65; Carbohydrates: 12g; Fat: 2g; Protein: 2g

238. Chilled Berry and Mint Soup

Preparation time: 5 minutes
Cooking time: 20 minutes
Servings: 1–2

There's no better way to cool down when it's hot outside than with this chilled, sweet mixed berry soup. It's light and showcases summer's berry bounty: raspberries, blackberries, and blueberries. The fresh mint brightens the soup and keeps the sweetness in check. This soup isn't just for lunch or dinner either—try it for a quick breakfast, too! If you like a thinner consistency for this, just add a little extra water.

Ingredients:
For The Sweetener
- ¼ cup unrefined whole cane sugar, such as Sucanat
- ¼ cup water, plus more if desired
- FOR THE SOUP
- 1 cup mixed berries (raspberries, blackberries, blueberries)
- ½ cup water
- 1 tsp. freshly squeezed lemon juice
- 8 fresh mint leaves

Directions:
1. To prepare the sweetener
2. In a small saucepan over medium-low, heat the sugar and water, stirring continuously for 1 to 2 minutes, until the sugar is dissolved. Cool.
3. To prepare the soup
4. In a blender, blend together the cooled sugar water with the berries, water, lemon juice, and mint leaves until well combined.
5. Transfer the mixture to the refrigerator and allow chilling completely, about 20 minutes.
6. Ladle into 1 large or 2 small bowls and enjoy.

Nutrition: Calories: 89; Carbohydrates: 12g; Fat: 6g; Protein: 2.2g

239. Blueberry and Chicken Salad

Preparation time: 10 minutes
Cooking time: 0 minute
Servings: 4
Ingredients:

- 2 cups chopped cooked chicken
- 1 cup fresh blueberries
- ¼ cup almonds
- 1 celery stalk
- ¼ cup red onion
- 1 tbsp. fresh basil
- 1 tbsp. fresh cilantro
- ½ cup plain, vegan mayonnaise
- ¼ tsp. salt
- ¼ tsp. freshly ground black pepper
- 8 cups salad greens

Directions:

1. Toss chicken, blueberries, almonds, celery, onion, basil, and cilantro.
2. Blend yogurt, salt, and pepper. Stir chicken salad to combine.
3. Situate 2 cups of salad greens on each of 4 plates and divide the chicken salad among the plates to serve.

Nutrition: Calories: 207; Carbohydrates: 11g; Sugars: 6g

240. Beef and Red Bean Chili

Preparation time: 10 minutes
Cooking time: 6 hours
Servings: 4
Ingredients:

- 1 cup dry red beans
- 1 tbsp. olive oil
- 2 pounds boneless beef chuck
- 1 large onion, coarsely chopped
- 1 (14 ounces) can beef broth
- 2 chipotle chili peppers in adobo sauce
- 2 tsp. dried oregano, crushed
- 1 tsp. ground cumin
- ½ tsp. salt

- 1 (14.5 ounces) can tomatoes with mild green chilis
- 1 (15 ounces) can tomato sauce
- ¼ cup snipped fresh cilantro
- 1 medium red sweet pepper

Directions:

1. Rinse out the beans and place them into a Dutch oven or big saucepan, then add in water enough to cover them. Allow the beans to boil then drop the heat down. Simmer the beans without a cover for 10 minutes. Take off the heat and keep covered for an hour.
2. In a big frypan, heat up the oil upon medium-high heat, then cook onion and half the beef until they brown a bit over medium-high heat. Move into a 3 ½- or 4-quart crockery cooker. Do this again with what's left of the beef. Add in tomato sauce, tomatoes (not drained), salt, cumin, oregano, adobo sauce, chipotle peppers, and broth, stirring to blend. Strain out and rinse beans and stir in the cooker.
3. Cook while covered on a low setting for around 10–12 hours or on a high setting for 5–6 hours. Spoon the chili into bowls or mugs and top with sweet pepper and cilantro.

Nutrition: Calories: 288; Carbohydrate: 24g; Sugar: 5

241. Berry Apple Cider

Preparation time: 15 minutes
Cooking time: 3 hours
Servings: 3
Ingredients:

- 4 cinnamon sticks, cut into 1-inch pieces
- 1½ tsp. whole cloves
- 4 cups apple cider
- 4 cups low-calorie cranberry-raspberry juice drink
- 1 medium apple

Directions:

1. To make the spice bag, cut out a 6-inch square from double-thick, pure cotton cheesecloth. Put in the cloves and cinnamon, then bring the corners up, tie it closed using a clean kitchen string that is pure cotton.
2. In a 3 ½- 5-quart slow cooker, combine cranberry-raspberry juice, apple cider, and the spice bag.

3. Cook while covered over low heat setting for around 4–6 hours or on a high heat setting for 2–2 ½ hours.
4. Throw out the spice bag. Serve right away or keep it warm while covered on warm or low-heat setting up to 2 hours, occasionally stirring. Garnish each serving with apples (thinly sliced).

Nutrition: Calories: 89; Carbohydrate: 22g; Sugar: 19g

242.   **Brunswick Stew**

Preparation time: 10 minutes
Cooking time: 45 minutes
Servings: 3
Ingredients:

- 4 ounces diced salt pork
- 2 pounds chicken parts
- 8 cups water
- 3 potatoes, cubed
- 3 onions, chopped
- 1 (28 ounces) can whole peeled tomatoes
- 2 cups canned whole kernel corn
- 1 (10 ounces) package frozen lima beans
- 1 tbsp. Worcestershire sauce
- ½ tsp. salt
- 1/4 tsp. ground black pepper

Directions:

1. Mix and boil water, chicken, and salt pork in a big pot on high heat. Lower heat to low. Cover then simmer until chicken is tender for 45 minutes.
2. Take out chicken. Let cool until easily handled. Take the meat out. Throw out bones and skin. Chop meat into bite-sized pieces. Put back in the soup.
3. Add ground black pepper, salt, Worcestershire sauce, lima beans, corn, tomatoes, onions, and potatoes. Mix well. Stir well and simmer for 1 hour, uncovered.

Nutrition: Calories: 368; Carbohydrate: 25.9g; Protein: 27.9g

243.   **Buffalo Chicken Salads**

Preparation time: 7 minutes
Cooking time: 3 hours
Servings: 5
Ingredients:

- 1½ pounds chicken breast halves
- ½ cup Wing Time® Buffalo chicken sauce
- 4 tsp. cider vinegar
- 1 tsp. Worcestershire sauce
- 1 tsp. paprika
- 1/3 cup light mayonnaise
- 2 tbsp. fat-free milk
- 2 tbsp. crumbled blue cheese
- 2 romaine hearts, chopped
- 1 cup whole-grain croutons
- ½ cup very thinly sliced red onion

Directions:

1. Place chicken in a 2-quarts slow cooker. Mix together Worcestershire sauce, 2 tsp. of vinegar, and Buffalo sauce in a small bowl; pour over chicken. Dust with paprika. Close and cook for 3 hours in a low-heat setting.
2. Mix the leftover 2 tsp. of vinegar with milk and light mayonnaise together in a small bowl at the serving time; mix in blue cheese. While chicken is still in the slow cooker, pull meat into bite-sized pieces using two forks.
3. Split the romaine among 6 dishes. Spoon sauce and chicken over lettuce. Pour with blue cheese dressing then add red onion slices and croutons on top.

Nutrition: Calories: 274; Carbohydrate: 11g; Fiber: 2g

244.   **Cacciatore Style Chicken**

Preparation time: 10 minutes
Cooking time: 4 hours
Servings: 6
Ingredients:

- 2 cups sliced fresh mushrooms
- 1 cup sliced celery
- 1 cup chopped carrot
- 2 medium onions, cut into wedges
- 1 green, yellow, or red sweet peppers
- 4 cloves garlic, minced
- 12 chicken drumsticks
- ½ cup chicken broth
- ¼ cup dry white wine
- 2 tbsp. quick-cooking tapioca
- 2 bay leaves
- 1 tsp. dried oregano, crushed
- 1 tsp. sugar

113

- ½ tsp. salt
- ¼ tsp. pepper
- 1 (14.5 ounces) can diced tomatoes
- 1/3 cup tomato paste
- Hot cooked pasta or rice

Directions:

1. Mix garlic, sweet pepper, onions, carrot, celery, and mushrooms in a 5- or 6-qt. slow cooker. Cover veggies with the chicken. Add pepper, salt, sugar, oregano, bay leaves, tapioca, wine, and broth.
2. Cover. Cook for 3–3 ½ hours in a high-heat setting.
3. Take chicken out; keep warm. Discard bay leaves. Turn to a high-heat setting if using a low-heat setting. Mix tomato paste and undrained tomatoes in. Cover. Cook on high-heat setting for 15 more minutes.
4. Put the veggie mixture on top of pasta and chicken.

Nutrition: Calories: 324; Sugar: 7g; Carbohydrate: 35g

245. Carnitas Tacos

Preparation time: 10 minutes
Cooking time: 5 hours
Servings: 4
Ingredients:

- 3 to 3½-pound bone-in pork shoulder roast
- ½ cup chopped onion
- 1/3 cup orange juice
- 1 tbsp. ground cumin
- 1½ tsp. kosher salt
- 1 tsp. dried oregano, crushed
- ¼ tsp. cayenne pepper
- 1 lime
- 2 (5.3 ounces) containers plain low-fat Greek yogurt
- 1 pinch kosher salt
- 16 (6 inches) soft yellow corn tortillas, such as Mission® brand
- 4 leaves green cabbage, quartered
- 1 cup very thinly sliced red onion
- 1 cup salsa (optional)

Directions:

1. Take off meat from the bone; throw away bone. Trim meat fat. Slice meat into 2 to 3-inch pieces; put in a slow cooker of 3 ½ or 4-quart in size.

Mix in cayenne, oregano, salt, cumin, orange juice, and onion.

2. Cover and cook for 4 to 5 hours on high. Take out the meat from the cooker. Shred meat with two forks. Mix in enough cooking liquid to moisten.
3. Take out 1 tsp. zest (put aside) for lime crema, then squeeze 2 tbsp. lime juice. Mix dash salt, yogurt, and lime juice in a small bowl.
4. Serve lime crema, salsa (if wished), red onion and cabbage with meat in tortillas. Scatter with lime zest.

Nutrition: Calories: 301; Carbohydrate: 28g; Sugar: 7g

246. Chicken Chili

Preparation time: 6 minutes
Cooking time: 1 hour
Servings: 4
Ingredients:

- 3 tbsp. vegetable oil
- 2 cloves garlic, minced
- 1 green bell pepper, chopped
- 1 onion, chopped
- 1 stalk celery, sliced
- 1/4-pound mushrooms, chopped
- 1-pound chicken breast
- 1 tbsp. chili powder
- 1 tsp. dried oregano
- 1 tsp. ground cumin
- ½ tsp. paprika
- ½ tsp. cocoa powder
- 1/4 tsp. salt
- 1 pinch crushed red pepper flakes
- 1 pinch ground black pepper
- 1 (14.5 oz) can tomatoes with juice
- 1 (19 oz) can kidney beans

Directions:

1. Fill 2 tbsp. of oil into a big skillet and heat it moderate heat. Add mushrooms, celery, onio bell pepper, and garlic, sautéing for 5 minute Put it to one side.
2. Insert the leftover 1 tbsp. of oil into the skill At high heat, cook the chicken until brown and its exterior turns firm. Transfer t vegetable mixture back into the skillet.
3. Stir in ground black pepper, hot pepper flak salt, cocoa powder, paprika, oregano, cum and chili powder. Continue stirring for seve

minutes to avoid burning. Pour in the beans and tomatoes and lead the entire mixture to boiling point then adjust the setting to low heat. Place a lid on the skillet and leave it simmering for 15 minutes. Uncover the skillet and leave it simmering for another 15 minutes.

Nutrition: Calories: 308; Carbohydrate: 25.9g; Protein: 29g

247.   Chicken Vera Cruz

Preparation time: 7 minutes
Cooking time: 10 hours
Servings: 5
Ingredients:

- 1 medium onion, cut into wedges
- 1-pound yellow-skin potatoes
- 6 skinless, boneless chicken thighs
- 2 (14.5 oz.) cans no-salt-added diced tomatoes
- 1 fresh jalapeño chili pepper
- 2 tbsp. Worcestershire sauce
- 1 tbsp. chopped garlic
- 1 tsp. dried oregano, crushed
- ¼ tsp. ground cinnamon
- 1/8 tsp. ground cloves
- ½ cup snipped fresh parsley
- ¼ cup chopped pimiento-stuffed green olives

Directions:

1. Put the onion in a 3 ½- or 4-quart slow cooker. Place chicken thighs and potatoes on top. Drain and discard juices from a can of tomatoes. Stir undrained and drained tomatoes, cloves, cinnamon, oregano, garlic, Worcestershire sauce, and jalapeño pepper together in a bowl. Pour over all in the cooker.
2. Cook with a cover for 10 hours in a low-heat setting.
3. To make the topping: Stir chopped pimiento-stuffed green olives and snipped fresh parsley together in a small bowl. Drizzle the topping over each serving of chicken.

Nutrition: Calories: 228; Sugar: 9g; Carbohydrate: 25g

248.   Chicken and Cornmeal Dumplings

Preparation time: 8 minutes
Cooking time: 8 hours
Servings: 4
Ingredients:

Chicken and Vegetable Filling

- 2 medium carrots, thinly sliced
- 1 stalk celery, thinly sliced
- 1/3 cup corn kernels
- ½ of a medium onion, thinly sliced
- 2 cloves garlic, minced
- 1 tsp. snipped fresh rosemary
- ¼ tsp. ground black pepper
- 2 chicken thighs, skinned
- 1 cup reduced-sodium chicken broth
- ½ cup fat-free milk
- 1 tbsp. all-purpose flour

Cornmeal Dumplings

- ¼ cup flour
- ¼ cup cornmeal
- ½ tsp. baking powder
- 1 egg white
- 1 tbsp. fat-free milk
- 1 tbsp. canola oil

Directions:

1. Mix 1/4 tsp. pepper, carrots, garlic, celery, rosemary, corn, and onion in a 1 ½ or 2-quart slow cooker. Place chicken on top. Pour the broth atop the mixture in the cooker.
2. Close and cook on low heat for 7 to 8 hours.
3. If cooking with the low-heat setting, switch to a high-heat setting (or if the heat setting is not available, continue to cook). Place the chicken onto a cutting board and let cool slightly. Once cool enough to handle, chop off the chicken from bones and get rid of the bones. Chop the chicken and place it back into the mixture in the cooker. Mix flour and milk in a small bowl until smooth. Stir into the mixture in the cooker.
4. Drop the Cornmeal Dumplings dough into 4 mounds atop hot chicken mixture using two spoons. Cover and cook for 20 to 25 minutes more or until a toothpick comes out clean when inserted into a dumpling. (Avoid lifting lid when cooking.) Sprinkle each of the servings with coarse pepper if desired.
5. Mix together ½ tsp. baking powder, 1/4 cup flour, a dash of salt, and 1/4 cup cornmeal in a medium bowl. Mix 1 tbsp. canola oil, 1 egg white, and 1 tbsp. fat-free milk in a small bowl. Pour the egg mixture into the flour mixture. Mix just until moistened.

249. Chicken and Pepperoni

Preparation time: 4 minutes
Cooking time: 4 hours
Servings: 5
Ingredients:

- 3½ to 4 pounds meaty chicken pieces
- 1/8 tsp. salt
- 1/8 tsp. black pepper
- 2 ounces sliced turkey pepperoni
- ¼ cup sliced pitted ripe olives
- ½ cup reduced-sodium chicken broth
- 1 tbsp. tomato paste
- 1 tsp. dried Italian seasoning, crushed
- ½ cup shredded part-skim mozzarella cheese (2 ounces)

Directions:

1. Put the chicken into a 3 ½ to 5-qt. slow cooker. Sprinkle pepper and salt on the chicken. Slice pepperoni slices in half. Put olives and pepperoni into the slow cooker. In a small bowl, blend Italian seasoning, tomato paste, and chicken broth together. Transfer the mixture into the slow cooker.
2. Cook with a cover for 3–3 ½ hours on high.
3. Transfer the olives, pepperoni, and chicken onto a serving platter with a slotted spoon. Discard the cooking liquid. Sprinkle cheese over the chicken. Use foil to loosely cover and allow to sit for 5 minutes to melt the cheese.

Nutrition: Calories: 243; Carbohydrate: 1g; Protein: 41g

250. Chicken and Sausage Gumbo

Preparation time: 6 minutes
Cooking time: 4 hours
Servings: 5
Ingredients:

- 1/3 cup all-purpose flour
- 1 (14 ounces) can reduced-sodium chicken broth
- 2 cups chicken breast
- 8 ounces smoked turkey sausage links
- 2 cups sliced fresh okra
- 1 cup water
- 1 cup coarsely chopped onion
- 1 cup sweet pepper
- ½ cup sliced celery
- 4 cloves garlic, minced
- 1 tsp. dried thyme
- ½ tsp. ground black pepper
- ¼ tsp. cayenne pepper
- 3 cups hot cooked brown rice

Directions:

1. To make the roux: Cook the flour upon a medium heat in a heavy medium-sized saucepan, stirring periodically, for roughly (minutes or until the flour browns. Take off the heat and slightly cool, then slowly stir in the broth. Cook the roux until it bubbles and thickens up.
2. Pour the roux in a 3 ½- or 4-quart slow cooker then add in cayenne pepper, black pepper thyme, garlic, celery, sweet pepper, onion water, okra, sausage, and chicken.
3. Cook the soup covered on a high setting for 3- 3 ½ hours. Take the fat off the top and serv atop hot cooked brown rice.

Nutrition: Calories: 230; Sugar: 3g; Protein: 19g

251. Chicken, Barley, and Leek Stew

Preparation time: 10 minutes
Cooking time: 3 hours
Servings: 2
Ingredients:

- 1-pound chicken thighs
- 1 tbsp. olive oil
- 1 (49 ounces) can reduced-sodium chicke broth
- 1 cup regular barley (not quick-cooking)
- 2 medium leeks, halved lengthwise and slice
- 2 medium carrots, thinly sliced
- 1½ tsp. dried basil or Italian seasoning, crushe
- ¼ tsp. cracked black pepper

Directions:

1. In the big skillet, cook the chicken in hot oil becoming brown on all sides. In the 4–5- slow cooker, whisk the pepper, dried bas carrots, leeks, barley, chicken broth, a chicken.

2. Keep covered and cooked over high heat setting for 2–2.5 hours or till the barley softens. As you wish, drizzle with the parsley or fresh basil prior to serving.

Nutrition: Calories: 248; Fiber: 6g; Carbohydrate: 27g

252. **Cider Pork Stew**

Preparation time: 9 minutes
Cooking time: 12 hours
Servings: 3
Ingredients:

- 2 pounds pork shoulder roast
- 3 medium cubed potatoes
- 3 medium carrots
- 2 medium onions, sliced
- 1 cup coarsely chopped apple
- ½ cup coarsely chopped celery
- 3 tbsp. quick-cooking tapioca
- 2 cups apple juice
- 1 tsp. salt
- 1 tsp. caraway seeds
- ¼ tsp. black pepper

Directions:

1. Chop the meat into 1-in. cubes. In the 3.5- 5.5 qt. slow cooker, mix the tapioca, celery, apple, onions, carrots, potatoes, and meat. Whisk in pepper, caraway seeds, salt, and apple juice.
2. Keep covered and cook over low heat setting for 10–12 hours. If you want, use the celery leaves to decorate each of the servings.

Nutrition: Calories: 244; Fiber: 5g; Carbohydrate: 33g

253. **Creamy Chicken Noodle Soup**

Preparation time: 7 minutes
Cooking time: 8 hours
Servings: 4
Ingredients:

- 1 (32 fluid ounce) container reduced-sodium chicken broth
- 3 cups water
- 2½ cups chopped cooked chicken
- 3 medium carrots, sliced
- 3 stalks celery
- 1½ cups sliced fresh mushrooms
- ¼ cup chopped onion
- 1½ tsp. dried thyme, crushed

- ¾ tsp. garlic-pepper seasoning
- 3 ounces reduced-fat cream cheese (Neufchâtel), cut up
- 2 cups dried egg noodles

Directions:

1. Mix together the garlic-pepper seasoning, thyme, onion, mushrooms, celery, carrots, chicken, water, and broth in a 5 to 6-quart slow cooker.
2. Put the cover and let it cook for 6–8 hours in a low-heat setting.
3. Increase to a high-heat setting if you are using a low-heat setting. Mix in the cream cheese until blended. Mix in uncooked noodles. Put the cover and let it cook for an additional 20–30 minutes or just until the noodles become tender.

Nutrition: Calories: 170; Sugar: 3g; Fiber: 2g

254. **Cuban Pulled Pork Sandwich**

Preparation time: 6 minutes
Cooking time: 5 hours
Servings: 5
Ingredients:

- 1 tsp. dried oregano, crushed
- ¾ tsp. ground cumin
- ½ tsp. ground coriander
- ¼ tsp. salt
- ¼ tsp. black pepper
- ¼ tsp. ground allspice
- 1 2 to 2½-pound boneless pork shoulder roast
- 1 tbsp. olive oil
- Nonstick cooking spray
- 2 cups sliced onions
- 2 green sweet peppers, cut into bite-size strips
- ½ to 1 fresh jalapeño pepper
- 4 cloves garlic, minced
- ¼ cup orange juice
- ¼ cup lime juice
- 6 heart-healthy wheat hamburger buns, toasted
- 2 tbsp. jalapeño mustard

Directions:

1. Mix allspice, oregano, black pepper, cumin, salt, and coriander together in a small bowl. Press each side of the roast into the spice mixture. On medium-high heat, heat oil in a big

non-stick pan; put in the roast. Cook for 5mins until both sides of the roast are light brown, turn the roast one time.

2. Using a cooking spray, grease a 3 ½ or 4qt slow cooker; arrange the garlic, onions, jalapeno, and green peppers in a layer. Pour in lime juice and orange juice. Slice the roast if needed to fit inside the cooker; put on top of the vegetables covered or 4 ½–5hrs on high heat setting.

3. Move roast to a cutting board using a slotted spoon. Drain the cooking liquid and keep the jalapeno, green peppers, and onions. Shred the roast with 2 forks then place it back in the cooker. Remove fat from the liquid. Mix half a cup of cooking liquid and reserved vegetables into the cooker. Pour in more cooking liquid if desired. Discard the remaining cooking liquid.

4. Slather mustard on rolls. Split the meat between the bottom roll halves. Add avocado on top if desired. Place the roll tops on sandwiches.

Nutrition: Calories: 379; Carbohydrate: 32g; Fiber: 4g

255.   Gazpacho

Preparation time: 15 minutes
Cooking time: 0 minute
Servings: 4
Ingredients:

- 3 pounds ripe tomatoes
- 1 cup low-sodium tomato juice
- ½ red onion, chopped
- 1 cucumber
- 1 red bell pepper
- 2 celery stalks
- 2 tbsp. parsley
- 2 garlic cloves
- 2 tbsp. extra-virgin olive oil
- 2 tbsp. red wine vinegar
- 1 tsp. honey
- ½ tsp. salt
- ¼ tsp. freshly ground black pepper

Directions:

1. In a blender jar, combine the tomatoes, tomato juice, onion, cucumber, bell pepper, celery, parsley, garlic, olive oil, vinegar, honey, salt, and pepper. Pulse until blended but still slightly chunky.

2. Adjust the seasonings as needed and serve.

Nutrition: Calories:170; Carbohydrates: 24g; Sugars: 16g

256.   Tomato and Kale Soup

Preparation time: 10 minutes
Cooking time: 15 minutes
Servings: 4
Ingredients:

- 1 tbsp. extra-virgin olive oil
- 1 medium onion
- 2 carrots
- 3 garlic cloves
- 4 cups low-sodium vegetable broth
- 1 (28-ounce) can crushed tomatoes
- ½ tsp. dried oregano
- ¼ tsp. dried basil
- 4 cups chopped baby kale leaves
- ¼ tsp. salt

Directions:

1. In a huge pot, heat up oil over medium heat. Sauté onion and carrots for 3 to 5 minutes. Add the garlic and sauté for 30 seconds more, until fragrant.

2. Add the vegetable broth, tomatoes, oregano, and basil to the pot and boil. Decrease the heat to low and simmer for 5 minutes.

3. Using an immersion blender, purée the soup.

4. Add the kale and simmer for 3 more minutes. Season with salt. Serve immediately.

Nutrition: Calories: 170; Carbohydrates: 31g; Sugar: 13g

257.   Comforting Summer Squash Soup with Crispy Chickpeas

Preparation time: 10 minutes
Cooking time: 20 minutes
Servings: 4
Ingredients:

- 1 (15-ounce) can low-sodium chickpeas
- 1 tsp. extra-virgin olive oil
- ¼ tsp. smoked paprika
- Pinch salt, plus ½ tsp.
- 3 medium zucchinis
- 3 cups low-sodium vegetable broth

- ½ onion
- 3 garlic cloves
- 2 tbsp. plain low-fat Greek yogurt
- Freshly ground black pepper

Directions:
1. Preheat the oven to 425°F. Line a baking sheet with parchment paper.
2. In a medium mixing bowl, toss the chickpeas with 1 tsp. of olive oil, the smoked paprika, and a pinch of salt. Transfer to the prepared baking sheet and roast until crispy, about 20 minutes, stirring once. Set aside.
3. Meanwhile, in a medium pot, heat the remaining 1 tbsp. of oil over medium heat.
4. Add the zucchini, broth, onion, and garlic to the pot, and boil. Simmer, and cook for 20 minutes.
5. In a blender jar, purée the soup. Return to the pot.
6. Add the yogurt, remaining ½ tsp. of salt, and pepper, and stir well. Serve topped with roasted chickpeas.

Nutrition: Calories: 188; Carbohydrates: 24g; Sugars: 7g

258. Curried Carrot Soup

Preparation time: 10 minutes
Cooking time: 5 minutes
Servings: 6
Ingredients:
- 1 tbsp. extra-virgin olive oil
- 1 small onion
- 2 celery stalks
- 1½ tsp. curry powder
- 1 tsp. ground cumin
- 1 tsp. minced fresh ginger
- 6 medium carrots
- 4 cups low-sodium vegetable broth
- ¼ tsp. salt
- 1 cup canned coconut milk
- ¼ tsp. freshly ground black pepper
- 1 tbsp. chopped fresh cilantro

Directions:
1. Heat an Instant Pot to high and add the olive oil.

2. Sauté the onion and celery for 2 to 3 minutes. Add the curry powder, cumin, and ginger to the pot and cook until fragrant, about 30 seconds.
3. Add the carrots, vegetable broth, and salt to the pot. Close and seal, and set for 5 minutes on high. Allow the pressure to release naturally.
4. In a blender jar, carefully purée the soup in batches and transfer it back to the pot.
5. Stir in the coconut milk and pepper, and heat through. Top with the cilantro and serve.

Nutrition: Calories: 145; Carbohydrates: 13g; Sugars: 4g

259. Thai Peanut, Carrot, and Shrimp Soup

Preparation time: 10 minutes
Cooking time: 10 minutes
Servings: 4
Ingredients:
- 1 tbsp. coconut oil
- 1 tbsp. Thai red curry paste
- ½ onion
- 3 garlic cloves
- 2 cups chopped carrots
- ½ cup whole unsalted peanuts
- 4 cups low-sodium vegetable broth
- ½ cup unsweetened plain almond milk
- ½ pound shrimp,
- Minced fresh cilantro, for garnish

Directions:
1. In a big pan, heat up oil over medium-high heat until shimmering.
2. Cook curry paste, stirring continuously, for 1 minute. Add the onion, garlic, carrots, and peanuts to the pan, and continue to cook for 2 to 3 minutes.
3. Boil broth. Reduce the heat to low and simmer for 5 to 6 minutes.
4. Purée the soup until smooth and return it to the pot. Over low heat, pour almond milk and stir to combine. Cook shrimp in the pot for 2 to 3 minutes.
5. Garnish with cilantro and serve.

Nutrition: Calories: 237; Carbohydrates: 17g; Sugars: 6g

260.   Chicken Tortilla Soup

Preparation time: 10 minutes
Cooking time: 35 minutes
Servings: 4
Ingredients:

- 1 tbsp. extra-virgin olive oil
- 1 onion, thinly sliced
- 1 garlic clove, minced
- 1 jalapeño pepper, diced
- 2 boneless, skinless chicken breasts
- 4 cups low-sodium chicken broth
- 1 Roma tomato, diced
- ½ tsp. salt
- 2 (6-inch) corn tortillas
- Juice of 1 lime
- Minced fresh cilantro, for garnish
- ¼ cup shredded cheddar cheese, for garnish

Directions:

1. In a medium pot, cook oil over medium-high heat. Add the onion and cook for 3 to 5 minutes until it begins to soften. Add the garlic and jalapeño, and cook until fragrant, about 1 minute more.
2. Add the chicken, chicken broth, tomato, and salt to the pot and boil. Lower heat to medium and simmer mildly for 20 to 25 minutes. Remove the chicken from the pot and set it aside.
3. Preheat a broiler too high.
4. Spray the tortilla strips with nonstick cooking spray and toss to coat. Spread in a single layer on a baking sheet and broil for 3 to 5 minutes, flipping once, until crisp.
5. Once the chicken is cooked, shred it with two forks and return to the pot.
6. Season the soup with lime juice. Serve hot, garnished with cilantro, cheese, and tortilla strips.

Nutrition: Calories: 191; Carbohydrates: 13g; Sugars: 2g

261.   Beef and Mushroom Barley Soup

Preparation time: 10 minutes
Cooking time: 80 minutes
Servings: 6

Ingredients:

- 1-pound beef stew meat, cubed
- ¼ tsp. salt
- ¼ tsp. freshly ground black pepper
- 1 tbsp. extra-virgin olive oil
- 8 ounces sliced mushrooms
- 1 onion, chopped
- 2 carrots, chopped
- 3 celery stalks, chopped
- 6 garlic cloves, minced
- ½ tsp. dried thyme
- 4 cups low-sodium beef broth
- 1 cup water
- ½ cup pearl barley

Directions:

1. Season the meat well.
2. In an Instant Pot, heat the oil over high heat. Cook meat on all sides. Remove from the pot and set aside.
3. Add the mushrooms to the pot and cook for 1 to 2 minutes. Remove the mushrooms and set them aside with the meat.
4. Sauté onion, carrots, and celery for 3 to 4 minutes. Add the garlic and continue to cook until fragrant, about 30 seconds longer.
5. Return the meat and mushrooms to the pot, then add the thyme, beef broth, and water. Adjust the pressure on high and cook for 1 minutes. Let the pressure release naturally.
6. Open the Instant Pot and add the barley. Use the slow cooker function on the Instant Pot, affix the lid (vent open), and continue to cook for 1 hour. Serve.

Nutrition: Calories: 245; Carbohydrates: 19g; Sugar: 3g

262.   Cucumber, Tomato, and Avocado Salad

Preparation time: 10 minutes
Cooking time: 0 minute
Servings: 4
Ingredients:

- 1 cup cherry tomatoes
- 1 large cucumber
- 1 small red onion
- 1 avocado

- 2 tbsp. chopped fresh dill
- 2 tbsp. extra-virgin olive oil
- Juice of 1 lemon
- ¼ tsp. salt
- ¼ tsp. freshly ground black pepper

Directions:

1. In a big mixing bowl, mix the tomatoes, cucumber, onion, avocado, and dill.
2. In a small bowl, combine the oil, lemon juice, salt, and pepper, and mix well.
3. Drizzle the dressing over the vegetables and toss to combine. Serve.

Nutrition: Calories: 151; Carbohydrates: 11g; Sugars:

263. Cabbage Slaw Salad

Preparation time: 15 minutes
Cooking time: 0 minute
Servings: 4
Ingredients:

- 2 cups green cabbage
- 2 cups red cabbage
- 2 cups grated carrots
- 3 scallions
- 2 tbsp. extra-virgin olive oil
- 2 tbsp. rice vinegar
- 1 tsp. honey
- 1 garlic clove
- ¼ tsp. salt

Directions:

1. Throw together the green and red cabbage, carrots, and scallions.
2. In a small bowl, whisk together the oil, vinegar, honey, garlic, and salt.
3. Pour the dressing over the veggies and mix to combine thoroughly.
4. Serve immediately, or cover and chill for several hours before serving.

Nutrition: Calories: 80; Carbohydrates: 10g; Sugars: 6g

264. Green Salad with Blackberries, Goat Cheese, and Sweet Potatoes

Preparation time: 15 minutes

Cooking time: 20 minutes
Servings: 4
Ingredients:
For the vinaigrette

- 1-pint blackberries
- 2 tbsp. red wine vinegar
- 1 tbsp. honey
- 3 tbsp. extra-virgin olive oil
- ¼ tsp. salt
- Freshly ground black pepper

For the salad

- 1 sweet potato, cubed
- 1 tsp. extra-virgin olive oil
- 8 cups salad greens (baby spinach, spicy greens, romaine)
- ½ red onion, sliced
- ¼ cup crumbled goat cheese

Directions:
For vinaigrette

1. In a blender jar, combine the blackberries, vinegar, honey, oil, salt, and pepper, and process until smooth.
2. Set aside.

For salad

2. Preheat the oven to 425°F. Line a baking sheet with parchment paper.
3. Mix the sweet potato with olive oil. Transfer to the prepared baking sheet and roast for 20 minutes, stirring once halfway through, until tender. Remove and cool for a few minutes.
4. In a large bowl, toss the greens with the red onion and cooled sweet potato, and drizzle with the vinaigrette. Serve topped with 1 tbsp. of goat cheese per serving.

Nutrition: Calories: 196; Carbohydrates: 21g; Sugars: 10g

265. Three Bean and Basil Salad

Preparation time: 10 minutes
Cooking time: 0 minute
Servings: 8
Ingredients:

- 1 (15-ounce) can low-sodium chickpeas
- 1 (15-ounce) can low-sodium kidney beans
- 1 (15-ounce) can low-sodium white beans
- 1 red bell pepper
- ¼ cup chopped scallions

- ¼ cup finely chopped fresh basil
- 3 garlic cloves, minced
- 2 tbsp. extra-virgin olive oil
- 1 tbsp. red wine vinegar
- 1 tsp. Dijon mustard
- ¼ tsp. freshly ground black pepper

Directions:
1. Toss chickpeas, kidney beans, white beans, bell pepper, scallions, basil, and garlic gently.
2. Blend together olive oil, vinegar, mustard, and pepper. Toss with the salad.
3. Wrap and chill for 1 hour.

Nutrition: Calories: 193; Carbohydrates: 29g; Sugars: 3g

266. Rainbow Black Bean Salad

Preparation time: 15 minutes
Cooking time: 0 minute
Servings: 5
Ingredients:

- 1 (15-ounce) can low-sodium black beans
- 1 avocado, diced
- 1 cup cherry
- tomatoes, halved
- 1 cup chopped baby spinach
- ½ cup red bell pepper
- ¼ cup jicama
- ½ cup scallions
- ¼ cup fresh cilantro
- 2 tbsp. lime juice
- 1 tbsp. extra-virgin olive oil
- 2 garlic cloves, minced
- 1 tsp. honey
- ¼ tsp. salt
- ¼ tsp. freshly ground black pepper

Directions:
1. Mix black beans, avocado, tomatoes, spinach, bell pepper, jicama, scallions, and cilantro.
2. Blend lime juice, oil, garlic, honey, salt, and pepper. Add to the salad and toss.
3. Chill for 1 hour before serving.

Nutrition: Calories: 169; Carbohydrates: 22g; Sugars: 3g

267. Warm Barley and Squash Salad

Preparation time: 20 minutes
Cooking time: 40 minutes
Servings: 8
Ingredients:

- 1 small butternut squash
- 3 tbsp. extra-virgin olive oil
- 2 cups broccoli florets
- 1 cup pearl barley
- 1 cup toasted chopped walnuts
- 2 cups baby kale
- ½ red onion, sliced
- 2 tbsp. balsamic vinegar
- 2 garlic cloves, minced
- ½ tsp. salt
- ¼ tsp. black pepper

Directions:
1. Preheat the oven to 400°F. Line a baking sheet with parchment paper.
2. Peel off the squash, and slice into dice. In large bowl, toss the squash with 2 tsp. of olive oil. Transfer to the prepared baking sheet and roast for 20 minutes.
3. While the squash is roasting, toss the broccoli in the same bowl with 1 tsp. of olive oil. After 20 minutes, flip the squash and push it to one side of the baking sheet. Add the broccoli to the other side and continue to roast for 20 more minutes until tender.
4. While the veggies are roasting, in a medium pot, cover the barley with several inches of water. Boil, then adjust heat, cover, and simmer for 30 minutes until tender. Drain and rinse.
5. Transfer the barley to a large bowl, and toss with the cooked squash and broccoli, walnuts, kale, and onion.
6. In a small bowl, mix the remaining 2 tbsp. of olive oil, balsamic vinegar, garlic, salt, and pepper. Drizzle dressing over the salad and toss.

Nutrition: Calories: 274; Carbohydrates: 32g; Sugars: 3g

268. Winter Chicken and Citrus Salad

Preparation time: 10 minutes

Cooking time: 0 minute
Servings: 4
Ingredients:

- 4 cups baby spinach
- 2 tbsp. extra-virgin olive oil
- 1 tbsp. lemon juice
- 1/8 tsp. salt
- 2 cups chopped cooked chicken
- 2 mandarin oranges
- ½ peeled grapefruit, sectioned
- ¼ cup sliced almonds

Directions:

1. Toss spinach with olive oil, lemon juice, salt, and pepper.
2. Add the chicken, oranges, grapefruit, and almonds to the bowl. Toss gently.
3. Arrange on 4 plates and serve.

Nutrition: Calories: 249; Carbohydrates: 11g; Sugars: 7g

269. Brussels Sprouts

Preparation time: 5 minutes
Cooking time: 3 minutes
Servings: 5
Ingredients:

- 1 tsp. extra-virgin olive oil
- 1 lb. halved Brussels sprouts
- 3 tbsps. apple cider vinegar
- 3 tbsps. gluten-free tamari soy sauce
- 3 tbsps. chopped sun-dried tomatoes

Directions:

1. Select the "Sauté" function on your Instant Pot, add oil and allow the pot to get hot.
2. Cancel the "Sauté" function and add the Brussels sprouts.
3. Stir well and allow the sprouts to cook in the residual heat for 2–3 minutes.
4. Add the tamari soy sauce and vinegar, and then stir.
5. Cover the Instant Pot, sealing the pressure valve by pointing it to "Sealing."
6. Select the "Manual, High Pressure" setting and cook for 3 minutes.
7. Once the cook cycle is done, do a quick pressure release, and then stir in the chopped sun-dried tomatoes.
8. Serve immediately.

Nutrition: Calories: 62; Carbohydrates: 10g; Fat: 1g

270. Garlic and Herb Carrots

Preparation time: 2 minutes
Cooking time: 18 minutes
Servings: 3
Ingredients:

- 2 tbsps. butter
- 1 lb. baby carrots
- 1 cup water
- 1 tsp. fresh thyme or oregano
- 1 tsp. minced garlic
- Black pepper
- Coarse sea salt

Directions:

1. Fill water into the inner pot of the Instant Pot, and then put it in a steamer basket.
2. Layer the carrots into the steamer basket.
3. Close and seal the lid, with the pressure vent in the "Sealing" position.
4. Select the "Steam" setting and cook for 2 minutes on high pressure.
5. Quick-release the pressure and then carefully remove the steamer basket with the steamed carrots, discarding the water.
6. Add butter to the inner pot of the Instant Pot and allow it to melt on the "Sauté" function.
7. Add garlic and sauté for 30 seconds, and then add the carrots. Mix well.
8. Stir in the fresh herbs, and cook for 2–3 minutes.
9. Season with salt and black pepper, and transfer to a serving bowl.
10. .Serve warm and enjoy!

Nutrition: Calories: 122; Carbohydrates: 12g; Fat: 7g

271. Cilantro Lime Drumsticks

Preparation time: 5 minutes
Cooking time: 15 minutes
Servings: 6
Ingredients:

- 1 tbsp. olive oil
- 6 chicken drumsticks
- 4 minced garlic cloves
- ½ cup low-sodium chicken broth
- 1 tsp. cayenne pepper
- 1 tsp. crushed red peppers
- 1 tsp. fine sea salt
- Juice of 1 lime

To Serve:

- 2 tbsp. chopped cilantro
- Extra lime zest

Directions:

1. Pour olive oil into the Instant Pot and set it on the "Sauté" function.
2. Once the oil is hot adding the chicken drumsticks and season them well.
3. Using tongs, stir the drumsticks and brown the drumsticks for 2 minutes per side.
4. Add the lime juice, fresh cilantro, and chicken broth to the pot.

5. Lock and seal the lid, turning the pressure valve to "Sealing."
6. Cook the drumsticks on the "Manual, High Pressure" setting for 9 minutes.
7. Once done let the pressure release naturally.
8. Carefully transfer the drumsticks to an aluminum-foiled baking sheet and broil them in the oven for 3–5 minutes until golden brown.
9. Serve warm, garnished with more cilantro and lime zest.

Nutrition: Calories: 480; Carbohydrates: 3.3g; Fat: 29g

72. Eggplant Spread

Preparation time: 5 minutes
Cooking time: 18 minutes
Servings: 5
Ingredients:

- 4 tbsps. extra-virgin olive oil
- 2 lbs. eggplant
- 4 skin-on garlic cloves
- ½ cup water
- ¼ cup pitted black olives
- 3 sprigs fresh thyme
- Juice of 1 lemon
- 1 tbsp. tahini
- 1 tsp. sea salt
- Fresh extra-virgin olive oil

Directions:

1. Peel the eggplant in alternating stripes, leaving some areas with skin and some with no skin.
2. Slice into big chunks and layer at the bottom of your Instant Pot.
3. Add olive oil to the pot, and on the "Sauté" function, fry and caramelize the eggplant on one side, about 5 minutes.
4. Add in the garlic cloves with the skin on.
5. Flip over the eggplant and then add in the remaining uncooked eggplant chunks, salt, and water.
6. Close the lid, ensure the pressure release valve is set to "Sealing."
7. Cook for 5 minutes on the "Manual, High Pressure" setting.
8. Once done, carefully open the pot by quickly releasing the pressure through the steam valve.
9. Discard most of the brown cooking liquid.
10. Remove the garlic cloves and peel them.
11. Add the lemon juice, tahini, cooked and fresh garlic cloves, and pitted black olives to the pot.
12. Using a hand-held immersion blender, process all the ingredients until smooth.
13. Pour out the spread into a serving dish and season with fresh thyme, whole black olives, and some extra-virgin olive oil, before serving.

Nutrition: Calories: 155; Carbohydrates: 16.8g; Fat: 11.7g

273. Carrot Hummus

Preparation time: 15 minutes
Cooking time: 10 minutes
Servings: 2
Ingredients:

- 1 chopped carrot
- 2 oz. cooked chickpeas
- 1 tsp. lemon juice
- 1 tsp. tahini
- 1 tsp. fresh parsley

Directions:

1. Place the carrot and chickpeas in your Instant Pot.
2. Add a cup of water, seal, cook for 10 minutes on Stew.
3. Depressurize naturally. Blend with the remaining ingredients.

Nutrition: Calories: 58; Carbohydrates: 8g; Fat: 2g

274. Vegetable Rice Pilaf

Preparation time: 5 minutes
Cooking time: 25 minutes
Servings: 6
Ingredients:

- 1 tbsp. olive oil
- ½ medium yellow onion, diced
- 1 cup uncooked long-grain brown rice
- 2 cloves minced garlic
- ½ tsp. dried basil
- Salt and pepper
- 2 cups fat-free chicken broth
- 1 cup frozen mixed veggies

Directions:

1. Cook oil in a large skillet over medium heat.
2. Add the onion and sauté for 3 minutes until translucent.
3. Stir in the rice and cook until lightly toasted.

4. Add the garlic, basil, salt, and pepper then stir to combine.
5. Stir in the chicken broth then bring to a boil.
6. Decrease heat and simmer, covered, for 10 minutes.
7. Stir in the frozen veggies then cover it and cook for another 10 minutes until heated through. Serve hot.

Nutrition: Calories: 90; Carbohydrates: 12.6g; Fiber: 2.2g

275. Curry Roasted Cauliflower Florets

Preparation time: 5 minutes
Cooking time: 25 minutes
Servings: 6
Ingredients:

- 8 cups cauliflower florets
- 2 tbsp. olive oil
- 1 tsp. curry powder
- ½ tsp. garlic powder
- Salt and pepper

Directions:

1. Prep the oven to 425°F and line a baking sheet with foil.
2. Toss the cauliflower with olive oil and spread it on the baking sheet.
3. Sprinkle with curry powder, garlic powder, salt, and pepper.
4. Roast for 25 minutes or until just tender. Serve hot.

Nutrition: Calories: 75; Carbohydrates: 7.4g; Fiber: 3.5g

276. Mushroom Barley Risotto

Preparation time: 5 minutes
Cooking time: 25 minutes
Servings: 8
Ingredients:

- 4 cups fat-free beef broth
- 2 tbsp. olive oil
- 1 small onion, diced well
- 2 cloves minced garlic
- 8 ounces thinly sliced mushrooms
- ¼ tsp. dried thyme
- Salt and pepper

- 1 cup pearled barley
- ½ cup dry white wine

Directions:

1. Heat the beef broth in a medium saucepan and keep it warm.
2. Heat the oil in a large, deep skillet over medium heat.
3. Add the onions and garlic and sauté for 2 minutes then stir in the mushrooms and thyme.
4. Season with salt and pepper and sauté for 2 minutes more.
5. Add the barley and sauté for 1 minute then pour in the wine.
6. Ladle about ½ cup of beef broth into the skillet and stir well to combine.
7. Cook until most of the broth has been absorbed then add another ladle.
8. Repeat until you have used all of the broth and the barley is cooked to al dente.
9. Season and serve hot.

Nutrition: Calories: 155; Carbohydrates: 21.9g; Fiber 4.4g

277. Braised Summer Squash

Preparation time: 10 minutes
Cooking time: 20 minutes
Servings: 6
Ingredients:

- 3 tbsp. olive oil
- 3 cloves minced garlic
- ¼ tsp. crushed red pepper flakes
- 1-pound summer squash, sliced
- 1-pound zucchini, sliced
- 1 tsp. dried oregano
- Salt and pepper

Directions:

1. Cook oil in a large skillet over medium heat.
2. Add the garlic and crushed red pepper and cook for 2 minutes.
3. Add the summer squash and zucchini and cook for 15 minutes, stirring often, until just tender.
4. Stir in the oregano then season with salt and pepper to taste. serve hot.

Nutrition: Calories: 90; Carbohydrates: 6.2g; Fiber 1.8g

78. Lemon Garlic Green Beans

Preparation time: 5 minutes
Cooking time: 10 minutes
Servings: 6
Ingredients:

- 1 ½ pounds green beans, trimmed
- 2 tbsp. olive oil
- 1 tbsp. fresh lemon juice
- 2 cloves minced garlic
- Salt and pepper

Directions:

1. Fill a large bowl with ice water and set it aside.
2. Bring a pot of salted water to boil then add the green beans.
3. Cook for 3 minutes then drain and immediately place in the ice water.
4. Cool the beans completely then drain them well.
5. Heat the oil in a large skillet over medium-high heat.
6. Add the green beans, tossing to coat, then add the lemon juice, garlic, salt, and pepper.
7. Sauté for 3 minutes until the beans are tender-crisp then serve hot.

Nutrition: Calories: 75; Total Fat: 4.8g; Saturated Fat: 'g; Total Carbs: 8.5g; Net Carbs: 4.6g; Protein: 2.1g; gar: 1.7g; Fiber: 3.9g; Sodium: 7mg

79. Brown Rice & Lentil Salad

Preparation time: 10 minutes
Cooking time: 10 minutes
Servings: 4
Ingredients:

- 1 cup water
- ½ cup instant brown rice
- 2 tbsp. olive oil
- 2 tbsp. red wine vinegar
- 1 tbsp. Dijon mustard
- 1 tbsp. minced onion
- ½ tsp. paprika
- Salt and pepper
- 1 (15-ounce) can brown lentils, rinsed and drained
- 1 medium carrot, shredded

- 2 tbsp. fresh chopped parsley

Directions:

1. Stir together the water and instant brown rice in a medium saucepan.
2. Bring to a boil then simmer for 10 minutes, covered.
3. Remove from heat and set aside while you prepare the salad.
4. Whisk together the olive oil, vinegar, Dijon mustard, onion, paprika, salt, and pepper in a medium bowl.
5. Toss in the cooked rice, lentils, carrots, and parsley.
6. Adjust seasoning to taste then stir well and serve warm.

Nutrition: Calories: 145; Total Fat: 7.7g; Saturated Fat: 1g; Total Carbs: 13.1g; Net Carbs: 10.9g; Protein: 6g; Sugar: 1g; Fiber: 2.2g; Sodium: 57mg

280. Mashed Butternut Squash

Preparation time: 5 minutes
Cooking time: 25 minutes
Servings: 6
Ingredients:

- 3 pounds whole butternut squash (about 2 medium)
- 2 tbsp. olive oil
- Salt and pepper

Directions:

1. Preheat the oven to 400F and line a baking sheet with parchment.
2. Cut the squash in half and remove the seeds.
3. Cut the squash into cubes and toss with oil then spread on the baking sheet.
4. Roast for 25 minutes until tender and then place it in a food processor.
5. Blend smooth then season with salt and pepper to taste.

Nutrition: Calories: 90; Total Fat: 4.8g; Saturated Fat: 0.7g; Total Carbs: 12.3g; Net Carbs: 10.2g; Protein: 1.1g; Sugar: 2.3g; Fiber: 2.1g; Sodium: 4mg

281. Cilantro Lime Quinoa

Preparation time: 5 minutes
Cooking time: 25 minutes
Servings: 6

Ingredients:

- 1 cup uncooked quinoa
- 1 tbsp. olive oil
- 1 medium yellow onion, diced
- 2 cloves minced garlic
- 1 (4-ounce) can diced green chiles, drained
- 1 ½ cups fat-free chicken broth
- ¾ cup fresh chopped cilantro
- ½ cup sliced green onion
- 2 tbsp. lime juice
- Salt and pepper

Directions:

1. Rinse the quinoa thoroughly in cool water using a fine-mesh sieve.
2. Heat the oil in a large saucepan over medium heat.
3. Add the onion and sauté for 2 minutes then stir in the chile and garlic.
4. Cook for 1 minute then stir in the quinoa and chicken broth.
5. Bring to a boil then reduce heat and simmer, covered, until the quinoa absorbs the liquid— about 20 to 25 minutes.
6. Remove from heat then stir in the cilantro, green onions, and lime juice.
7. Season with salt and pepper to taste and serve hot.

Nutrition: Calories: 150; Total Fat: 4.1g; Saturated Fat: 0.5g; Total Carbs: 22.5g; Net Carbs: 19.8g; Protein: 6g; Sugar: 1.7g; Fiber: 2.7g; Sodium: 179mg

282. Oven-Roasted Veggies

Preparation time: 5 minutes
Cooking time: 25 minutes
Servings: 6
Ingredients:

- 1 pound cauliflower florets
- ½ pound broccoli florets
- 1 large yellow onion, cut into chunks
- 1 large red pepper, cored and chopped
- 2 medium carrots, peeled and sliced
- 2 tbsp. olive oil
- 2 tbsp. apple cider vinegar
- Salt and pepper

Directions:

1. Preheat the oven to 425F and line a large rimmed baking sheet with parchment.
2. Spread the veggies on the baking sheet and drizzle with oil and vinegar.
3. Toss well and season with salt and pepper.
4. Spread the veggies in a single layer then roast for 20 to 25 minutes, stirring every 10 minutes, until tender.
5. Adjust seasoning to taste and serve hot.

Nutrition: Calories: 100; Total Fat: 5g; Saturated Fat: 0.7g; Total Carbs: 12.4g; Net Carbs: 8.2g; Protein: 3.2g; Sugar: 5.5g; Fiber: 4.2g; Sodium: 51mg

283. Parsley Tabbouleh

Preparation time: 5 minutes
Cooking time: 25 minutes
Servings: 6
Ingredients:

- 1 cup water
- ½ cup bulgur
- ¼ cup fresh lemon juice
- 2 tbsp. olive oil
- 2 cloves minced garlic
- Salt and pepper
- 2 cups fresh chopped parsley
- 2 medium tomatoes, died
- 1 small cucumber, diced
- ¼ cup fresh chopped mint

Directions:

1. Bring the water and bulgur to a boil in a small saucepan then remove from heat.
2. Cover and let stand until the water is fully absorbed, about 25 minutes.
3. Meanwhile, whisk together the lemon juice, olive oil, garlic, salt, and pepper in a medium bowl.
4. Toss in the cooked bulgur along with the parsley, tomatoes, cucumber, and mint.
5. Season with salt and pepper to taste and serve.

Nutrition: Calories: 110; Total Fat: 5.3g; Saturated Fat: 0.9g; Total Carbs: 14.4g; Net Carbs: 10.5g; Protein: 3; Sugar: 2.4g; Fiber: 3.9g; Sodium: 21mg

284. Garlic Sautéed Spinach

Preparation time: 5 minutes
Cooking time: 10 minutes
Servings: 4

Ingredients:
- 1 ½ tbsp. olive oil
- 4 cloves minced garlic
- 6 cups fresh baby spinach
- Salt and pepper

Directions:
1. Heat the oil in a large skillet over medium-high heat.
2. Add the garlic and cook for 1 minute.
3. Stir in the spinach and season with salt and pepper.
4. Sauté for 1 to 2 minutes until just wilted. Serve hot.

Nutrition: Calories: 60; Total Fat: 5.5g; Saturated Fat: 0.8g; Total Carbs: 2.6g; Net Carbs: 1.5g; Protein: 1.5g; Sugar: 0.2g; Fiber: 1.1g; Sodium: 36mg

285. French Lentils

Preparation time: 5 minutes
Cooking time: 25 minutes
Servings: 10
Ingredients:
- 2 tbsp. olive oil
- 1 medium onion, diced
- 1 medium carrot, peeled and diced
- 2 cloves minced garlic
- 5 ½ cups water
- 2 ¼ cups French lentils, rinsed and drained
- 1 tsp. dried thyme
- 2 small bay leaves
- Salt and pepper

Directions:
1. Heat the oil in a large saucepan over medium heat.
2. Add the onions, carrot, and garlic and sauté for 3 minutes.
3. Stir in the water, lentils, thyme, and bay leaves—season with salt.
4. Bring to a boil then reduce to a simmer and cook until tender, about 20 minutes.
5. Drain any excess water and adjust seasoning to taste. Serve hot.

Nutrition: Calories: 185; Total Fat: 3.3g; Saturated Fat: 5g; Total Carbs: 27.9g; Net Carbs: 14.2g; Protein: 4g; Sugar: 1.7g; Fiber: 13.7g; Sodium: 11mg

286. Grain-Free Berry Cobbler

Preparation time: 5 minutes
Cooking time: 25 minutes
Servings: 10
Ingredients:
- 4 cups fresh mixed berries
- ½ cup ground flaxseed
- ¼ cup almond meal
- ¼ cup unsweetened shredded coconut
- ½ tbsp. baking powder
- 1 tsp. ground cinnamon
- ¼ tsp. salt
- Powdered stevia, to taste
- 6 tbsp. coconut oil

Directions:
1. Preheat the oven to 375F and lightly grease a 10-inch cast-iron skillet.
2. Spread the berries on the bottom of the skillet.
3. Whisk together the dry ingredients in a mixing bowl.
4. Cut in the coconut oil using a fork to create a crumbled mixture.
5. Spread the crumble over the berries and bake for 25 minutes until hot and bubbling.
6. Cool the cobbler for 5 to 10 minutes before serving.

Nutrition: Calories: 215; Total Fat: 16.8g; Saturated Fat: 10.4g; Total Carbs: 13.1g; Net Carbs: 6.7g; Protein: 3.7g; Sugar: 5.3g; Fiber: 6.4g; Sodium: 61mg

287. Coffee-Steamed Carrots

Preparation time: 10 minutes
Cooking time: 3 minutes
Servings: 4
Ingredients:
- 1 cup brewed coffee
- 1 tsp. light brown sugar
- ½ tsp. kosher salt
- Freshly ground black pepper
- 1-pound baby carrots
- Chopped fresh parsley
- 1 tsp. grated lemon zest

Directions:

1. Pour the coffee into the electric pressure cooker. Stir in the brown sugar, salt, and pepper. Add the carrots.
2. Close the pressure cooker. Set to sealing.
3. Cook on high pressure for minutes.
4. Once complete, click Cancel and quickly release the pressure.
5. Once the pin drops, open and remove the lid.
6. Using a slotted spoon, portion carrots to a serving bowl. Topped with the parsley and lemon zest, and serve.

Nutrition: Calories:51; Carbohydrates: 12g; Fiber: 4g

288. Rosemary Potatoes

Preparation time: 5 minutes
Cooking time: 25 minutes
Servings: 2
Ingredients:

- 1 lb. red potatoes
- 1 cup vegetable stock
- 2tbsp. olive oil
- 2tbsp. rosemary sprigs

Directions:

1. Situate potatoes in the steamer basket and add the stock into the Instant Pot.
2. Steam the potatoes in your Instant Pot for 15 minutes.
3. Depressurize and pour away the remaining stock.
4. Set to sauté and add the oil, rosemary, and potatoes.
5. Cook until brown.

Nutrition: Calories: 195; Carbohydrates: 31g; Fat: 1g

289. Corn on the Cob

Preparation time: 10 minutes
Cooking time: 5 minutes
Servings: 12
Ingredients:

- 6 ears corn

Directions:

1. Take off husks and silk from the corn. Cut or break each ear in half.
2. Pour 1 cup of water into the bottom of the electric pressure cooker. Insert a wire rack or trivet.
3. Place the corn upright on the rack, cut-side down. Seal lid of the pressure cooker.

4. Cook on high pressure for 5 minutes.
5. When it's complete, select Cancel and quick release the pressure.
6. When the pin drops, unlock and take off the lid.
7. Pull out the corn from the pot. Season as desired and serve immediately.

Nutrition: Calories: 62; Carbohydrates: 14g; Fiber: 1g

290. Chili Lime Salmon

Preparation time: 6 minutes
Cooking time: 10 minutes
Servings: 2
Ingredients:
For Sauce:

- 1 jalapeno pepper
- 1 tbsp. chopped parsley
- 1 tsp. minced garlic
- ½ tsp. cumin
- ½ tsp. paprika
- ½ tsp. lime zest
- 1 tbsp. honey
- 1 tbsp. lime juice
- 1 tbsp. olive oil
- 1 tbsp. water

For Fish:

- 2 salmon fillets, each about 5 ounces
- 1 cup water
- ½ tsp. salt
- 1/8 tsp. ground black pepper

Directions:

1. Prepare salmon and for this, season salmon with salt and black pepper until evenly coated.
2. Plugin instant pot, insert the inner pot, pour water, then place steamer basket and place seasoned salmon on it.
3. Seal the instant pot with its lid, press the 'steam' button, then press the 'timer' to set the cooking time to 5 minutes and cook on high pressure, for 5 minutes.
4. Transfer all the ingredients for the sauce to bowl, whisk until combined, and set aside until required.
5. When the timer beeps, press the 'cancel' button and do a quick pressure release until the pressure nob drops down.

6. Open the instant pot, then transfer salmon to a serving plate and drizzle generously with prepared sauce.
7. Serve straight away.

Nutrition: Calories: 305; Carbohydrates: 29g; Fiber: 6g

291. **Collard Greens**

Preparation time: 5 minutes
Cooking time: 6 hours
Servings: 12
Ingredients:

- 2 pounds chopped collard greens
- ¾ cup chopped white onion
- 1 tsp. onion powder
- 1 tsp. garlic powder
- 1 tsp. salt
- 2 tsp. brown sugar
- ½ tsp. ground black pepper
- ½ tsp. red chili powder
- ¼ tsp. crushed red pepper flakes
- 3 tbsp. apple cider vinegar
- 2 tbsp. olive oil
- 14.5-ounce vegetable broth
- ½ cup water

Directions:

1. Plugin instant pot, insert the inner pot, add onion and collard, and then pour in vegetable broth and water.
2. Close instant pot with its lid, seal, press the 'slow cook' button, then press the 'timer' to set the cooking time to 6 hours at high heat setting.
3. When the timer beeps, press the 'cancel' button and do natural pressure release until the pressure nob drops down.
4. Open the instant pot, add remaining ingredients and stir until mixed.
5. Then press the 'sauté/simmer' button and cook for 3 to minutes or more until collards reach to desired texture.
6. Serve straight away.

Nutrition: Calories: 49; Carbohydrates: 2. 3g; Fiber: 5g

292. **Mashed Pumpkin**

Preparation time: 9 minutes
Cooking time: 15 minutes
Servings: 2
Ingredients:

- 2 cups chopped pumpkin
- 0.5 cup water
- 2 tbsp. powdered sugar-free sweetener of choice
- 1 tbsp. cinnamon

Directions:

1. Place the pumpkin and water in your Instant Pot.
2. Seal and cook on Stew for 15 minutes.
3. Remove and mash with the sweetener and cinnamon.

Nutrition: Calories: 12; Carbohydrates: 3g; Sugar: 1g

293. **Parmesan-Topped Acorn Squash**

Preparation time: 8 minutes
Cooking time: 20 minutes
Servings: 4
Ingredients:

- 1 acorn squash (about 1 pound)
- 1 tbsp. extra-virgin olive oil
- 1 tsp. dried sage leaves, crumbled
- ¼ tsp. freshly grated nutmeg
- 1/8 tsp. kosher salt
- 1/8 tsp. freshly ground black pepper
- 2 tbsp. freshly grated Parmesan cheese

Directions:

1. Chop acorn squash in half lengthwise and remove the seeds. Cut each half in half for a total of 4 wedges. Snap off the stem if it's easy to do.
2. In a small bowl, combine the olive oil, sage, nutmeg, salt, and pepper. Brush the cut sides of the squash with the olive oil mixture.
3. Fill 1 cup of water into the electric pressure cooker and insert a wire rack or trivet.
4. Place the squash on the trivet in a single layer, skin-side down.
5. Set the lid of the pressure cooker on sealing.
6. Cook on high pressure for 20 minutes.
7. Once done, press Cancel and quickly release the pressure.
8. Once the pin drops, open it.
9. Carefully remove the squash from the pot, sprinkle with the Parmesan, and serve.

Nutrition: Calories: 85; Carbohydrates: 12g; Fiber: 2g

294.   Quinoa Tabbouleh

Preparation time: 8 minutes
Cooking time: 16 minutes
Servings: 6
Ingredients:

- 1 cup quinoa, rinsed
- 1 large English cucumber
- 2 scallions, sliced
- 2 cups cherry tomatoes, halved
- 2/3 cup chopped parsley
- ½ cup chopped mint
- ½ tsp. minced garlic
- ½ tsp. salt
- ½ tsp. ground black pepper
- 2 tbsp. lemon juice
- ½ cup olive oil

Directions:

1. Plugin instant pot, insert the inner pot, add quinoa, then pour in water and stir until mixed.
2. Close the instant pot with its lid and turn the pressure knob to seal the pot.
3. Select the 'manual' button, then set the 'timer' to 1 minute and cook in high pressure, it may take 7 minutes.
4. Once the timer stops, select the 'cancel' button and do natural pressure release for 10 minutes, and then do quick pressure release until pressure nob drops down.
5. Open the instant pot, fluff quinoa with a fork, then spoon it on a rimmed baking sheet, spread quinoa evenly and let cool.
6. Meanwhile, place lime juice in a small bowl, add garlic, and stir until just mixed.
7. Then add salt, black pepper, and olive oil and whisk until combined.
8. Transfer cooled quinoa to a large bowl, add remaining ingredients, then drizzle generously with the prepared lime juice mixture and toss until evenly coated.
9. Taste quinoa to adjust seasoning and then serve.

Nutrition: Calories: 283; Carbohydrates: 30.6g; Fiber: 3.4g

295.   Wild Rice Salad with Cranberries and Almonds

Preparation time: 6 minutes
Cooking time: 25 minutes
Servings: 18
Ingredients:
For the rice:

- 2 cups wild rice blend, rinsed
- 1 tsp. kosher salt
- 2½ cups Vegetable Broth

For the dressing:

- ¼ cup extra-virgin olive oil
- ¼ cup white wine vinegar
- 1½ tsp. grated orange zest
- Juice of 1 medium orange (about ¼ cup)
- 1 tsp. honey or pure maple syrup

For the salad:

- ¾ cup unsweetened dried cranberries
- ½ cup sliced almonds, toasted
- Freshly ground black pepper

Directions:
To make the rice:

1. In the electric pressure cooker, combine rice, salt, and broth.
2. Close and lock the lid. Set the valve to sealing
3. Cook on high pressure for 25 minutes.
4. When the cooking is complete, hit Cancel a allow the pressure to release naturally 1minutes, then quick release any remaini pressure.
5. Once the pin drops, unlock and remove the l
6. Let the rice cool briefly, then fluff it with fork.

To make the dressing:

7. While the rice cooks, make the dressing: I small jar with a screw-top lid, combine olive oil, vinegar, zest, juice, and honey. (If y don't have a jar, whisk the ingredients togeth in a small bowl.) Shake to combine.
8. To make the salad
9. Mix rice, cranberries, and almonds.
10. Add the dressing and season with pepper.
11. Serve warm or refrigerate.

Nutrition: Calories: 126; Carbohydrates: 18g; Fiber:

96. Low Fat Roasties

Preparation time: 8 minutes
Cooking time: 25 minutes
Servings: 2
Ingredients:

- 1 lb. roasting potatoes
- 1 garlic clove
- 1 cup vegetable stock
- 2tbsp. olive oil

Directions:

1. Position potatoes in the steamer basket and add the stock into the Instant Pot.
2. Steam the potatoes in your Instant Pot for 15 minutes.
3. Depressurize and pour away the remaining stock.
4. Set to sauté and add the oil, garlic, and potatoes. Cook until brown.

Nutrition: Calories: 201; Carbohydrates: 3g; Fat: 6g

97. Roasted Parsnips

Preparation time: 9 minutes
Cooking time: 25 minutes
Servings: 2
Ingredients:

- 1 lb. parsnips
- 1 cup vegetable stock
- 2tbsp. herbs
- 2tbsp. olive oil

Directions:

1. Put the parsnips in the steamer basket and add the stock into the Instant Pot.
2. Steam the parsnips in your Instant Pot for 15 minutes.
3. Depressurize and pour away the remaining stock.
4. Set to sauté and add the oil, herbs, and parsnips.
5. Cook until golden and crisp.

Nutrition: Calories: 130; Carbohydrates: 14g; Protein:

98. Lower Carb Hummus

Preparation time: 9 minutes
Cooking time: 60 minutes
Servings: 2

Ingredients:

- 0.5 cup dry chickpeas
- 1 cup vegetable stock
- 1 cup pumpkin puree
- 2tbsp. smoked paprika
- salt and pepper to taste

Directions:

1. Soak the chickpeas overnight.
2. Place the chickpeas and stock in the Instant Pot.
3. Cook on Beans for 60 minutes.
4. Depressurize naturally.
5. Blend the chickpeas with the remaining ingredients.

Nutrition: Calories: 135; Carbohydrates: 18g; Fat: 3g

299. Sweet and Sour Red Cabbage

Preparation time: 7 minutes
Cooking time: 10 minutes
Servings: 8
Ingredients:

- 2 cups Spiced Pear Applesauce
- 1 small onion, chopped
- ½ cup apple cider vinegar
- ½ tsp. kosher salt
- 1 head red cabbage

Directions:

1. In the electric pressure cooker, combine the applesauce, onion, vinegar, salt, and a cup of water. Stir in the cabbage.
2. Seal lid of the pressure cooker.
3. Cook on high pressure for 10 minutes.
4. When the cooking is complete, hit Cancel and quickly release the pressure.
5. Once the pin drops, unlock and remove the lid.
6. Spoon into a bowl or platter and serve.

Nutrition: Calories: 91; Carbohydrates: 18g; Fiber: 4g

300. Pinto Beans

Preparation time: 6 minutes
Cooking time: 55 minutes
Servings: 10
Ingredients:

- 2 cups pinto beans, dried
- 1 medium white onion
- 1 ½ tsp. minced garlic

- ¾ tsp. salt
- 1/4 tsp. ground black pepper
- 1 tsp. red chili powder
- 1/4 tsp. cumin
- 1 tbsp. olive oil
- 1 tsp. chopped cilantro
- 5 ½ cup vegetable stock

Directions:

1. Plugin instant pot, insert the inner pot, press sauté/simmer button, add oil and when hot, add onion and garlic and cook for 3 minutes or until onions begin to soften.
2. Add remaining ingredients, stir well, then press the cancel button, shut the instant pot with its lid, and seal the pot.
3. Click the 'manual' button, then press the 'timer' to set the cooking time to 45 minutes and cook at high pressure.
4. Once done, click the 'cancel' button and do a natural pressure release for 10 minutes until the pressure nob drops down.
5. Open the instant pot, spoon beans into plates, and serve.

Nutrition: Calories: 107; Carbohydrates: 11.7g; Fiber: 4g

301. Parmesan Cauliflower Mash

Preparation time: 19 minutes
Cooking time: 5 minutes
Servings: 4
Ingredients:

- 1 head cauliflower
- ½ tsp. kosher salt
- ½ tsp. garlic pepper
- 2 tbsp. plain Greek yogurt
- ¾ cup freshly grated Parmesan cheese
- 1 tbsp. unsalted butter or ghee (optional)
- Chopped fresh chives

Directions:

1. Pour a cup of water into the electric pressure cooker and insert a steamer basket or wire rack.
2. Place the cauliflower in the basket.
3. Cover the lid of the pressure cooker to seal.
4. Cook on high pressure for 5 minutes.
5. Once complete, hit Cancel and quick-release the pressure.
6. When the pin drops, remove the lid.

7. Remove the cauliflower from the pot and p͏ out the water. Return the cauliflower to the͏ and add the salt, garlic pepper, yogurt, ͏ cheese. Use an immersion blender to purée͏ mash the cauliflower in the pot.
8. Spoon into a serving bowl, and garnish w͏ butter (if using) and chives.

Nutrition: Calories: 141; Carbohydrates: 12g; Fiber͏

302. Steamed Asparagus

Preparation time: 3 minutes
Cooking time: 2 minutes
Servings: 4
Ingredients:

- 1 lb. fresh asparagus, rinsed and tough e͏ trimmed
- 1 cup water

Directions:

1. Place the asparagus into a wire steamer ra͏ and set it inside your Instant Pot.
2. Add water to the pot. Close and seal the͏ turning the steam release valve to the "Seali͏ position.
3. Select the "Steam" function to cook on h͏ pressure for 2 minutes.
4. Once done, do a quick pressure release of͏ steam.
5. Lift the wire steamer basket out of the pot ͏ place the asparagus onto a serving plate.
6. Season as desired and serve.

Nutrition: Calories: 22; Carbohydrates: 4g; Protein͏

303. Squash Medley

Preparation time: 10 minutes
Cooking time: 20 minutes.
Servings: 2
Ingredients:

- 2 lbs. mixed squash
- ½ cup mixed veg
- 1 cup vegetable stock
- 2 tbsps. olive oil
- 2 tbsps. mixed herbs

Directions:

1. Put the squash in the steamer basket and ͏ the stock into the Instant Pot.
2. Steam the squash in your Instant Pot for͏ minutes.

3. Depressurize and pour away the remaining stock.
4. Set to sauté and add the oil and remaining ingredients.
5. Cook until a light crust forms.

Nutrition: Calories: 100; Carbohydrates: 10g; Fat: 6g

304. Eggplant Curry

Preparation time: 15 minutes
Cooking time: 20 minutes
Servings: 2
Ingredients:

- 3 cups chopped eggplant
- 1 thinly sliced onion
- 1 cup coconut milk
- 3 tbsps. curry paste
- 1 tbsp. oil or ghee

Directions:

1. Select Instant Pot to sauté and put the onion, oil, and curry paste.
2. Once the onion is soft, stir in the remaining ingredients and seal.
3. Cook on Stew for 20 minutes. Release the pressure naturally.

Nutrition: Calories: 350; Carbohydrates: 15g; Fat: 25g

305. Lentil and Eggplant Stew

Preparation time: 15 minutes
Cooking time: 35 minutes
Servings: 2
Ingredients:

- 1 lb. eggplant
- 1 lb. dry lentils
- 1 cup chopped vegetables
- 1 cup low sodium vegetable broth

Directions:

1. Incorporate all the ingredients in your Instant Pot, cook on Stew for 35 minutes.
2. Release the pressure naturally and serve.

Nutrition: Calories: 310; Carbohydrates: 22g; Fat: 10g

306. Tofu Curry

Preparation time: 15 minutes
Cooking time: 20 minutes
Servings: 2
Ingredients:

- 2 cups cubed extra firm tofu
- 2 cups mixed stir fry vegetables
- ½ cup soy yogurt
- 3 tbsps. curry paste
- 1 tbsp. oil or ghee

Directions:

1. Set the Instant Pot to sauté and add the oil and curry paste.
2. Once soft, place the remaining ingredients except for the yogurt and seal.
3. Cook on Stew for 20 minutes.
4. Release the pressure naturally and serve with a scoop of soy yogurt.

Nutrition: Calories: 300; Carbohydrates: 9g; Fat: 14g

307. Lentil and Chickpea Curry

Preparation time: 15 minutes
Cooking time: 20 minutes
Servings: 2
Ingredients:

- 2 cups dry lentils and chickpeas
- 1 thinly sliced onion
- 1 cup chopped tomato
- 3 tbsps. curry paste
- 1 tbsp. oil or ghee

Directions:

1. Press Instant Pot to sauté and mix onion, oil, and curry paste.
2. Once the onion is cooked, stir the remaining ingredients and seal.
3. Cook on Stew for 20 minutes.
4. Release the pressure naturally and serve.

Nutrition: Calories: 360; Carbohydrates: 26g; Fat: 19g

308. Split Pea Stew

Preparation time: 5 minutes
Cooking time: 35 minutes
Servings: 2
Ingredients:

- 1 cup dry split peas
- 1 lb. chopped vegetables
- 1 cup mushroom soup
- 2 tbsps. old bay seasoning

Directions:

1. Incorporate all the ingredients in Instant Pot, cook for 33 minutes.

2. Release the pressure naturally.
Nutrition: Calories: 300; Carbohydrates: 7g; Fat: 2g

309.   Fried Tofu Hotpot

Preparation time: 15 minutes
Cooking time: 15 minutes
Servings: 2
Ingredients:
- ½ lb. fried tofu
- 1 lb. chopped Chinese vegetable mix
- 1 cup low sodium vegetable broth
- 2 tbsps. 5 spice seasoning
- 1 tbsp. smoked paprika

Directions:
1. Combine all the ingredients in your Instant Pot, set on Stew for 15 minutes.
2. Release the pressure naturally and serve.

Nutrition: Calories: 320; Carbohydrates: 11g; Fat: 23g

310.   Chili Sin Carne

Preparation time: 15 minutes
Cooking time: 35 minutes
Servings: 2
Ingredients:
- 3 cups mixed cooked beans
- 2 cups chopped tomatoes
- 1 tbsp. yeast extract
- 2 squares very dark chocolate
- 1 tbsp. red chili flakes

Directions:
1. Combine all the ingredients in your Instant Pot, cook for 35 minutes.
2. Release the pressure naturally and serve.

Nutrition: Calories: 240; Carbohydrates: 20g; Fat: 3g

311. Peanut Butter Cups

Preparation time: 5 minutes
Cooking time: 10 minutes
Servings: 4
Ingredients:

- 1 packet plain gelatin
- ¼ cup sugar substitute
- 2 cups nonfat cream
- ½ tsp. vanilla
- ¼ cup low-fat peanut butter
- 2 tbsp. unsalted peanuts, chopped

Directions:

1. Mix gelatin; Sugar: substitute and cream in a pan.
2. Let sit for 5 minutes.
3. Place over medium heat and cook until gelatin has been dissolved.
4. Stir in vanilla and peanut butter.
5. Pour into custard cups. Chill for 3 hours.
6. Top with the peanuts and serve.

Nutrition: Calories: 171; Carbohydrate: 21g; Protein: .8g

312. Fruit Pizza

Preparation time: 5 minutes
Cooking time: 10 minutes
Servings: 4
Ingredients:

- 1 tsp. maple syrup
- ¼ tsp. vanilla extract
- ½ cup coconut milk yogurt
- 2 round slices watermelon
- ½ cup blackberries, sliced
- ½ cup strawberries, sliced
- 2 tbsp. coconut flakes (unsweetened)

Directions:

1. Mix maple syrup, vanilla, and yogurt in a bowl.
2. Spread the mixture on top of the watermelon slice.
3. Top with the berries and coconut flakes.

Nutrition: Calories: 70; Carbohydrate: 14.6g; Protein: ?g

313. Choco Peppermint Cake

Preparation time: 5 minutes
Cooking time: 10 minutes
Servings: 4
Ingredients:

- Cooking spray
- 1/3 cup oil
- 15 oz. package chocolate cake mix
- 3 eggs, beaten
- 1 cup water
- ¼ tsp. peppermint extract

Directions:

1. Spray slow cooker with oil.
2. Mix all the ingredients in a bowl.
3. Use an electric mixer on a medium-speed setting to mix ingredients for 2 minutes.
4. Pour the mixture into the slow cooker.
5. Cover the pot and cook on low for 3 hours.
6. Let cool before slicing and serving.

Nutrition: Calories: 185; Carbohydrate: 27g; Protein: 3.8g

314. Roasted Mango

Preparation time: 5 minutes
Cooking time: 10 minutes
Servings: 4
Ingredients:

- 2 mangoes, sliced
- 2 tsp. crystallized ginger, chopped
- 2 tsp. orange zest
- 2 tbsp. coconut flakes (unsweetened)

Directions:

1. Preheat your oven to 350°F.
2. Add mango slices in custard cups.
3. Top with ginger, orange zest, and coconut flakes.
4. Bake in the oven for 10 minutes.

Nutrition: Calories: 89; Carbohydrate: 20g; Protein: 0.8g

315. Roasted Plums

Preparation time: 5 minutes
Cooking time: 10 minutes

Servings: 4
Ingredients:

- Cooking spray
- 6 plums, sliced
- ½ cup pineapple juice (unsweetened)
- 1 tbsp. brown sugar
- 2 tbsp. brown sugar
- ¼ tsp. ground cardamom
- ½ tsp. ground cinnamon
- 1/8 tsp. ground cumin

Directions:

1. Combine all the ingredients in a baking pan.
2. Roast in the oven at 450°F for 20 minutes.

Nutrition: Calories: 102; Carbohydrate: 18.7g; Protein: 2g

316.   Figs with Honey & Yogurt

Preparation time: 5 minutes
Cooking time: 10 minutes
Servings: 4
Ingredients:

- ½ tsp. vanilla
- 8 oz. nonfat yogurt
- 2 figs, sliced
- 1 tbsp. walnuts, chopped and toasted
- 2 tsp. honey

Directions:

1. Stir vanilla into yogurt.
2. Mix well.
3. Top with the figs and sprinkle with walnuts.
4. Drizzle with honey and serve.

Nutrition: Calories: 157; Carbohydrate: 24g; Protein: 7g

317.   Flourless Chocolate Cake

Preparation time: 10 minutes
Cooking time: 45 minutes
Servings: 6
Ingredients:

- ½ Cup of stevia
- 12 ounces of unsweetened baking chocolate
- 2/3 Cup of ghee
- 1/3 Cup of warm water
- ¼ tsp. of salt

- 4 large pastured eggs
- 2 cups of boiling water

Directions:

1. Line the bottom of a 9-inch pan of a springform with parchment paper.
2. Heat the water in a small pot; then add the salt and the stevia over the water until wait until the mixture becomes completely dissolved.
3. Melt the baking chocolate into a double boiler or simply microwave it for about 30 seconds.
4. Mix the melted chocolate and the butter in a large bowl with an electric mixer.
5. Beat in your hot mixture; then crack in the eggs and whisk after adding each of the eggs.
6. Pour the obtained mixture into your prepared springform tray.
7. Wrap the springform tray with foil paper.
8. Place the springform tray in a large cake tray and add boiling water right to the outside make sure the depth doesn't exceed 1 inch.
9. Bake the cake into the water bath for about 4 minutes at a temperature of about 350°F.
10. Remove the tray from the boiling water and transfer it to a wire to cool.
11. Let the cake chill overnight in the refrigerator.

Nutrition: Calories: 295; Carbohydrates: 6g; Fiber: 4

318.   Lava Cake

Preparation time: 10 minutes
Cooking time: 10 minutes
Servings: 2
Ingredients:

- 2 Oz of dark chocolate; you should at least u chocolate of 85% cocoa solids
- 1 Tbsp. of super-fine almond flour
- 2 Oz of unsalted almond butter
- 2 large eggs

Directions:

1. Heat your oven to a temperature of about 350°F.
2. Grease 2 heat-proof ramekins with almo butter.
3. Now, melt the chocolate and the almo butter and stir very well.
4. Beat the eggs very well with a mixer.
5. Add the eggs to the chocolate and the but mixture and mix very well with almond fl and the swerve; then stir.
6. Pour the dough into 2 ramekins.

7. Bake for about 9 to 10 minutes.
8. Turn the cakes over plates and serve with pomegranate seeds!

Nutrition: Calories: 459; Carbohydrates: 3.5g; Fiber: 0.8g

319. <u>Cheese Cake</u>

Preparation time: 15 minutes
Cooking time: 50 minutes
Servings: 6
Ingredients:

For Almond Flour Cheesecake Crust:

- 2 Cups Blanched almond flour
- 1/3 cup almond butter
- 3 Tbsp. Erythritol (powdered or granular)
- 1 tsp. Vanilla extract

For Keto Cheesecake Filling:

- 32 Oz softened Cream cheese
- 1 and ¼ cups powdered erythritol
- 3 Large Eggs
- 1 Tbsp. Lemon juice
- 1 tsp. Vanilla extract

Directions:

1. Preheat your oven to a temperature of about 350°F.
2. Grease a springform pan of 9" with cooking spray or just line its bottom with parchment paper.
3. In order to make the cheesecake crust, stir in the melted butter, the almond flour, the vanilla extract, and the erythritol in a large bowl.
4. The dough will get will be a bit crumbly; so, press it into the bottom of your prepared tray.
5. Bake for about 12 minutes; then let cool for about 10 minutes.
6. In the meantime, beat the softened cream cheese and the powdered sweetener at a low speed until it becomes smooth.
7. Crack in the eggs and beat them in at a low to medium speed until it becomes fluffy. Make sure to add one at a time.
8. Add in the lemon juice and the vanilla extract and mix at a low to medium speed with a mixer.
9. Pour your filling into your pan right on top of the crust. You can use a spatula to smooth the top of the cake.
10. Bake for about 45 to 50 minutes.
11. Remove the baked cheesecake from your oven and run a knife around its edge.

12. Let the cake cool for about 4 hours in the refrigerator.
13. Serve and enjoy your delicious cheesecake!

Nutrition: Calories: 325; Carbohydrates: 6g; Fiber: 1g

320. **Orange Cake**

Preparation time: 10 minutes
Cooking time: 50minutes
Servings: 8
Ingredients:

- 2 and ½ cups of almond flour
- 2 Unwaxed washed oranges
- 5 Large separated eggs
- 1 tsp. of baking powder
- 2 tsp. s of orange extract
- 1 tsp. of vanilla bean powder
- 6 Seeds of cardamom pods crushed
- 16 drops of liquid stevia; about 3 tsp.
- 1 Handful of flaked almonds to decorate

Directions:

1. Preheat your oven to a temperature of about 350°F.
2. Line a rectangular bread baking tray with parchment paper.
3. Place the oranges into a pan filled with cold water and cover it with a lid.
4. Bring the saucepan to a boil, then let simmer for about 1 hour and make sure the oranges are totally submerged.
5. Make sure the oranges are always submerged to remove any taste of bitterness.
6. Cut the oranges into halves; then remove any seeds; and drain the water and set the oranges aside to cool down.
7. Cut the oranges in half and remove any seeds, then puree it with a blender or a food processor.
8. Separate the eggs; then whisk the egg whites until you see stiff peaks forming.
9. Add all your ingredients except for the egg whites to the orange mixture and add in the egg whites; then mix.
10. Pour the batter into the cake tin and sprinkle with the flaked almonds right on top.
11. Bake your cake for about 50 minutes.
12. Remove the cake from the oven and set it aside to cool for 5 minutes.

Nutrition: Calories: 164 Carbohydrates: 7.1g; Fiber: 2.7g

321. Madeleine

Preparation time: 10 minutes
Cooking time: 15 minutes
Servings: 12
Ingredients:

- 2 large pastured eggs
- ¾ Cup of almond flour
- 1 and ½ Tbsp. of Swerve
- ¼ Cup of cooled, melted coconut oil
- 1 tsp. of vanilla extract
- 1 tsp. of almond extract
- 1 tsp. of lemon zest
- ¼ tsp. of salt

Directions:

1. Preheat your oven to a temperature of about 350°F.
2. Combine the eggs with the salt and whisk at a high speed for about 5 minutes.
3. Slowly add in the Swerve and keep mixing on high for 2 additional minutes.
4. Stir in the almond flour until it is very well incorporated; then add in the vanilla and the almond extracts.
5. Add in the melted coconut oil and stir all your ingredients together.
6. Pour the obtained batter into equal parts in a greased Madeleine tray.
7. Bake your Ketogenic Madeleine for about 13 minutes or until the edges start to have a brown color.
8. Flip the Madeleines out of the baking tray.

Nutrition: Calories: 87 Carbohydrates: 3g; Fiber: 3g

322. Waffles

Preparation time: 20 minutes
Cooking time: 30 minutes
Servings: 3
Ingredients:
For Ketogenic waffles:

- 8 Oz of cream cheese
- 5 large pastured eggs
- 1/3 Cup of coconut flour
- ½ tsp. of Xanthan gum
- 1 Pinch of salt
- ½ tsp. of vanilla extract
- 2 Tbsp. of Swerve
- ¼ tsp. of baking soda
- 1/3 Cup of almond milk

Optional Ingredients:

- ½ tsp. of cinnamon pie spice
- ¼ tsp. of almond extract

For low-carb Maple Syrup:

- 1 Cup of water
- 1 Tbsp. of Maple flavor
- ¾ Cup of powdered Swerve
- 1 Tbsp. of almond butter
- ½ tsp. of Xanthan gum

Directions:
For the waffles:

1. Make sure all your ingredients are exactly at room temperature.
2. Place all your ingredients for the waffles from cream cheese to pastured eggs, coconut flour, Xanthan gum, salt, vanilla extract, the Swerve, the baking soda, and the almond milk except for the almond milk with the help of a processor.
3. Blend your ingredients until it becomes smooth and creamy; then transfer the batter to a bowl.
4. Add the almond milk and mix your ingredients with a spatula.
5. Heat a waffle maker to a temperature of high.
6. Spray your waffle maker with coconut oil and add about ¼ of the batter in it evenly with spatula into your waffle iron.
7. Close your waffle and cook until you get the color you want.
8. Carefully remove the waffles to a platter.

For the Ketogenic Maple Syrup:

9. Place 1 and ¼ cups of water, the swerve, and the maple in a small pan and bring to a boil over low heat; then let simmer for about 1 minutes.
10. Add the coconut oil.
11. Sprinkle the Xanthan gum over the top of the waffle and use an immersion blender to blend smoothly.
12. Serve and enjoy your delicious waffles!

Nutrition: Calories: 316 Carbohydrates: 7g; Fiber: 3

323. Pretzels

Preparation time: 10 minutes
Cooking time: 20 minutes
Servings: 8
Ingredients:

- 1 and ½ cups of pre-shredded mozzarella
- 2 Tbsp. of full-fat cream cheese
- 1 large egg
- ¾ Cup of almond flour+ 2 tbsp. of ground almonds or almond meal
- ½ tsp. of baking powder
- 1 Pinch of coarse sea salt

Directions:

1. Heat your oven to a temperature of about 180 C/356 F.
2. Melt the cream cheese and the mozzarella cheese and stir over low heat until the cheeses are perfectly melted.
3. If you choose to microwave the cheese, just do that for about 1 minute no more and if you want to do it on the stove, turn off the heat as soon as the cheese is completely melted.
4. Add the large egg to the prepared warm dough; then stir until your ingredients are very well combined. If the egg is cold; you will need to heat it gently.
5. Add in the ground almonds or the almond flour and the baking powder and stir until your ingredients are very well combined.
6. Take one pinch of the dough of cheese and toll it or stretch it in your hands until it is about 18 to 20 cm in length; if your dough is sticky, you can oil your hands to avoid that.
7. Now, form pretzels from the cheese dough and nicely shape it; then place it over a baking sheet.
8. Sprinkle with a little bit of salt and bake for about 17 minutes.

Nutrition: Calories: 113 Carbohydrates: 2.5g; Fiber: 8g

324. **Cheesy Taco Bites**

Preparation time: 5 minutes
Cooking time: 10minutes
Servings: 12
Ingredients:

- 2 Cups of Packaged Shredded Cheddar Cheese
- 2 Tbsp. of Chili Powder
- 2 Tbsp. of Cumin
- 1 tsp. of Salt
- 8 tsp. s of coconut cream for garnishing
- Use Pico de Gallo for garnishing as well

Directions:

1. Preheat your oven to a temperature of about 350°F.
2. Over a baking sheet lined with parchment paper, place 1 tbsp. piles of cheese and make sure to a space of 2 inches between each.
3. Place the baking sheet in your oven and bake for about 5 minutes.
4. Remove from the oven and let the cheese cool down for about 1 minute; then carefully lift up and press each into the cups of a mini muffin tin.
5. Make sure to press the edges of the cheese to form the shape of muffins mini.
6. Let the cheese cool completely; then remove it.
7. While you continue to bake the cheese and create your cups.
8. Fill the cheese cups with coconut cream, then top with the Pico de Gallo.

Nutrition: Calories: 73 Carbohydrates: 3g; Protein: 4g

325. **Nut Squares**

Preparation time: 30 minutes
Cooking time: 10 minutes
Servings: 10
Ingredients:

- 2 cups almonds, pumpkin seeds, sunflower seeds, and walnuts
- ½ Cup desiccated coconut
- 1 Tbsp. chia seeds
- ¼ tsp. salt
- 2 Tbsp. coconut oil
- 1 tsp. vanilla extract
- 3 Tbsp. almond or peanut butter
- 1/3 cup Sukrin Gold Fiber: Syrup

Directions:

1. Line a square baking tin with baking paper; then lightly grease it with cooking spray
2. Chop all the nuts roughly; then slightly grease it too, you can also leave them as whole
3. Mix the nuts in a large bowl; then combine them in a large bowl with the coconut, the chia seeds, and the salt
4. In a microwave-proof bowl; add the coconut oil; then add the vanilla, the coconut butter or oil, the almond butter, and the Fiber: syrup and microwave the mixture for about 30 seconds
5. Stir your ingredients together very well; then pour the melted mixture right on top of the nuts

6. Press the mixture into your prepared baking tin with the help of the back of a measuring cup and push very well
7. Freeze your treat for about 1 hour before cutting it
8. Cut your frozen nut batter into small cubes or squares of the same size

Nutrition: Calories: 268 Carbohydrates: 14g; Fiber: 1g

326. Pumpkin & Banana Ice Cream

Preparation time: 5 minutes
Cooking time: 10 minutes
Servings: 4
Ingredients:

- 15 oz. pumpkin puree
- 4 bananas, sliced and frozen
- 1 tsp. pumpkin pie spice
- Chopped pecans

Directions:
1. Add pumpkin puree, bananas, and pumpkin pie spice in a food processor.
2. Pulse until smooth.
3. Chill in the refrigerator.
4. Garnish with pecans.

Nutrition: Calories: 71; Carbohydrate: 18g; Protein: 1.2g

327. Brulee Oranges

Preparation time: 5 minutes
Cooking time: 10 minutes
Servings: 4
Ingredients:

- 4 oranges, sliced into segments
- 1 tsp. ground cardamom
- 6 tsp. brown sugar
- 1 cup nonfat Greek yogurt

Directions:
1. Preheat your broiler.
2. Arrange orange slices in a baking pan.
3. In a bowl, mix the cardamom and sugar.
4. Sprinkle mixture on top of the oranges. Broil for 5 minutes.
5. Serve oranges with yogurt.

Nutrition: Calories: 168; Carbohydrate: 26.9g; Protein: 6.8g

328. Frozen Lemon & Blueberry

Preparation time: 5 minutes
Cooking time: 10 minutes
Servings: 4
Ingredients:

- 6 cup fresh blueberries
- 8 sprigs fresh thyme
- ¾ cup light brown sugar
- 1 tsp. lemon zest
- ¼ cup lemon juice
- 2 cups water

Directions:
1. Add blueberries, thyme, and sugar to a pan over medium heat.
2. Cook for 6 to 8 minutes.
3. Transfer mixture to a blender.
4. Remove thyme sprigs.
5. Stir in the remaining ingredients.
6. Pulse until smooth.
7. Strain mixture and freeze for 1 hour.

Nutrition: Calories: 78; Carbohydrate: 20g; Protein: 3

329. Peanut Butter Choco Chip Cookies

Preparation time: 5 minutes
Cooking time: 10 minutes
Servings: 4
Ingredients:

- 1 egg
- ½ cup light brown sugar
- 1 cup natural unsweetened peanut butter
- Pinch salt
- ¼ cup dark chocolate chips

Directions:
1. Preheat your oven to 375°F.
2. Mix egg, sugar, peanut butter, salt, and chocolate chips in a bowl.
3. Form into cookies and place in a baking pan.
4. Bake the cookie for 10 minutes.
5. Let cool before serving.

Nutrition: Calories: 159; Carbohydrate: 12g; Protein 4.3g

330. Watermelon Sherbet

Preparation time: 5 minutes
Cooking time: 3 minutes
Servings: 4
Ingredients:

- 6 cups watermelon, sliced into cubes
- 14 oz. almond milk
- 1 tbsp. honey
- ¼ cup lime juice
- Salt to taste

Directions:

1. Freeze watermelon for 4 hours.
2. Add frozen watermelon and other ingredients to a blender.
3. Blend until smooth.
4. Transfer to a container with a seal.
5. Seal and freeze for 4 hours.

Nutrition: Calories: 132; Carbohydrate: 24.5g; Protein: 3.1g

331. Strawberry & Mango Ice Cream

Preparation time: 5 minutes
Cooking time: 10 minutes
Servings: 4
Ingredients:

- 8 oz. strawberries, sliced
- 12 oz. mango, sliced into cubes
- 1 tbsp. lime juice

Directions:

1. Add all ingredients to a food processor.
2. Pulse for 2 minutes.
3. Chill before serving.

Nutrition: Calories: 70 Carbohydrate: 17.4g; Protein: 1g

332. Sparkling Fruit Drink

Preparation time: 5 minutes
Cooking time: 10 minutes
Servings: 4
Ingredients:

- 8 oz. unsweetened grape juice
- 8 oz. unsweetened apple juice
- 8 oz. unsweetened orange juice
- 1 qt. homemade ginger ale
- Ice

Directions:

1. Makes 7 servings. Mix the first 4 ingredients together in a pitcher. Stir in ice cubes and 9 ounces of the beverage to each glass. Serve immediately.

Nutrition: Calories: 60; Protein: 1.1g

333. Tiramisu Shots

Preparation time: 5 minutes
Cooking time: 10 minutes
Servings: 4
Ingredients:

- 1 pack silken tofu
- 1 oz. dark chocolate, finely chopped
- ¼ cup sugar substitute
- 1 tsp. lemon juice
- ¼ cup brewed espresso
- Pinch salt
- 24 slices angel food cake
- Cocoa powder (unsweetened)

Directions:

1. Add tofu, chocolate; Sugar: substitute, lemon juice, espresso, and salt in a food processor.
2. Pulse until smooth.
3. Add angel food cake pieces into shot glasses.
4. Drizzle with the cocoa powder.
5. Pour the tofu mixture on top.
6. Top with the remaining angel food cake pieces.
7. Chill for 30 minutes and serve.

Nutrition: Calories: 75; Carbohydrate: 12g; Protein: 2.9g

334. Ice Cream Brownie Cake

Preparation time: 5 minutes
Cooking time: 10 minutes
Servings: 4
Ingredients:

- Cooking spray
- 12 oz. no-sugar brownie mix
- ¼ cup oil
- 2 egg whites
- 3 tbsp. water
- 2 cups sugar-free ice cream

Directions:

1. Preheat your oven to 325°F.
2. Spray your baking pan with oil.
3. Mix brownie mix, oil, egg whites, and water in a bowl.
4. Pour into the baking pan.
5. Bake for 25 minutes.
6. Let cool.
7. Freeze brownie for 2 hours.
8. Spread ice cream over the brownie.
9. Freeze for 8 hours.

Nutrition: Calories: 198; Carbohydrate: 33g; Protein: 3g

335.   **Berry Sorbet**

Preparation time: 10 minutes
Cooking time: 20 minutes
Servings: 6
Ingredients:

- 2 cup Water
- 2 cup Blend strawberries
- 1½ tsp. Spelt Flour
- ½ cup Date sugar

Directions:
1. Add the water into a large pot and let the water begin to warm. Add the flour and date sugar and stir until dissolved. Allow this mixture to start boiling and continue to cook for around ten minutes. It should have started to thicken. Take off the heat and set it to the side to cool.
2. Once the syrup has cooled off, add in the strawberries, and stir well to combine.
3. Pour into a container that is freezer safe and put it into the freezer until frozen.
4. Take sorbet out of the freezer, cut into chunks, and put it either into a blender or a food processor. Hit the pulse button until the mixture is creamy.
5. Pour this into the same freezer-safe container and put it back into the freezer for four hours.

Nutrition: Calories: 99; Carbohydrates: 8g

336.   **Quinoa Porridge**

Preparation time: 5 minutes
Cooking time: 15 minutes
Servings: 04
Ingredients:

- Zest of one lime
- ½ cup Coconut milk
- ½ tsp. Cloves

- 1½ tsp. Ground ginger
- 2 cup Springwater
- 1 cup Quinoa
- 1 Grated apple

Directions:
1. Cook the quinoa. Follow the instructions on the package. When the quinoa has been cooked, drain well. Place it back into the pot and stir in spices.
2. Add coconut milk and stir well to combine.
3. Grate the apple now and stir well.
4. Divide equally into bowls and add the lime zest on top. Sprinkle with nuts and seeds of choice.

Nutrition: Calories: 180g; Fat: 3 g; Carbohydrates: 40g; Protein: 10 g

337.   **Apple Quinoa**

Preparation time: 15 minutes
Cooking time: 30 minutes
Servings: 04
Ingredients:

- Coconut oil, 1 tbsp.
- Ginger
- Key lime .5
- Apple, 1
- Quinoa, .5 c
- Optional toppings
- Seeds
- Nuts
- Berries

Directions:
1. Fix the quinoa according to the instructions on the package. When you are getting close to the end of the cooking time, grate in the apple and cook for 30 seconds.
2. Zest the lime into the quinoa and squeeze the juice in. Stir in the coconut oil.
3. Divide evenly into bowls and sprinkle with some ginger.
4. You can add in some berries, nuts, and seeds right before you eat.

Nutrition: Calories: 146; Fiber: 2.3g; Fat: 8.3 g

338.   **Kamut Porridge**

Preparation time: 10 minutes
Cooking time: 25 minutes
Servings: 04
Ingredients:

- Agave syrup, 4 tbsp.
- Coconut oil, 1 tbsp.
- Sea salt, .5 tsp.
- Coconut milk, 3.75 c
- Kamut berries, 1 c
- Optional toppings
- Berries
- Coconut chips
- Ground nutmeg
- Ground cloves

Directions:
1. You need to "crack" the Kamut berries. You can try this by placing the berries into a food processor and pulsing until you have 1.25 cups of Kamut.
2. Place the cracked Kamut in a pot with salt and coconut milk. Give it a good stir to combine everything. Allow this mixture to come to a full rolling boil and then turn the heat down until the mixture is simmering. Stir every now and then until the Kamut has thickened to your likeness. This normally takes about ten minutes.
3. Take off heat, stir in agave syrup and coconut oil.
4. Garnish with toppings of choice and enjoy.

Nutrition: Calories: 114g; Protein: 5 g; Carbohydrates: 4g; Fiber: 4 g

339. Hot Kamut With Peaches, Walnuts, And Coconut

Preparation time: 10 minutes
Cooking time: 35 minutes
Servings: 04
Ingredients:
- 4 tbsp. Toasted coconut
- ½ cup Toasted and chopped walnuts
- 8 Chopped dried peaches
- 3 cup Coconut milk
- 1 cup Kamut cereal

Directions:
1. Mix the coconut milk into a saucepan and allow it to warm up. When it begins simmering, add in the Kamut. Let this cook for about 15 minutes, while stirring every now and then.

2. When done, divide evenly into bowls and top with the toasted coconut, walnuts, and peaches.
3. You could even go one more and add some fresh berries.

Nutrition: Calories: 156g; Protein: 5.8 g; Carbohydrates: 25g; Fiber: 6 g

340. Overnight "Oats"

Preparation time: 5 minutes
Cooking time: 0 minutes
Servings: 04
Ingredients:
- Berry of choice, .5 c
- Walnut butter, .5 tbsp.
- Burro banana, .5
- Ginger, .5 tsp.
- Coconut milk, .5 c
- Hemp seeds, .5 c

Directions:
1. Put the hemp seeds, salt, and coconut milk into a glass jar. Mix well.
2. Place the lid on the jar then put it in the refrigerator to sit overnight.
3. The next morning, add the ginger, berries, and banana. Stir well and enjoy.

Nutrition: Calories: 139g; Fat: 4.1g; Protein: 9 g; Sugar: 7 g

341. Blueberry Cupcakes

Preparation time: 15 minutes
Cooking time: 40 minutes
Servings: 04
Ingredients:
- Grapeseed oil
- Sea salt, .5 tsp.
- Sea moss gel, .25 c
- Agave, .3 c
- Blueberries, .5 c
- Teff flour, .75 c
- Spelt flour, .75 c
- Coconut milk, 1 c

Directions:
1. Warm your oven to 365. Place paper liners into a muffin tin.

2. Place sea moss gel, sea salt, agave, flour, and milk in a large bowl. Mix well to combine. Gently fold in blueberries.
3. Gently pour batter into paper liners. Place in oven and bake 30 minutes.
4. They are done if they have turned a nice golden color, and they spring back when you touch them.

Nutrition: Calories: 85g; Fat: 0.7 g; Carbohydrates: 12g; Protein: 1.4g; Fiber: 5 g

342. Brazil Nut Cheese

Preparation time: 2 hours
Cooking time: 0 minutes
Servings: 04
Ingredients:

- Grapeseed oil, 2 tsp.
- Water, 1.5 c
- Hemp milk, 1.5 c
- Cayenne, .5 tsp.
- Onion powder, 1 tsp.
- Juice of .5 lime
- Sea salt, 2 tsp.
- Brazil nuts, 1 lb.
- Onion powder, 1 tsp.

Directions:
1. You will need to start the process by soaking the Brazil nuts in some water. You just put the nuts into a bowl and make sure the water covers them. Soak no less than two hours or overnight. Overnight would be best.
2. Now you need to put everything except water into a food processor or blender.
3. Add just .5 cups water and blend for two minutes
4. Continue adding .5 cup water and blending until you have the consistency you want.
5. Scrape into an airtight container and enjoy.

Nutrition: Calories: 187; Protein: 4.1g; Fat: 19 g; Carbs: 3.3g; Fiber: 2.1 g

343. Slow Cooker Peaches

Preparation time: 10 minutes
Cooking time: 4 hours 20 minutes
Servings: 4–6
Ingredients:

- 4 cups peaches, sliced

- 2/3 cup rolled oats
- 1/3 cup Bisques
- 1/4 tsp. cinnamon
- ½ cup brown sugar
- ½ cup granulated sugar

Directions:
1. Spray the slow cooker pot with a cook spray.
2. Mix oats, Bisques, cinnamon, and all the sug in the pot.
3. Add peaches and stir well to combine. Cook low for 4–6 hours.

Nutrition: Calories: 617; Fat: 3.6g; Total Carbs: 1 Protein: 9 g

344. Pumpkin Custard

Preparation time: 10 minutes
Cooking time: 2 hours 30 minutes
Servings: 6
Ingredients:

- ½ cup almond flour
- 4 eggs
- 1 cup pumpkin puree
- ½ cup stevia/erythritol blend, granulated
- 1/8 tsp. sea salt
- 1 tsp. vanilla extract or maple flavoring
- 4 tbsp. butter, ghee, or coconut oil melted
- 1 tsp. pumpkin pie spice

Directions:
1. Grease or spray a slow cooker with butter coconut oil spray.
2. In a medium mixing bowl, beat the eggs u smooth. Then add in the sweetener.
3. To the egg mixture, add in the pumpkin pu along with vanilla or maple extract.
4. Then add almond flour to the mixture alc with the pumpkin pie spice and salt. A melted butter, coconut oil, or ghee.
5. Transfer the mixture into a slow cooker. Cl the lid. Cook for 2–2 ¾ hours on low.
6. When through, serve with whipped cream, a then sprinkle with little nutmeg if need Enjoy!
7. Set slow-cooker to the low setting. Cook for 2.45 hours, and begin checking at the two-h mark. Serve warm with stevia-sweeten whipped cream and a sprinkle of nutmeg.

Nutrition: Calories: 147; Fat: 12g; Total Carbs: Protein: 5 g

146

345. Blueberry Lemon Custard Cake

Preparation time: 10 minutes
Cooking time: 3 hours
Servings: 12
Ingredients:

- 6 eggs, separated
- 2 cups light cream
- ½ cup coconut flour
- ½ tsp. salt
- 2 tsp. lemon zest
- ½ cup granulated sugar substitute
- 1/3 cup lemon juice
- ½ cup blueberries fresh
- 1 tsp. lemon liquid stevia

Directions:

1. Into a stand mixer, add the egg whites and whip them well until stiff peaks have formed; set aside.
2. Whisk the yolks together with the remaining ingredients except for blueberries, to form a batter.
3. When done, fold egg whites into the formed batter a little at a time until slightly combined.
4. Grease the crockpot and then pour in the mixture. Then sprinkle batter with the blueberries.
5. Close the lid then cook for 3 hours on low. When the cooking time is over, open the lid and let cool for an hour, and then let chill in the refrigerator for at least 2 hours or overnight.
6. Serve cold with little sugar-free whipped cream and enjoy!

Nutrition: Calories: 165; Fat: 10g; Total Carbs: 14g; Protein: 4 g

346. Sugar-Free Carrot Cake

Preparation time: 25 minutes
Cooking time: 4 hours
Servings: 8
Ingredients:
For Carrot cake:

- 2 eggs
- 1 ½ almond flour
- ½ cup butter, melted
- ¼ cup heavy cream
- 1 tsp. baking powder
- 1 tsp. vanilla extract or almond extract, optional
- 1 cup sugar substitute
- 1 cup carrots, finely shredded
- 1 tsp. cinnamon
- ¼ tsp. nutmeg
- 1/8 tsp. allspice
- 1 tsp. ginger
- ½ tsp. baking soda

For cream cheese frosting:

- 1 cup confectioner's sugar substitute
- ¼ cup butter, softened
- 1 tsp. almond extract
- 4 oz. cream cheese, softened

Directions:

1. Grease a loaf pan well and then set it aside.
2. Using a mixer, combine butter together with eggs, vanilla; Sugar: substitute and heavy cream in a mixing bowl, until well blended.
3. Combine almond flour together with baking powder, spices, and baking soda in another bowl until well blended.
4. When done, combine the wet ingredients together with the dry ingredients until well blended, and then stir in carrots.
5. Pour the mixer into the prepared loaf pan, and then place the pan into a slow cooker on a trivet. Add 1 cup water inside.
6. Cook for about 4–5 hours on low. Be aware that the cake will be very moist.
7. When the cooking time is over, let the cake cool completely.
8. To prepare the cream cheese frosting: blend the cream cheese together with extract, butter, and powdered sugar substitute until frosting is formed.
9. Top the cake with the frosting.

Nutrition: Calories: 299; Fat: 25.4g; Total Carbs: 15g; Protein: 4 g

347. Sugar-Free Chocolate Molten Lava Cake

Preparation time: 10 minutes
Cooking time: 3 hours
Servings: 12

Ingredients:

- 3 egg yolks
- 1 ½ cups Swerve sweetener, divided
- 1 tsp. baking powder
- ½ cup flour, gluten-free
- 3 whole eggs
- 5 tbsp. cocoa powder, unsweetened, divided
- 4 oz. chocolate chips; Sugar: free
- ½ tsp. salt
- ½ tsp. vanilla liquid stevia
- ½ cup butter, melted, cooled
- 2 cups hot water
- 1 tsp. vanilla extract

Directions:

1. Grease the crockpot well with cooking spray.
2. Whisk 1 ¼ cups of swerving together with flour, salt, baking powder, and 3 tbsp. cocoa powder in a bowl.
3. Stir the cooled melted butter together with eggs, yolks, liquid stevia, and the vanilla extract in a separate bowl.
4. When done, add the wet ingredients to the dry ingredient until nicely combined, and then pour the mixture into the prepared crockpot.
5. Then top the mixture in the crockpot with chocolate chips.
6. Whisk the rest of the swerve sweetener and the remaining cocoa powder with the hot water, and then pour this mixture over the chocolate chips top.
7. Close the lid and cook for 3 hours on low. When the cooking time is over, let cool a bit and then serve. Enjoy!

Nutrition: Calories: 157; Fat: 13g; Total Carbs: 10.5g; Protein: 3.9 g

348. Chocolate Quinoa Brownies

Preparation time: 10 minutes
Cooking time: 2 hours
Servings: 16
Ingredients:

- 2 eggs
- 3 cups quinoa, cooked
- 1 tsp. vanilla liquid stevia
- 1 ¼ chocolate chips; Sugar: free
- 1 tsp. vanilla extract

- 1/3 cup flaxseed ground
- ¼ tsp. salt
- 1/3 cup cocoa powder, unsweetened
- ½ tsp. baking powder
- 1 tsp. pure stevia extract
- ½ cup applesauce, unsweetened

Sugar-free frosting:

- ¼ cup heavy cream
- 1 tsp. chocolate liquid stevia
- ¼ cup cocoa powder, unsweetened
- ½ tsp. vanilla extract

Directions:

1. Add all the ingredients to a food processor. Then process until well incorporated.
2. Line a crockpot with parchment paper, and then spread the batter into the lined pot.
3. Close the lid and cook for 4 hours on LOW or 2 hours on HIGH. Let cool.
4. Prepare the frosting. Whisk all the ingredients together and then microwave for 20 seconds. Taste and adjust on sweetener if desired.
5. When the frosting is ready, stir it well again and then pour it over the sliced brownies.
6. Serve and enjoy!

Nutrition: Calories: 133; Fat: 7.9g; Total Carbs: 18.4 Protein:4.3 g

349. Blueberry Crisp

Preparation time: 10 minutes
Cooking time: 3–4 hours
Servings: 10
Ingredients:

- 1/4 cup butter, melted
- 24 oz. blueberries, frozen
- 3/4 tsp. salt
- 1 ½ cups rolled oats, coarsely ground
- 3/4 cup almond flour, blanched
- 1/4 cup coconut oil, melted
- 6 tbsp. sweetener
- 1 cup pecans or walnuts, coarsely chopped

Directions:

1. Using a non-stick cooking spray, spray the slo cooker pot well.
2. Into a bowl, add ground oats and chopped n along with salt, blanched almond flour, brov sugar, stevia granulated sweetener, and th stir in the coconut/butter mixture. Stir well combine.

3. When done, spread crisp topping over blueberries. Cook for 3–4 hours, until the mixture, has become bubbling hot and you can smell the blueberries.
4. Serve while still hot with whipped cream or ice cream if desired. Enjoy!

Nutrition: Calories: 261; Fat: 16.6g; Total Carbs: 32g; Protein: 4 g

350.   Maple Custard

Preparation time: 10 minutes
Cooking time: 2 hours
Servings: 6
Ingredients:

- 1 tsp. maple extract
- 2 egg yolks
- 1 cup heavy cream
- 2 eggs
- ½ cup whole milk
- 1/4 tsp. salt
- 1/4 cup Sukrin Gold or any sugar-free brown sugar substitute
- ½ tsp. cinnamon

Directions:

1. Combine all ingredients together in a blender, process well.
2. Grease 6 ramekins and then pour the batter evenly into each ramekin.
3. To the bottom of the slow cooker, add 4 ramekins and then arrange the remaining 2 against the side of a slow cooker, and not at the top of the bottom ramekins.
4. Close the lid and cook on high for 2 hours, until the center is cooked through but the middle is still jiggly.
5. Let cool at room temperature for an hour after removing from the slow cooker, and then chill in the fridge for at least 2 hours.
6. Serve and enjoy with a sprinkle of cinnamon and little sugar-free whipped cream.

Nutrition: Calories: 190; Fat: 18g; Total Carbs: 2g; Protein: 4 g

51.   Raspberry Cream Cheese Coffee Cake

Preparation time: 10 minutes
Cooking time: 4 hours
Servings: 12

Ingredients:

- 1 1/4 almond flour
- 2/3 cup water
- ½ cup Swerve
- 3 eggs
- 1/4 cup coconut flour
- 1/4 cup; Protein: powder
- 1/4 tsp. salt
- ½ tsp. vanilla extract
- 1 ½ tsp. baking powder
- 6 tbsp. butter, melted

For the Filling:

- 1 ½ cup fresh raspberries
- 8 oz. cream cheese
- 1 large egg
- 1/3 cup powdered Swerve
- 2 tbsp. whipping cream

Directions:

1. Grease the slow cooker pot. Prepare the cake batter. In a bowl, combine almond flour together with coconut flour, sweetener, baking powder; Protein: powder and salt, and then stir in the melted butter along with eggs and water until well combined. Set aside.
2. Prepare the filling. Beat cream cheese thoroughly with the sweetener until have smoothened, and then beat in whipping cream along with the egg and vanilla extract until well combined.
3. Assemble the cake. Spread around 2/3 of batter in the slow cooker as you smoothen the top using a spatula or knife.
4. Pour cream cheese mixture over the batter in the pan, evenly spread it, and then sprinkle with raspberries. Add the rest of the batter.
5. Cook for 3–4 hours on low. Let cool completely.
6. Serve and enjoy!

Nutrition: Calories: 239; Fat: 19.18g; Total Carbs: 6.9 g; Protein: 7.5 g

352.   Pumpkin Pie Bars

Preparation time: 10 minutes
Cooking time: 3 hours
Servings: 16
Ingredients:
For the Crust:

- 3/4 cup coconut, shredded

- 4 tbsp. butter, unsalted, softened
- 1/4 cup cocoa powder, unsweetened
- 1/4 tsp. salt
- ½ cup raw sunflower seeds or sunflower seed flour
- 1/4 cup confectioners Swerve

Filling:
- 2 tsp. cinnamon liquid stevia
- 1 cup heavy cream
- 1 can pumpkin puree
- 6 eggs
- 1 tbsp. pumpkin pie spice
- ½ tsp. salt
- 1 tbsp. vanilla extract
- ½ cup sugar-free chocolate chips, optional

Directions:
1. Add all the crust ingredients to a food processor. Then process until fine crumbs are formed.
2. Grease the slow cooker pan well. When done, press crust mixture onto the greased bottom.
3. In a stand mixer, combine all the ingredients for the filling, and then blend well until combined.
4. Top the filling with chocolate chips if using, and then pour the mixture onto the prepared crust.
5. Close the lid and cook for 3 hours on low. Open the lid and let cool for at least 30 minutes, and then place the slow cooker into the refrigerator for at least 3 hours.
6. Slice the pumpkin pie bar and serve it with sugar-free whipped cream. Enjoy!

Nutrition: Calories: 169; Fat: 15g; Total Carbs: 6g; Protein: 4 g

353.   Dark Chocolate Cake

Preparation time: 10 minutes
Cooking time: 3 hours
Servings: 10
Ingredients:
- 1 cup almond flour
- 3 eggs
- 2 tbsp. almond flour
- 1/4 tsp. salt
- ½ cup Swerve Granular
- 3/4 tsp. vanilla extract
- 2/3 cup almond milk, unsweetened

- ½ cup cocoa powder
- 6 tbsp. butter, melted
- 1 ½ tsp. baking powder
- 3 tbsp. unflavored whey; Protein: powder or egg white; Protein: powder
- 1/3 cup sugar-free chocolate chips, optional

Directions:
1. Grease the slow cooker well.
2. Whisk the almond flour together with cocoa powder, sweetener, whey; Protein: powder salt, and baking powder in a bowl. Then stir in butter along with almond milk, eggs, and the vanilla extract until well combined, and then stir in the chocolate chips if desired.
3. When done, pour into the slow cooker. Allow cooking for 2–2½ hours on low.
4. When through, turn off the slow cooker and let the cake cool for about 20–30 minutes.
5. When cooled, cut the cake into pieces and serve warm with lightly sweetened whipped cream. Enjoy!

Nutrition: Calories: 205; Fat: 17g; Total Carbs: 8.4g Protein: 12 g

354.   Lemon Custard

Preparation time: 10 minutes
Cooking time: 3 hours
Servings: 4
Ingredients:
- 2 cups whipping cream or coconut cream
- 5 egg yolks
- 1 tbsp. lemon zest
- 1 tsp. vanilla extract
- 1/4 cup fresh lemon juice, squeezed
- ½ tsp. liquid stevia
- Lightly sweetened whipped cream

Directions:
1. Whisk egg yolks together with lemon zest liquid stevia, lemon zest, and vanilla in a bowl and then whisk in heavy cream.
2. Divide the mixture among 4 small jars ramekins.
3. To the bottom of a slow cooker add a rack, a then add ramekins on top of the rack and a enough water to cover half of the ramekins.
4. Close the lid and cook for 3 hours on lo Remove ramekins.

5. Let cool to room temperature, and then place into the refrigerator to cool completely for about 3 hours.
6. When through, top with the whipped cream and serve. Enjoy!

Nutrition: Calories: 319; Fat: 30g; Total Carbs: 3g; Protein: 7 g

355. Baked Stuffed Pears

Preparation time: 15 minutes
Cooking time: 35 minutes
Servings: 04
Ingredients:

- Agave syrup, 4 tbsp.
- Cloves, .25 tsp.
- Chopped walnuts, 4 tbsp.
- Currants, 1 c
- Pears, 4

Directions:

1. Make sure your oven has been warmed to 375.
2. Slice the pears in two lengthwise and remove the core. To get the pear to lay flat, you can slice a small piece off the backside.
3. Place the agave syrup, currants, walnuts, and cloves in a small bowl and mix well. Set this to the side to be used later.
4. Put the pears on a cookie sheet that has parchment paper on it. Make sure the cored sides are facing up. Sprinkle each pear half with about ½ tbsp. of the chopped walnut mixture.
5. Place into the oven and cook for 25 to 30 minutes. Pears should be tender.

Nutrition: Calories: 103.9; Fiber: 3.1 g; Carbohydrates: 2 g

356. Butternut Squash Pie

Preparation time: 25 minutes
Cooking time: 35 minutes
Servings: 04
Ingredients:

- For the Crust
- Coldwater
- Agave, splash
- Sea salt, pinch
- Grapeseed oil, .5 c

- Coconut flour, .5 c
- Spelt Flour, 1 c
- For the Filling
- Butternut squash, peeled, chopped
- Water
- Allspice, to taste
- Agave syrup, to taste
- Hemp milk, 1 c
- Sea moss, 4 tbsp.

Directions:

1. You will need to warm your oven to 350.
2. For the Crust
3. Place the grapeseed oil and water into the refrigerator to get it cold. This will take about one hour.
4. Place all ingredients into a large bowl. Now you need to add in the cold water a little bit in small amounts until a dough forms. Place this onto a surface that has been sprinkled with some coconut flour. Knead for a few minutes and roll the dough as thin as you can get it. Carefully, pick it up and place it inside a pie plate.
5. Place the butternut squash into a Dutch oven and pour in enough water to cover. Bring this to a full rolling boil. Let this cook until the squash has become soft.
6. Completely drain and place into a bowl. Using a potato masher, mash the squash. Add in some allspice and agave to taste. Add in the sea moss and hemp milk. Using a hand mixer, blend well. Pour into the pie crust.
7. Place into an oven and bake for about one hour.

Nutrition: Calories: 245; Carbohydrates: 50g; Fat: 10 g

357. Coconut Chia Cream Pot

Preparation time: 5 minutes
Cooking time: 5 minutes
Servings: 04
Ingredients:

- Date, one (1)
- Coconut milk (organic), one (1) cup
- Coconut yogurt, one (1) cup
- Vanilla extract, ½ tsp.
- Chia seeds, ¼ cup

- Sesame seeds, one (1) tsp.
- Flaxseed (ground), one (1) tbsp. or flax meal, one (1) tbsp.
- Toppings:
- Fig, one (1)
- Blueberries, one(1) handful
- Mixed nuts (brazil nuts, almonds, pistachios, macadamia, etc.)
- Cinnamon (ground), one tsp.

Directions:
1. First, blend the date with coconut milk (the idea is to sweeten the coconut milk).
2. Get a mixing bowl and add the coconut milk with the vanilla, sesame seeds, chia seeds, and flax meal.
3. Refrigerate for between twenty to thirty minutes or wait till the chia expands.
4. To serve, pour a layer of coconut yogurt in a small glass, then add the chia mix, followed by pouring another layer of coconut yogurt.
5. It's alkaline, creamy, and delicious.

Nutrition: Calories: 310; Carbohydrates: 39g; Protein: 4g; Fiber: 8.1 g

358. Chocolate Avocado Mousse

Preparation time: 10 minutes
Cooking time: 5 minutes
Servings: 04
Ingredients:

- Coconut water, 2/3 cup
- Avocado, ½ Hass
- Raw cacao, 2 tsp.
- Vanilla, 1 tsp.
- Dates, three (3)
- Sea salt, 0ne (1) tsp.
- Dark chocolate shavings

Directions:
1. Blend all ingredients.
2. Blast until it becomes thick and smooth, as you wish.
3. Put in a fridge and allow it to get firm.

Nutrition: Calories: 181.8g; Fat: 151.g; Protein: 12 g

359. Chia Vanilla Coconut Pudding

Preparation time: 5 minutes

Cooking time: 5 minutes
Servings: 2
Ingredients:

- Coconut oil, 2 tbsp.
- Raw cashew, ½ cup
- Coconut water, ½ cup
- Cinnamon, 1 tsp.
- Dates (pitted), 3
- Vanilla, 2 tsp.
- Coconut flakes (unsweetened), 1 tsp.
- Salt (Himalayan or Celtic Grey)
- Chia seeds, 6 tbsp.
- Cinnamon or pomegranate seeds for garnish (optional)

Directions:
1. Get a blender, add all the ingredients (minus the pomegranate and chia seeds), and blend for about forty to sixty seconds.
2. Reduce the blender speed to the lowest and add the chia seeds.
3. Pour the content into an airtight container and put it in a refrigerator for five to six hours.
4. To serve, you can garnish with the cinnamon powder of pomegranate seeds.

Nutrition: Calories: 201g; Fat: 10 g; Sodium: 32.8 mg

360. Sweet Tahini Dip with Ginger Cinnamon Fruit

Preparation time: 10 minutes
Cooking time: 5 minutes
Servings: 2
Ingredients:

- Cinnamon, one (1) tsp.
- Green apple, one (1)
- Pear, one (1)
- Fresh ginger, two (2)–three (3)
- Celtic sea salt, one (1) tsp.
- Ingredient for sweet Tahini
- Almond butter (raw), three (3) tsp.
- Tahini (one big scoop), three (3) tsp.
- Coconut oil, two (2) tsp.
- Cayenne (optional), ¼ tsp.
- Wheat-free tamari, two (2) tsp.
- Liquid coconut nectar, one (1) tsp.

Directions:

1. Get a clean mixing bowl.
2. Grate the ginger, add cinnamon, sea salt and mix together in the bowl.
3. Dice apple and pear into little cubes, turn into the bowl, and mix.
4. Get a mixing bowl and mix all the ingredients.
5. Then add the Sprinkle the Sweet Tahini Dip all over the Ginger Cinnamon Fruit.
6. Serve.

Nutrition: Calories: 109g; Fat: 10.8 g; Sodium: 258 mg

361.   Coconut Butter and Chopped Berries with Mint

Preparation time: 5 minutes
Cooking time: 5 minutes
Servings: 04
Ingredients:

- Chopped mint, one (1) tbsp.
- Coconut butter (melted), two (2) tbsp.
- Mixed berries (strawberries, blueberries, and raspberries)

Directions:

1. Get a small bowl and add the berries.
2. Drizzle the melted coconut butter and sprinkle the mint.
3. Serve.

Nutrition: Calories: 159g; Fat: 12 g; Carbohydrates: 18

362.   Alkaline Raw Pumpkin Pie

Preparation time: 5 minutes
Cooking time: 5 minutes
Servings: 04
Ingredients:
For Pie Crust:

- Cinnamon, one (1) tsp.
- Dates/Turkish apricots, one (1) cup
- Raw almonds, one (1) cup
- Coconut flakes (unsweetened), one (1) cup

For Pie Filling:

- Dates, six (6)
- Cinnamon, ½ tsp.
- Nutmeg, ½ tsp.
- Pecans (soaked overnight), one (1) cup
- Organic pumpkin Blends (12 oz.), 1 ¼ cup

- Nutmeg, ½ tsp.
- Sea salt (Himalayan or Celtic Sea Salt), ¼ tsp.
- Vanilla, 1 tsp.
- Gluten-free tamari

Directions:
Directions for pie crust:

1. Get a food processor and blend all the pie crust ingredients at the same time.
2. Make sure the mixture turns oily and sticky before you stop mixing.
3. Put the mixture in a pie pan and mold it against the sides and floor, to make it stick properly.

Directions for the pie filling:

1. Mix the ingredients together in a blender.
2. Add the mixture to fill in the pie crust.
3. Pour some cinnamon on top.
4. Then refrigerate till it's cold.
5. Then mold.

Nutrition: Calories: 135; Fat 41.4g; Total Fat: 4.6g; Cholesterol: 11.3 mg

363.   Strawberry Sorbet

Preparation time: 5 minutes
Cooking time: 4 Hours
Servings: 4
Ingredients:

- 2 cups of Strawberries*
- 1 ½ tsp. of Spelt Flour
- ½ cup of Date Sugar
- 2 cups of Spring Water

Directions:

- Add Date Sugar, Spring Water, and Spelt Flour to a medium pot and boil on low heat for about ten minutes. The mixture should thicken, like syrup.
- Remove the pot from the heat and allow it to cool.
- After cooling, add Blend Strawberry and mix gently.
- Put the mixture in a container and freeze.
- Cut it into pieces, put the sorbet into a processor, and blend until smooth.
- Put everything back in the container and leave it in the refrigerator for at least four hours.
- Serve and enjoy your Strawberry Sorbet!

Nutrition: Calories: 198; Carbohydrates: 28 g

364. Blueberry Muffins

Preparation time: 5 minutes
Cooking time: 1 Hour
Servings: 3
Ingredients:

- ½ cup of Blueberries
- 3/4 cup of Teff Flour
- 3/4 cup of Spelt Flour
- 1/3 cup of Agave Syrup
- ½ tsp. of Pure Sea Salt
- 1 cup of Coconut Milk
- 1/4 cup of Sea Moss Gel (optional, check information)
- Grape Seed Oil

Directions:

1. Preheat your oven to 365°F.
2. Grease or line 6 standard muffin cups.
3. Add Teff, Spelt flour, Pure Sea Salt, Coconut Milk, Sea Moss Gel, and Agave Syrup to a large bowl. Mix them together.
4. Add Blueberries to the mixture and mix well.
5. Divide muffin batter among the 6 muffin cups.
6. Bake for 30 minutes until golden brown.
7. Serve and enjoy your Blueberry Muffins!

Nutrition: Calories: 65g; Fat: 0.7 g; Carbohydrates: 12g; Protein: 1.4g; Fiber: 5 g

365. Banana Strawberry Ice Cream

Preparation time: 5 minutes
Cooking time: 4 Hours
Servings: 5
Ingredients:

- 1 cup of Strawberry*
- 5 quartered Baby Bananas*
- ½ Avocado, chopped
- 1 tbsp. of Agave Syrup
- 1/4 cup of Homemade Walnut Milk

Directions:

1. Mix the ingredients into the blender and blend them well.
2. Taste. If it is too thick, add extra Milk or Agave Syrup if you want it sweeter.
3. Put in a container with a lid and allow to freeze for at least 5 to 6 hours.
4. Serve it and enjoy your Banana Strawberry Ice Cream!

Nutrition: Calories: 200g; Fat: 0.5 g; Carbohydrates: 44 g

366. Homemade Whipped Cream

Preparation time: 5 minutes
Cooking time: 10 Minutes
Servings: 1 Cup
Ingredients:

- 1 cup of Aquafaba
- 1/4 cup of Agave Syrup

Directions:

1. Add Agave Syrup and Aquafaba into a bowl.
2. Mix at high speed around 5 minutes with a stand mixer or 10 to 15 minutes with a hand mixer.
3. Serve and enjoy your Homemade Whipped Cream!

Nutrition: Calories: 21; Fat: 0g; Sodium: 0.3g; Carbohydrates: 5.3g; Fiber: 0g; Sugars: 4.7g; Protein: 0g

367. Chocolate Crunch Bars

Preparation time: 5 minutes
Cooking time: 5 minutes
Servings: 4
Ingredients:

- 1 ½ cups sugar-free chocolate chips
- 1 cup almond butter
- Stevia to taste
- 1/4 cup coconut oil
- 3 cups pecans, chopped

Directions:

1. Layer an 8-inch baking pan with parchment paper.
2. Mix chocolate chips with butter, coconut oil and sweetener in a bowl.
3. Melt it by heating in a microwave for 2 to minutes until well mixed.
4. Stir in nuts and seeds. Mix gently.
5. Pour this batter carefully into the baking pan and spread evenly.
6. Refrigerate for 2 to 3 hours.
7. Slice and serve.

Nutrition: Calories: 316; Total Fat: 30.9g; Saturated Fat: 8.1g; Cholesterol: 0mg; Total Carbs: 8.3g; Sugar 1.8g; Fiber: 3.8g; Sodium: 8mg; Protein: 6.4 g

368.   Homemade; Protein: Bar

Preparation time: 5 minutes
Cooking time: 10 minutes
Servings: 4
Ingredients:

- 1 cup nut butter
- 4 tbsp. coconut oil
- 2 scoops vanilla; Protein:
- Stevia, to taste
- ½ tsp. sea salt
- Optional ingredients
- 1 tsp. cinnamon

Directions:

1. Mix coconut oil with butter, protein, stevia, and salt in a dish.
2. Stir in cinnamon and chocolate chip.
3. Press the mixture firmly and freeze until firm.
4. Cut the crust into small bars.
5. Serve and enjoy.

Nutrition: Calories: 179; Total Fat: 15.7g; Saturated Fat: 8g; Cholesterol: 0mg; Total Carbs: 4.8g; Sugar: .6g; Fiber: 0.8g; Sodium: 43mg; Protein: 5.6 g

369.   Shortbread Cookies

Preparation time: 10 minutes
Cooking time: 70 minutes
Servings: 6
Ingredients:

- 2 ½ cups almond flour
- 6 tbsp. nut butter
- ½ cup erythritol
- 1 tsp. vanilla essence

Directions:

1. Preheat your oven to 350°F.
2. Layer a cookie sheet with parchment paper.
3. Beat butter with erythritol until fluffy.
4. Stir in vanilla essence and almond flour. Mix well until becomes crumbly.
5. Spoon out a tbsp. of cookie dough onto the cookie sheet.
6. Add more dough to make as many cookies.
7. Bake for 15 minutes until brown.
8. Serve.

Nutrition: Calories: 288; Total Fat: 25.3g; Saturated Fat: 6.7g; Cholesterol: 23mg; Total Carbs: 9.6g; Sugar: 0.1 g Fiber: 3.8g; Sodium: 74mg; Potassium: 3mg; Protein: 7.6 g

370.   Coconut Chip Cookies

Preparation time: 10 minutes
Cooking time: 15 minutes
Servings: 4
Ingredients:

- 1 cup almond flour
- ½ cup cacao nibs
- ½ cup coconut flakes, unsweetened
- 1/3 cup erythritol
- ½ cup almond butter
- ¼ cup nut butter, melted
- ¼ cup almond milk
- Stevia, to taste
- ¼ tsp. sea salt

Directions:

1. Preheat your oven to 350°F.
2. Layer a cookie sheet with parchment paper.
3. Add and then combine all the dry ingredients in a glass bowl.
4. Whisk in butter, almond milk, vanilla essence, stevia, and almond butter.
5. Beat well then stir in dry mixture. Mix well.
6. Spoon out a tbsp. of cookie dough on the cookie sheet.
7. Add more dough to make as many as 16 cookies.
8. Flatten each cookie using your fingers.
9. Bake for 25 minutes until golden brown.
10. Let them sit for 15 minutes.
11. Serve.

Nutrition: Calories: 192; Total Fat: 17.44g; Saturated Fat: 11.5g; Cholesterol: 125mg; Total Carbs: 2.2g; Sugar: 1.4g; Fiber: 2.1g; Sodium: 135mg; Protein: 4.7 g

371.   Peanut Butter Bars

Preparation time: 10 minutes
Cooking time: 10 minutes
Servings: 6
Ingredients:

- 3/4 cup almond flour
- 2 oz. almond butter
- 1/4 cup Swerve

- ½ cup peanut butter
- ½ tsp. vanilla

Directions:
1. Combine all the ingredients for bars.
2. Transfer this mixture to a 6-inch small pan. Press it firmly.
3. Refrigerate for 30 minutes.
4. Slice and serve.

Nutrition: Calories: 214; Total Fat: 19g; Saturated Fat: 5.8g; Cholesterol: 15mg; Total Carbs: 6.5g; Sugar: 1.9g; Fiber: 2.1g; Sodium: 123mg; Protein: 6.5 g

372. Zucchini Bread Pancakes

Preparation time: 15 minutes
Cooking time: 35 minutes
Servings: 3
Ingredients:
- Grapeseed oil, 1 tbsp.
- Chopped walnuts, .5 c
- Walnut milk, 2 c
- Shredded zucchini, 1 c
- Mashed burro banana, .25 c
- Date sugar, 2 tbsp.
- Kamut flour or spelt, 2 c

Directions:
1. Place the date sugar and flour into a bowl. Whisk together.
2. Add in the mashed banana and walnut milk. Stir until combined. Remember to scrape the bowl to get all the dry mixture. Add in walnuts and zucchini. Stir well until combined.
3. Place the grapeseed oil onto a griddle and warm.
4. Pour .25 cup batter on the hot griddle. Leave it along until bubbles begin forming on to surface. Carefully turn over the pancake and cook another four minutes until cooked through.
5. Place the pancakes onto a serving plate and enjoy with some agave syrup.

Nutrition: Calories: 246; Carbohydrates: 49.2g; Fiber: 4.6g; Protein: 7.8g

373. Raspberry Cake With White Chocolate Sauce

Preparation time: 15 minutes
Cooking time: 60 minutes
Servings: 6
Ingredients:
- 5 Ounces of melted cacao butter
- 2 Ounces of grass-fed ghee
- ½ Cup of coconut cream
- 1 Cup of green banana flour
- 3 tsp. s of pure vanilla
- 4 large eggs
- ½ Cup of as Lakanto Monk Fruit
- 1 tsp. of baking powder
- 2 tsp. s of apple cider vinegar
- 2 Cup of raspberries

For the white chocolate sauce:
- 3 and ½ ounces of cacao butter
- ½ Cup of coconut cream
- 2 tsp. s of pure vanilla extract
- 1 Pinch of salt

Directions:
1. Preheat your oven to a temperature of abo 280°F.
2. Combine the green banana flour with the pu vanilla extract, the baking powder, the cocon cream, the eggs, the cider vinegar, and the mon fruit and mix very well.
3. Leave the raspberries aside and line a cake lo tin with baking paper.
4. Pour the batter into the baking tray and scatt the raspberries over the top of the cake.
5. Place the tray in your oven and bake it for abo 60 minutes; in the meantime, prepare the sauc

6. Combine the cacao cream, the vanilla extract, the cacao butter, and the salt in a saucepan over low heat.
6. Mix all your ingredients with a fork to make sure the cacao butter mixes very well with the cream.
7. Remove from the heat and set aside to cool a little bit, but don't let it harden.
8. Drizzle with the chocolate sauce.
9. Scatter the cake with more raspberries.
10. Slice your cake; then serve and enjoy it!

Nutrition: Calories: 323g; Fat: 31.5g; Carbohydrates: 0.9g; Fiber: 4g; Protein: 5g

374. Cake with Whipped Cream Icing

Preparation time: 20 minutes
Cooking time: 25 minutes
Servings: 7
Ingredients:

- ¾ Cup Coconut flour
- ¾ Cup of Swerve Sweetener
- ½ Cup of Cocoa powder
- 2 tsp. s of Baking powder
- 6 Large Eggs
- 2/3 Cup of Heavy Whipping Cream
- ½ Cup of Melted almond Butter

For the whipped cream Icing:

- 1 Cup of Heavy Whipping Cream
- ¼ Cup of Swerve Sweetener
- 1 tsp. of Vanilla extract
- 1/3 Cup of Sifted Cocoa Powder

Directions:

1. Pre-heat your oven to a temperature of about 350°F.
2. Grease an 8x8 cake tray with cooking spray.

3. Add the coconut flour, the Swerve sweetener; the cocoa powder, the baking powder, the eggs, the melted butter; and combine very well with an electric or a hand mixer.
4. Pour your batter into the cake tray and bake for about 25 minutes.
5. Remove the cake tray from the oven and let cool for about 5 minutes.

For the Icing:

6. Whip the cream until it becomes fluffy; then add in the Swerve, the vanilla, and the cocoa powder.
7. Add the Swerve, the vanilla, and the cocoa powder; then continue mixing until your ingredients are very well combined.
8. Frost your baked cake with the icing; then slice it; serve and enjoy your delicious cake!

Nutrition: Calories: 357; Fat: 33g; Carbohydrates: 11g; Fiber: 2g; Protein: 8g

375. Walnut-Fruit Cake

Preparation time: 15 minutes
Cooking time: 20 minutes
Servings: 6
Ingredients:

- ½ cup almond butter (softened)
- ¼ Cup so Nourished granulated erythritol
- 1 Tbsp. ground cinnamon
- ½ tsp. ground nutmeg
- ¼ tsp. ground cloves
- 4 large pastured eggs
- 1 tsp. vanilla extract
- ½ tsp. almond extract
- 2 cups almond flour
- ½ cup chopped walnuts
- ¼ cup dried unsweetened cranberries
- ¼ cup seedless raisins

Directions:

1. Preheat your oven to a temperature of about 350°F and grease an 8-inch baking tin of round shape with coconut oil.
2. Beat the granulated erythritol at a high speed until it becomes fluffy.
3. Add the cinnamon, the nutmeg, and the cloves; then blend your ingredients until they become smooth.
4. Crack in the eggs and beat very well by adding one at a time, plus the almond extract and the vanilla.
5. Whisk in the almond flour until it forms a smooth batter then fold in the nuts and the fruit.
6. Spread your mixture into your prepared baking pan and bake it for about 20 minutes.
7. Remove the cake from the oven and let cool for about 5 minutes.
8. Dust the cake with powdered erythritol.
9. Serve and enjoy your cake!

Nutrition: Calories: 250; Fat: 11g; Carbohydrates: 12g; Fiber: 2g; Protein: 7g

376. Ginger Cake

Preparation time: 15 minutes
Cooking time: 20 minutes
Servings: 9
Ingredients:

- ½ Tbsp. of unsalted almond butter to grease the pan
- 4 large eggs
- ¼ Cup coconut milk
- 2 Tbsp. of unsalted almond butter
- 1 and ½ tsp. of stevia
- 1 Tbsp. of ground cinnamon
- 1 Tbsp. of natural unweeded cocoa powder
- 1 Tbsp. of fresh ground ginger
- ½ tsp. of kosher salt
- 1 and ½ cups of blanched almond flour
- ½ tsp. of baking soda

Directions:

1. Preheat your oven to a temperature of 325 F.
2. Grease a glass baking tray of about 8X8 inches generously with almond butter.
3. In a large bowl, whisk all together with the coconut milk, the eggs, the melted almond butter, the stevia, the cinnamon, the cocoa powder, the ginger, and the kosher salt.
4. Whisk in the almond flour, then the baking soda, and mix very well.
5. Pour the batter into the prepared pan and bake for about 20 to 25 minutes.
6. Let the cake cool for about 5 minutes; then slice; serve and enjoy your delicious cake.

Nutrition: Calories: 175; Fat: 15g; Carbohydrates: 5g Fiber: 1.9g; Protein: 5g

377. Lemon Cake

Preparation time: 20 minutes
Cooking time: 20minutes
Servings: 6
Ingredients:

- 2 medium lemons
- 4 large eggs
- 2 Tbsp. of almond butter
- 2 Tbsp. of avocado oil
- 1/3 cup of coconut flour
- 4–5 tbsp. of honey (or another sweetener your choice)
- ½ tbsp. of baking soda

Directions:

1. Preheat your oven to a temperature of about 350°F.

2. Crack the eggs in a large bowl and set two egg whites aside.
3. Whisk the 2 whites of eggs with the egg yolks, the honey, the oil, the almond butter, the lemon zest, and the juice and whisk very well together.
4. Combine the baking soda with the coconut flour and gradually add this dry mixture to the wet ingredients and keep whisking for a couple of minutes.
5. Beat the two eggs with a hand mixer and beat the egg into foam.
6. Add the white egg foam gradually to the mixture with a silicone spatula.
7. Transfer your obtained batter to a tray covered with baking paper.
8. Bake your cake for about 20 to 22 minutes.
9. Let the cake cool for 5 minutes; then slice your cake.
10. Serve and enjoy your delicious cake!

Nutrition: Calories: 164; Fat: 12g; Carbohydrates: 7.1 Fiber: 2.7g; Protein: 10.9g

378. <u>Cinnamon Cake</u>

Preparation time: 15 minutes
Cooking time: 35minutes
Servings: 6

Ingredients:
For the Cinnamon Filling:
- 3 Tbsp. of Swerve Sweetener
- 2 tsp. s of ground cinnamon

For the Cake:
- 3 cups of almond flour
- ¾ Cup of Swerve Sweetener
- ¼ Cup of unflavored whey; Protein: powder
- 2 tsp. of baking powder

- ½ tsp. of salt
- 3 large pastured eggs
- ½ Cup of melted coconut oil
- ½ tsp. of vanilla extract
- ½ Cup of almond milk
- 1 Tbsp. of melted coconut oil

For the cream cheese Frosting:
- 3 Tbsp. of softened cream cheese
- 2 Tbsp. of powdered Swerve Sweetener
- 1 Tbsp. of coconut heavy whipping cream
- ½ tsp. of vanilla extract

Directions:
1. Preheat your oven to a temperature of about 325 F and grease a baking tray of 8x8 inches.
2. For the filling, mix the Swerve and the cinnamon in a mixing bowl and mix very well; then set it aside.
3. For the preparation of the cake; whisk it all together with the almond flour, the sweetener, the; Protein: powder, the baking powder, and the salt in a mixing bowl.
4. Add in the eggs, the melted coconut oil, and the vanilla extract and mix very well.
5. Add in the almond milk and keep stirring until your ingredients are very well combined.
6. Spread about half of the batter in the prepared pan; then sprinkle with about two-thirds of the filling mixture.
7. Spread the remaining mixture of the batter over the filling and smooth it with a spatula.
8. Bake for about 35 minutes in the oven.
9. Brush with the melted coconut oil and sprinkle with the remaining cinnamon filling.
10. Prepare the frosting by beating the cream cheese, the powdered erythritol, the cream, and the vanilla extract in a mixing bowl until it becomes smooth.
11. Drizzle frost over the cooled cake.
12. Slice the cake; then serve and enjoy your cake!

Nutrition: Calories: 222; Fat: 19.2g; Carbohydrates: 5.4g; Fiber: 1.5g; Protein: 7.3g

379. <u>Banana Nut Muffins</u>

Preparation time: 5 minutes
Cooking time: 1 Hour
Servings: 6
Ingredients

Dry Ingredients:
- 1 ½ cups of Spell or Teff Flour
- ½ tsp. of Pure Sea Salt
- 3/4 cup of Date Syrup

Wet Ingredients:
- 2 medium Blend Burro Bananas
- ¼ cup of Grape Seed Oil
- ¾ cup of Homemade Walnut Milk (see recipe)*
- 1 tbsp. of Key Lime Juice

Filling Ingredients:
- ½ cup of chopped Walnuts (plus extra for decorating)
- 1 chopped Burro Banana

Directions:
1. Preheat your oven to 400°F.
2. Take a muffin tray and grease 12 cups or line with cupcake liners.
3. Put all dry ingredients in a large bowl and mix them thoroughly.
4. Add all wet ingredients to a separate, smaller bowl and mix well with Blend Bananas.
5. Mix ingredients from the two bowls in one large container. Be careful not to over mix.
6. Add the filling ingredients and fold in gently.
7. Pour muffin batter into the 12 prepared muffin cups and garnish with a couple of Walnuts.
8. Bake it for 22 to 26 minutes until golden brown.
9. Allow cooling for 10 minutes.
10. Serve and enjoy your Banana Nut Muffins!

Nutrition: Calories: 150; Fat: 10 g; Carbohydrates: 30g; Protein: 2.4g; Fiber: 2 g

380. Mango Nut Cheesecake

Preparation time: 20 minutes
Cooking time: 4 Hours 30 Minutes
Servings: 8
Ingredients:
Filling:
- 2 cups of Brazil Nuts
- 5 to 6 Dates
- 1 tbsp. of Sea Moss Gel (check information)
- 1/4 cup of Agave Syrup
- 1/4 tsp. of Pure Sea Salt
- 2 tbsp. of Lime Juice
- 1 ½ cups of Homemade Walnut Milk (see recipe)*

Crust:
- 1 ½ cups of quartered Dates
- 1/4 cup of Agave Syrup
- 1 ½ cups of Coconut Flakes
- 1/4 tsp. of Pure Sea Salt

Toppings:
- Sliced Mango
- Sliced Strawberries

Directions:
1. Put all crust ingredients, in a food processor and blend for 30 seconds.
2. With parchment paper, cover a baking form and spread out the blended crust Ingredients.
3. Put sliced Mango across the crust and freeze for 10 minutes.
4. Mix all filling ingredients, using a blender until it becomes smooth
5. Pour the filling above the crust, cover with foil or parchment paper and let it stand for about to 4 hours in the refrigerator.
6. Take out from the baking form and garnish with toppings.
7. Serve and enjoy your Mango Nut Cheesecake

Nutrition: Calories: 164; Fat: 12g; Carbohydrates: 7. Fiber: 2.7g; Protein: 10.9g

381. Blackberry Jam

Preparation time: 5 minutes
Cooking time: 4 Hours 30 Minutes
Servings: 1 Cup
Ingredients:
- 3/4 cup of Blackberries
- 1 tbsp. of Key Lime Juice
- 3 tbsp. of Agave Syrup
- ¼ cup of Sea Moss Gel + extra 2 tbsp. (check information)

Directions:
1. Put rinsed Blackberries into a medium pot and cook on medium heat.
2. Stir Blackberries until liquid appears.
3. Once berries soften, use your immersion blender to chop up any large pieces. If you don't have a blender put the mixture in a food processor, mix it well, then return to the pot.
4. Add Sea Moss Gel, Key Lime Juice, and Agave Syrup to the blended mixture. Boil on medium heat and stir well until it becomes thick.

5. Remove from the heat and leave it to cool for 10 minutes.
6. Serve it with bread pieces or Flatbread (see recipe).
7. Enjoy your Blackberry Jam!

Nutrition: Calories: 43; Fat: 0.5 g; Carbohydrates: 13 g

382. Blackberry Bars

Preparation time: 5 minutes
Cooking time: 1 Hour 20 Minutes
Servings: 4
Ingredients:

- 3 Burro Bananas or 4 Baby Bananas
- 1 cup of Spelt Flour
- 2 cups of Quinoa Flakes
- 1/4 cup of Agave Syrup
- 1/4 tsp. of Pure Sea Salt
- ½ cup of Grape Seed Oil
- 1 cup of prepared Blackberry Jam

Directions:

1. Preheat your oven to 350°F.
2. Remove the skin of the Bananas and mash with a fork in a large bowl.
3. Combine Agave Syrup and Grape Seed Oil with the Blend and mix well.
4. Add Spelt Flour and Quinoa Flakes. Knead the dough until it becomes sticky to your fingers.
5. Cover a 9x9-inch baking pan with parchment paper.
6. Take 2/3 of the dough and smooth it out over the parchment pan with your fingers.
7. Spread Blackberry Jam over the dough.
8. Crumble the remaining dough and sprinkle on the top.
9. Bake for 20 minutes.
10. Remove from the oven and let it cool for 10 to 15 minutes.
11. Cut into small pieces.
12. Serve and enjoy your Blackberry Bars!

Nutrition: Calories: 43; Fat: 0.5 g; Carbohydrates: 10g; Protein: 1.4g; Fiber: 5 g

383. Detox Berry Smoothie

Preparation time: 15 minutes
Cooking time: 0
Servings: 1
Ingredients:

- Springwater
- 1/4 avocado, pitted
- One medium burro banana
- One Seville orange
- Two cups of fresh lettuce
- One tbsp. of hemp seeds
- One cup of berries (blueberries or an aggregate of blueberries, strawberries, and raspberries)

Directions:

1. Add the spring water to your blender.
2. Put the fruits and veggies right inside the blender.
3. Blend all ingredients till smooth.

Nutrition: Calories: 202.4; Fat: 4.5g; Carbohydrates: 32.9g; Protein: 13.3g

APPETIZER RECIPES

384. Aromatic Toasted Pumpkin Seeds

Preparation time: 5 minutes
Cooking time: 45 minutes
Servings: 4
Ingredients:

- 1 cup pumpkin seeds
- 1 tsp. cinnamon
- 2 packets stevia
- 1 tbsp. canola oil
- ¼ tsp. sea salt

Directions:

1. Prep the oven to 300°F (150°C).
2. Combine the pumpkin seeds with cinnamon, stevia, canola oil, and salt in a bowl. Stir to mix well.
3. Pour the seeds in a single layer on a baking sheet, then arrange the sheet in the preheated oven.
4. Bake for 45 minutes or until well toasted and fragrant. Shake the sheet twice to bake the seeds evenly.
5. Serve immediately.

Nutrition: Calories: 202 Carbohydrates: 5.1g Fiber: 2.3g;

385. Bacon-Wrapped Shrimps

Preparation time: 10 minutes
Cooking time: 6 minutes
Servings: 10
Ingredients:

- 20 shrimps, peeled and deveined
- 7 slices bacon
- 4 leaves romaine lettuce

Directions:

1. Set the oven to 205°C.
2. Wrap each shrimp with each bacon strip, then arrange the wrapped shrimps in a single layer on a baking sheet, seam side down.
3. Broil for 6 minutes. Flip the shrimps halfway through the cooking time.
4. Take out from the oven and serve on lettuce leaves.

Nutrition: Calories: 70; Fat: 4.5g; Protein: 7g

386. Cheesy Broccoli Bites

Preparation time: 10 minutes
Cooking time: 25 minutes
Servings: 6
Ingredients:

- 2 tbsp. olive oil
- 2 heads broccoli, trimmed
- 1 egg
- 1/3 cup reduced-fat shredded Cheddar cheese
- 1 egg white
- ½ cup onion, chopped
- 1/3 cup bread crumbs
- ¼ tsp. salt
- ¼ tsp. black pepper

Directions:

1. Ready the oven at 400°F (205°C). Coat a large baking sheet with olive oil.
2. Arrange a colander in a saucepan, then place the broccoli in the colander. Pour the water into the saucepan to cover the bottom. Boil then reduce the heat to low. Close and simmer for 6 minutes. Allow cooling for 10 minutes.
3. Blend broccoli and the remaining ingredients in a food processor. Let sit for 10 minutes.
4. Make the bites: Drop 1 tbsp. of the mixture on the baking sheet. Repeat with the remaining mixture.
5. Bake in the preheated oven for 25 minutes. Flip the bites halfway through the cooking time.
6. Serve immediately.

Nutrition: Calories: 100; Carbohydrates: 13g; Fiber 3g

387. Easy Caprese Skewers

Preparation time: 5 minutes
Cooking time: 0 minute
Servings: 2
Ingredients:

- 12 cherry tomatoes
- 8 (1-inch) pieces Mozzarella cheese
- 12 basil leaves
- ¼ cup Italian Vinaigrette, for serving

162

Directions:

1. Thread the tomatoes, cheese, and bay leave alternatively through the skewers.
2. Place the skewers on a huge plate and baste with the Italian Vinaigrette. Serve immediately.

Nutrition: Calories: 230 Carbohydrates: 8.5g; Fiber: 1.9g

388. Grilled Tofu with Sesame Seeds

Preparation time: 45 minutes
Cooking time: 20 minutes
Servings: 6
Ingredients:

- 1½ tbsp. brown rice vinegar
- 1 scallion
- 1 tbsp. ginger root
- 1 tbsp. no-sugar-added applesauce
- 2 tbsp. naturally brewed soy sauce
- ¼ tsp. dried red pepper flakes
- 2 tsp. sesame oil, toasted
- 1 (14-ounce / 397-g) package extra-firm tofu
- 2 tbsp. fresh cilantro
- 1 tsp. sesame seeds

Directions:

1. Combine the vinegar, scallion, ginger, applesauce, soy sauce, red pepper flakes, and sesame oil in a large bowl. Stir to mix well.
2. Dunk the tofu pieces in the bowl, then refrigerate to marinate for 30 minutes.
3. Preheat a grill pan over medium-high heat.
4. Place the tofu on the grill pan with tongs, reserve the marinade, then grill for 8 minutes or until the tofu is golden brown and have deep grilled marks on both sides. Flip the tofu halfway through the cooking time. You may need to work in batches to avoid overcrowding.
5. Transfer the tofu to a large plate and sprinkle with cilantro leaves and sesame seeds. Serve with the marinade alongside.

Nutrition: Calories: 90; Carbohydrates: 3g; Fiber: 1g

89. Kale Chips

Preparation time: 5 minutes
Cooking time: 15 minutes
Servings: 1
Ingredients:

- ¼ tsp. garlic powder
- Pinch cayenne to taste
- 1 tbsp. extra-virgin olive oil
- ½ tsp. sea salt, or to taste
- 1 (8-ounce) bunch kale

Directions:

1. Prepare oven at 180°C. Line two baking sheets with parchment paper.
2. Toss the garlic powder, cayenne pepper, olive oil, and salt in a large bowl, then dunk the kale in the bowl.
3. Situate kale in a single layer on one of the baking sheets.
4. Arrange the sheet in the preheated oven and bake for 7 minutes. Remove the sheet from the oven and pour the kale into the single layer of the other baking sheet.
5. Move the sheet of kale back to the oven and bake for another 7 minutes.
6. Serve immediately.

Nutrition: Calories: 136 Carbohydrates: 3g; Fiber: 1.1g

390. Simple Deviled Eggs

Preparation time: 5 minutes
Cooking time: 8 minutes
Servings: 12
Ingredients:

- 6 large eggs
- 1/8 tsp. mustard powder
- 2 tbsp. light mayonnaise

Directions:

1. Sit the eggs in a saucepan, then pour in enough water to cover the egg. Bring to a boil, then boil the eggs for another 8 minutes. Turn off the heat and cover, then let sit for 15 minutes.
2. Transfer the boiled eggs to a pot of cold water and peel them under the water.
3. Transfer the eggs to a large plate, then cut them in half. Remove the egg yolks and place them in a bowl, then mash with a fork.
4. Add the mustard powder, mayo, salt, and pepper to the bowl of yolks, then stir to mix well.
5. Spoon the yolk mixture in the egg white on the plate. Serve immediately.

Nutrition: Calories: 45 Carbohydrates: 1g; Fiber: 0.9g

391. Sautéed Collard Greens and Cabbage

Preparation time: 10 minutes
Cooking time: 10 minutes
Servings: 8
Ingredients:
- 2 tbsp. extra-virgin olive oil
- 1 collard greens bunch
- ½ small green cabbage
- 6 garlic cloves
- 1 tbsp. low-sodium soy sauce

Directions:
1. Cook olive oil in a large skillet over medium-high heat.
2. Sauté the collard greens in the oil for about 2 minutes, or until the greens start to wilt.
3. Toss in the cabbage and mix well. Set to medium-low, cover, and cook for 5 to 7 minutes, stirring occasionally, or until the greens are softened.
4. Fold in the garlic and soy sauce and stir to combine. Cook for about 30 seconds more until fragrant.
5. Remove from the heat to a plate and serve.

Nutrition: Calories: 73 Carbohydrates: 5.9g; Fiber: 2.9g

392. Roasted Delicata Squash with Thyme

Preparation time: 10 minutes
Cooking time: 20 minutes
Servings: 4
Ingredients:
- 1 (1½-pound) Delicata squash
- 1 tbsp. extra-virgin olive oil
- ½ tsp. dried thyme
- ¼ tsp. salt
- ¼ tsp. freshly ground black pepper

Directions:
1. Prep the oven to 400°F (205°C). Ready baking sheet with parchment paper and set aside.
2. Add the squash strips, olive oil, thyme, salt, and pepper in a large bowl, and toss until the squash strips are fully coated.
3. Place the squash strips on the prepared baking sheet in a single layer. Roast for about 20 minutes, flipping the strips halfway through.

4. Remove from the oven and serve on plates.

Nutrition: Calories: 78 Carbohydrates: 11.8g; Fiber: 2.1g

393. Roasted Asparagus and Red Peppers

Preparation time: 5 minutes
Cooking time: 15 minutes
Servings: 4
Ingredients:
- 1-pound (454 g) asparagus
- 2 red bell peppers, seeded
- 1 small onion
- 2 tbsp. Italian dressing

Directions:
1. Ready oven to (205°C). Wrap baking sheet with parchment paper and set aside.
2. Combine the asparagus with the peppers, onion, dressing in a large bowl, and toss well.
3. Arrange the vegetables on the baking sheet and roast for about 15 minutes. Flip the vegetable with a spatula once during cooking.
4. Transfer to a large platter and serve.

Nutrition: Calories: 92 Carbohydrates: 10.7g; Fiber 4g

394. Tarragon Spring Peas

Preparation time: 10 minutes
Cooking time: 12 minutes
Servings: 6
Ingredients:
- 1 tbsp. unsalted butter
- ½ Vidalia onion
- 1 cup low-sodium vegetable broth
- 3 cups fresh shelled peas
- 1 tbsp. minced fresh tarragon

Directions:
1. Cook butter in a pan at medium heat.
2. Sauté the onion in the melted butter for abo 3 minutes, stirring occasionally.
3. Pour in the vegetable broth and whisk we Add the peas and tarragon to the skillet and s to combine.
4. Reduce the heat to low, cover, cook for abc 8 minutes more, or until the peas are tender

5. Let the peas cool for 5 minutes and serve warm.

Nutrition: Calories: 82 Carbohydrates: 12g; Fiber: 3.8g

395. Butter-Orange Yams

Preparation time: 7 minutes
Cooking time: 45 minutes
Servings: 8
Ingredients:

- 2 medium jewel yams
- 2 tbsp. unsalted butter
- Juice of 1 large orange
- 1½ tsp. ground cinnamon
- ¼ tsp. ground ginger
- ¾ tsp. ground nutmeg
- 1/8 tsp. ground cloves

Directions:

1. Set oven at 180°C.
2. Arrange the yam dices on a rimmed baking sheet in a single layer. Set aside.
3. Add the butter, orange juice, cinnamon, ginger, nutmeg, and garlic cloves to a medium saucepan over medium-low heat. Cook for 3 to 5 minutes, stirring continuously.
4. Spoon the sauce over the yams and toss to coat well.
5. Bake in the prepared oven for 40 minutes.
6. Let the yams cool for 8 minutes on the baking sheet before removing and serving.

Nutrition: Calories: 129 Carbohydrates: 24.7g; Fiber:

396. Roasted Tomato Brussels Sprouts

Preparation time: 15 minutes
Cooking time: 20 minutes
Servings: 4
Ingredients:

- 1-pound (454 g) Brussels sprouts
- 1 tbsp. extra-virgin olive oil
- ½ cup sun-dried tomatoes
- 2 tbsp. lemon juice
- 1 tsp. lemon zest

Directions:

1. Set oven 205°C. Prep large baking sheet with aluminum foil.
2. Toss the Brussels sprouts in the olive oil in a large bowl until well coated. Sprinkle with salt and pepper.
3. Spread out the seasoned Brussels sprouts on the prepared baking sheet in a single layer.
4. Roast for 20 minutes, shake halfway through.
5. Remove from the oven then situate in a bowl. Whisk tomatoes, lemon juice, and lemon zest, to incorporate. Serve immediately.

Nutrition: Calories: 111 Carbohydrates: 13.7g; Fiber: 4.9g

397. Simple Sautéed Greens

Preparation time: 10 minutes
Cooking time: 10 minutes
Servings: 4
Ingredients:

- 2 tbsp. extra-virgin olive oil
- 1 pound (454 g) Swiss chard
- 1-pound (454 g) kale
- ½ tsp. ground cardamom
- 1 tbsp. lemon juice

Directions:

1. Heat up olive oil in a big skillet over medium-high heat.
2. Stir in Swiss chard, kale, cardamom, lemon juice to the skillet, and stir to combine. Cook for about 10 minutes, stirring continuously, or until the greens are wilted.
3. Sprinkle with salt and pepper and stir well.
4. Serve the greens on a plate while warm.

Nutrition: Calories: 139 Carbohydrates: 15.8g; Fiber: 3.9g

398. Garlicky Mushrooms

Preparation time: 10 minutes
Cooking time: 12 minutes
Servings: 4
Ingredients:

- 1 tbsp. butter
- 2 tsp. extra-virgin olive oil
- 2 pounds button mushrooms
- 2 tsp. minced fresh garlic

- 1 tsp. chopped fresh thyme

Directions:

1. Warm-up butter and olive oil in a huge skillet over medium-high heat.
2. Add the mushrooms and sauté for 10 minutes, stirring occasionally.
3. Stir in the garlic and thyme and cook for an additional 2 minutes.
4. Season and serve on a plate.

Nutrition: Calories: 96 Carbohydrates: 8.2g; Fiber: 1.7g

399.   Green Beans in Oven

Preparation time: 5 minutes
Cooking time: 17 minutes
Servings: 3
Ingredients:

- 12 oz. green bean pods
- 1 tbsp. olive oil
- ½ tsp. onion powder
- 1/8 tsp. pepper
- 1/8 tsp. salt

Directions:

1. Preheat oven to 350°F. Mix green beans with onion powder, pepper, and oil.
2. Spread the seeds on the baking sheet.
3. Bake for 17 minutes or until you have a delicious aroma in the kitchen.

Nutrition: Calories: 37; Protein: 1.4g; Carbohydrates: 5.5g

400.   Parmesan Broiled Flounder

Preparation time: 10 minutes
Cooking time: 7 minutes
Servings: 2
Ingredients:

- 2 (4-oz) flounder
- 1,5 tbsp. Parmesan cheese
- 1,5 tbsp. mayonnaise
- 1/8 tsp. soy sauce
- 1/4 tsp. chili sauce
- 1/8 tsp. salt-free lemon-pepper seasoning

Directions:

1. Preheat flounder.

2. Mix cheese, reduced-fat mayonnaise, soy sauce, chili sauce, seasoning.
3. Put fish on a baking sheet coated with cooking spray, sprinkle with salt and pepper.
4. Spread Parmesan mixture over flounder.
5. Broil for 6 to 8 minutes or until a crust appears on the fish.

Nutrition: Calories: 200; Fat: 17g; Carbohydrate: 7g

401.   Fish with Fresh Tomato—Basil Sauce

Preparation time: 10 minutes
Cooking time: 15 minutes
Servings: 2
Ingredients:

- 2 (4-oz) tilapia fillets
- 1 tbsp. fresh basil, chopped
- 1/8 tsp. salt
- 1 pinch of crushed red pepper
- 1 cup cherry tomatoes, chopped
- 2 tsp. extra virgin olive oil

Directions:

1. Preheat oven to 400°F.
2. Arrange rinsed and patted dry fish fillets on fo (coat a foil baking sheet with cooking spray).
3. Sprinkle tilapia fillets with salt and red peppe
4. Bake for 12–15 minutes.
5. Meanwhile, mix leftover ingredients in saucepan.
6. Cook over medium-high heat until tomatoe are tender.
7. Top fish fillets properly with tomato mixture

Nutrition: Calories: 130; Protein: 30g; Carbohydrate 1g

402.   Baked Chicken

Preparation time: 15 minutes
Cooking time: 25 minutes
Servings: 4
Ingredients:

- 2 (6-oz) bone-in chicken breasts
- 1/8 tsp. salt
- 1/8 tsp. pepper
- 3 tsp. extra virgin olive oil
- ½ tsp. dried oregano
- 7 pitted kalamata olives
- 1 cup cherry tomatoes

- ½ cup onion
- 1 (9-oz) pkg frozen artichoke hearts
- 1 lemon

Directions:

1. Preheat oven to 400°F.
2. Sprinkle chicken with pepper, salt, and oregano.
3. Heat oil, add chicken, and cook until it browned.
4. Place chicken in a baking dish. Arrange tomatoes, coarsely chopped olives, and onion, artichokes and lemon cut into wedges around the chicken.
5. Bake 20 minutes or until chicken is done and vegetables are tender.

Nutrition: Calories: 160; Fat: 3g; Carbohydrates: 1g

403. Seared Chicken with Roasted Vegetables

Preparation time: 20 minutes
Cooking time: 30 minutes
Servings: 1
Ingredients:

- 1 (8-oz) boneless, skinless chicken breasts
- 3/4 lb. small Brussels sprouts
- 2 large carrots
- 1 large red bell pepper
- 1 small red onion
- 2 cloves garlic halved
- 2 tbsp. extra virgin olive oil
- ½ tsp. dried dill
- 1/4 tsp. pepper
- 1/4 tsp. salt

Directions:

1. Preheat oven to 425°F.
2. Match Brussels sprouts cut in half, red onion cut into wedges, sliced carrots, bell pepper cut into pieces, and halved garlic on a baking sheet.
3. Sprinkle with 1 tbsp. oil and with 1/8 tsp. salt and 1/8 tsp. pepper. Bake until well-roasted, cool slightly.
4. In the Meantime, sprinkle chicken with dill, remaining 1/8 tsp. salt, and 1/8 tsp. pepper. Cook until the chicken is done. Put roasted vegetables with drippings over chicken.

Nutrition: Calories: 170; Fat 7g; Protein: 12g

404. Fish Simmered in Tomato-Pepper Sauce

Preparation time: 5 minutes
Cooking time: 10 minutes
Servings: 2
Ingredients:

- 2 (4-oz) cod fillets
- 1 big tomato
- 1/3 cup red peppers (roasted)
- 3 tbsp. almonds
- 2 cloves garlic
- 2 tbsp. fresh basil leaves
- 2 tbsp. extra virgin olive oil
- 1/4 tsp. salt
- 1/8 tsp. pepper

Directions:

1. Toast sliced almonds in a pan until fragrant.
2. Grind almonds, basil, minced garlic, 1–2 tsp. oil in a food processor until finely ground.
3. Add coarsely-chopped tomato and red peppers; grind until smooth.
4. Season fish with salt and pepper.
5. Cook in hot oil in a large pan over medium-high heat until fish is browned. Pour sauce around fish. Cook 6 minutes more.

Nutrition: Calories: 90; Fat: 5g; Carbohydrates: 7g

405. Cheese Potato and Pea Casserole

Preparation time: 10 minutes
Cooking time: 35 minutes
Servings: 3
Ingredients:

- 1 tbsp. olive oil
- ¾ lb. red potatoes
- ¾ cup green peas
- ½ cup red onion
- ¼ tsp. dried rosemary
- ¼ tsp. salt
- 1/8 tsp. pepper

Directions:

1. Prepare oven to 350°F.
2. Cook 1 tsp. oil in a skillet. Stir in thinly sliced onions and cook. Remove from pan.
3. Situate half of the thinly sliced potatoes and onions in the bottom of the skillet; top with

peas, crushed dried rosemary, and 1/8 tsp. each salt and pepper.

4. Place remaining potatoes and onions on top. Season with remaining 1/8 tsp. salt.
5. Bake 35 minutes, pour the remaining 2 tsp. oil, and sprinkle with cheese.

Nutrition: Calories: 80; Protein: 2g; Carbohydrates: 18g

406.   Oven-Fried Tilapia

Preparation time: 7 minutes
Cooking time: 15 minutes
Servings: 2
Ingredients:

- 2 (4-oz) tilapia fillets
- 1/4 cup yellow cornmeal
- 2 tbsp. light ranch dressing
- 1 tbsp. canola oil
- 1 tsp. dill (dried)
- 1/8 tsp. salt

Directions:

1. Preheat oven to 425°F. Brush both sides of rinsed and patted dry tilapia fish fillets with dressing.
2. Combine cornmeal, oil, dill, and salt.
3. Sprinkle fish fillets with cornmeal mixture.
4. Put fish on a prepared baking sheet.
5. Bake 15 minutes.

Nutrition: Calories: 96; Protein: 21g; Fat: 2g

407.   Chicken with Coconut Sauce

Preparation time: 15 minutes
Cooking time: 20 minutes
Servings: 2
Ingredients:

- ½ lb. chicken breasts
- 1/3 cup red onion
- 1 tbsp. paprika (smoked)
- 2 tsp. cornstarch
- ½ cup light coconut milk
- 1 tsp. extra virgin olive oil
- 2 tbsp. fresh cilantro
- 1 (10-oz) can tomatoes and green chilis
- 1/4 cup water

Directions:

1. Cut chicken into little cubes; sprinkle with 1,5 tsp. paprika.
2. Heat oil, add chicken, and cook for 3 to 5 minutes.
3. Remove from skillet, and fry the finely chopped onion for 5 minutes.
4. Return chicken to pan. Add tomatoes,1,5 tsp. paprika, and water. Bring to a boil, and then simmer for 4 minutes.
5. Mix cornstarch and coconut milk; stir into the chicken mixture, and cook until it has been done.
6. Sprinkle with chopped cilantro.

Nutrition: Calories: 200; Protein: 13g; Fat: 10g

408.   Fish with Fresh Herb Sauce

Preparation time: 10 minutes
Cooking time: 10 minutes
Servings: 2
Ingredients:

- 2 (4-oz) cod fillets
- 1/3 cup fresh cilantro
- 1/4 tsp. cumin
- 1 tbsp. red onion
- 2 tsp. extra virgin olive oil
- 1 tsp. red wine vinegar
- 1 small clove garlic
- 1/8 tsp. salt
- 1/8 black pepper

Directions:

1. Combine chopped cilantro, finely chopped onion, oil, red wine vinegar, minced garlic, and salt.
2. Sprinkle both sides of fish fillets with cumin and pepper.
3. Cook fillets 4 minutes per side. Top each fillet with cilantro mixture.

Nutrition: Calories: 90 Fat 4g; Carbohydrates: 3g

409.   Skillet Turkey Patties

Preparation time: 7 minutes
Cooking time: 8 minutes
Servings: 2
Ingredients:

- ½ lb. lean ground turkey

- ½ cup low-sodium chicken broth
- 1/4 cup red onion
- ½ tsp. Worcestershire sauce
- 1 tsp. extra virgin olive oil
- 1/4 tsp. oregano (dried)
- 1/8 tsp. pepper

Directions:
1. Combine turkey, chopped onion, Worcestershire sauce, dried oregano, and pepper; make 2 patties.
2. Warm-up oil and cook patties 4 minutes per side; set aside.
3. Add broth to skillet, bring to a boil. Boil 2 minutes, spoon sauce over patties.

Nutrition: Calories: 180; Fat: 11g; Carbohydrates: 9g

410. Turkey Loaf

Preparation time: 10 minutes
Cooking time: 50 minutes
Servings: 2
Ingredients:
- ½ lb. 93% lean ground turkey
- 1/3 cup panko breadcrumbs
- ½ cup green onion
- 1 egg
- ½ cup green bell pepper
- 1 tbsp. ketchup
- 1/4 cup sauce (Picante)
- ½ tsp. cumin (ground)

Directions:
1. Preheat oven to 350°F. Mix lean ground turkey, 3 tbsp. Picante sauce, panko breadcrumbs, egg, chopped green onion, chopped green bell pepper, and cumin in a bowl (mix well);
2. Put the mixture into a baking sheet; shape into an oval (about 1,5 inches thick). Bake 45 minutes.
3. Mix remaining Picante sauce and the ketchup; apply over the loaf. Bake 5 minutes longer. Let stand 5 minutes.

Nutrition: Calories: 161; Protein: 20g; Fat: 8g

11. Mushroom Pasta

Preparation time: 7 minutes
Cooking time: 10 minutes
Servings: 4
Ingredients:

- 4 oz whole-grain linguine
- 1 tsp. extra virgin olive oil
- ½ cup light sauce
- 2 tbsp. green onion
- 1 (8-oz) pkg mushrooms
- 1 clove garlic
- 1/8 tsp. salt
- 1/8 tsp. pepper

Directions:
1. Cook pasta according to package directions, drain.
2. Fry sliced mushrooms for 4 minutes.
3. Stir in fettuccine minced garlic, salt, and pepper. Cook 2 minutes.
4. Heat light sauce until heated; top pasta mixture properly with sauce and with finely-chopped green onion.

Nutrition: Calories: 300; Fat: 1g; Carbohydrates: 15g

412. Chicken Tikka Masala

Preparation time: 5 minutes
Cooking time: 15 minutes
Servings: 2
Ingredients:
- ½ lb. chicken breasts
- 1/4 cup onion
- 1.5 tsp. extra virgin olive oil
- 1 (14.5-oz) can tomatoes
- 1 tsp. ginger
- 1 tsp. fresh lemon juice
- 1/3 cup plain Greek yogurt (fat-free)
- 1 tbsp. garam masala
- 1/4 tsp. salt
- 1/4 tsp. pepper

Directions:
1. Flavor chicken cut into 1-inch cubes with 1,5 tsp. garam masala,1/8 tsp. salt, and pepper.
2. Cook chicken and diced onion for 4 to 5 minutes.
3. Add diced tomatoes, grated ginger, 1.5 tsp. garam masala, 1/8 tsp. salt. Cook 8 to 10 minutes.
4. Add lemon juice and yogurt until blended.

Nutrition: Calories: 200; Protein: 26g; Fat: 10g

413. Tomato and Roasted Cod

Preparation time: 10 minutes
Cooking time: 35 minutes
Servings: 2
Ingredients:

- 2 (4-oz) cod fillets
- 1 cup cherry tomatoes
- 2/3 cup onion
- 2 tsp. orange rind
- 1 tbsp. extra virgin olive oil
- 1 tsp. thyme (dried)
- 1/4 tsp. salt, divided
- 1/4 tsp. pepper, divided

Directions:

1. Preheat oven to 400°F. Mix in half tomatoes, sliced onion, grated orange rind, extra virgin olive oil, dried thyme, and 1/8 salt and pepper. Fry 25 minutes. Remove from oven.
2. Arrange fish on pan, and flavor with remaining 1/8 tsp. each salt and pepper. Put reserved tomato mixture over fish. Bake 10 minutes.

Nutrition: Calories: 120; Protein: 9g; Fat: 2g

414. French Broccoli Salad

Preparation time: 10 minutes,
Cooking time: 10 minutes;
Servings: 10
Ingredients:

- 8 cups broccoli florets
- 3 strips of bacon, cooked and crumbled
- ¼ cup sunflower kernels
- 1 bunch of green onion, sliced

What you will need from the store cupboard:

- 3 tbsp. seasoned rice vinegar
- 3 tbsp. canola oil
- ½ cup dried cranberries

Directions:

1. Combine the green onion, cranberries, and broccoli in a bowl.
2. Whisk the vinegar, and oil in another bowl. Blend well.
3. Now drizzle over the broccoli mix.
4. Coat well by tossing.

5. Sprinkle bacon and sunflower kernels before serving.

Nutrition: Calories: 121; Carbohydrates: 14g; Cholesterol: 2mg; Fiber: 3g; Sugar: 1g; Fat: 7g; Protein 3g; Sodium: 233mg

415. Tenderloin Grilled Salad

Preparation time: 10 minutes,
Cooking time: 20 minutes;
Servings: 5
Ingredients:

- 1 lb. pork tenderloin
- 10 cups mixed salad greens
- 2 oranges, seedless, cut into bite-sized pieces
- 1 tbsp. orange zest, grated

What you will need from the store cupboard:

- 2 tbsp. of cider vinegar
- 2 tbsp. olive oil
- 2 tsp. Dijon mustard
- ½ cup juice of an orange
- 2 tsp. honey
- ½ tsp. ground pepper

Directions:

1. Bring together all the dressing ingredients in bowl.
2. Grill each side of the pork covered ov medium heat for 9 minutes.
3. Slice after 5 minutes.
4. Slice the tenderloin thinly.
5. Keep the greens on your serving plate.
6. Top with the pork and oranges.
7. Sprinkle nuts (optional).

Nutrition: Calories: 211; Carbohydrates: 1 Cholesterol: 51mg; Fiber: 3g; Sugar: 0.8g; Fat: Protein: 20g; Sodium: 113mg

416.   Barley Veggie Salad

Preparation time: 10 minutes,
Cooking time: 20 minutes;
Servings: 6
Ingredients:

- 1 tomato, seeded and chopped
- 2 tbsp. parsley, minced
- 1 yellow pepper, chopped
- 1 tbsp. basil, minced
- ¼ cup almonds, toasted

What you will need from the store cupboard:

- 1–1/4 cups vegetable broth
- 1 cup barley
- 1 tbsp. lemon juice
- 2 tbsp. of white wine vinegar
- 3 tbsp. olive oil
- ¼ tsp. pepper
- ½ tsp. salt
- 1 cup of water

Directions:

1. Boil the broth, barley, and water in a saucepan.
2. Reduce heat. Cover and let it simmer for 10 minutes.
3. Take out from the heat.
4. In the meantime, bring together the parsley, yellow pepper, and tomato in a bowl.
5. Stir the barley in.
6. Whisk the vinegar, oil, basil, lemon juice, water, pepper, and salt in a bowl.
7. Pour this over your barley mix. Toss to coat well.
8. Stir the almonds in before serving.

Nutrition: Calories: 211; Carbohydrates: 27g; Cholesterol: 0mg; Fiber: 7g; Sugar: 0g; Fat: 10g; Protein: 6g; Sodium: 334mg

417.   Spinach Shrimp Salad

Preparation time: 10 minutes,
Cooking time: 10 minutes;
Servings: 4
Ingredients:

- 1 lb. uncooked shrimp, peeled and deveined
- 2 tbsp. parsley, minced
- ¾ cup halved cherry tomatoes
- 1 medium lemon
- 4 cups baby spinach

What you will need from the store cupboard:

- 2 tbsp. butter
- 3 minced garlic cloves
- ¼ tsp. pepper
- ¼ tsp. salt

Directions:

1. Melt the butter over the medium temperature in a nonstick skillet.
2. Add the shrimp.
3. Now cook the shrimp for 3 minutes until your shrimp becomes pink.
4. Add the parsley and garlic.
5. Cook for another minute. Take out from the heat.
6. Keep the spinach in your salad bowl.
7. Top with the shrimp mix and tomatoes.
8. Drizzle lemon juice on the salad.
9. Sprinkle pepper and salt.

Nutrition: Calories: 201; Carbohydrates: 6g; Cholesterol: 153mg; Fiber: 2g; Sugar: 0g; Fat: 10g; Protein: 21g; Sodium: 350mg

418. Sweet Potato and Roasted Beet Salad

Preparation time: 10 minutes,
Cooking time: 10 minutes;
Servings: 4
Ingredients:

- 2 beets
- 1 sweet potato, peeled and cubed
- 1 garlic clove, minced
- 2 tbsp. walnuts, chopped and toasted
- 1 cup fennel bulb, sliced

What you will need from the store cupboard:

- 3 tbsp. balsamic vinegar
- 1 tsp. Dijon mustard
- 1 tbsp. honey
- 3 tbsp. olive oil
- ¼ tsp. pepper
- ¼ tsp. salt
- 3 tbsp. water

Directions:

1. Scrub the beets. Trim the tops to 1 inch.
2. Wrap in foil and keep on a baking sheet.
3. Bake until tender. Take off the foil.
4. Combine water and sweet potato in a bowl.
5. Cover. Microwave for 5 minutes. Drain off.
6. Now peel the beets. Cut into small wedges.
7. Arrange the fennel, sweet potato, and beets on 4 salad plates.
8. Sprinkle nuts.
9. Whisk the honey, mustard, vinegar, water, garlic, pepper, and salt.
10. Whisk in oil gradually.
11. Drizzle over the salad.

Nutrition: Calories: 270; Carbohydrates: 37g; Cholesterol: 0mg; Fiber: 6g; Sugar: 0.3g; Fat: 13g; Protein: 5g; Sodium: 309mg

419. Potato Calico Salad

Preparation time: 15 minutes,
Cooking time: 5 minutes;
Servings: 14
Ingredients:

- 4 red potatoes, peeled and cooked
- 1½ cups kernel corn, cooked
- ½ cup green pepper, diced
- ½ cup red onion, chopped
- 1 cup carrot, shredded

What you will need from the store cupboard:

- ½ cup olive oil
- ¼ cup vinegar
- 1½ tsp. chili powder
- 1 tsp. salt
- Dash of hot pepper sauce

Directions:

1. Keep all the ingredients together in a jar.
2. Close it and shake well.
3. Cube the potatoes. Combine with the carr onion, and corn in your salad bowl.
4. Pour the dressing over.
5. Now toss lightly.

Nutrition: Calories: 146; Carbohydrates: 1 Cholesterol: 0mg; Fiber: 0g; Sugar: 0g; Fat: 9g; Prote 2g; Sodium: 212mg

420. Mango and Jicama Salad

Nutrition: Calories: 143; Carbohydrates: 20g; Cholesterol: 0mg; Fiber: 3g; Sugar: 1.6g; Fat: 7g; Protein: 1g; Sodium: 78mg

421. Asian Crispy Chicken Salad

Preparation time: 15 minutes,
Cooking time: 5 minutes;
Servings: 8
Ingredients:

- 1 jicama, peeled
- 1 mango, peeled
- 1 tsp. ginger root, minced
- 1/3 cup chives, minced
- ½ cup cilantro, chopped

What you will need from the store cupboard:

- ¼ cup canola oil
- ½ cup white wine vinegar
- 2 tbsp. of lime juice
- ¼ cup honey
- 1/8 tsp. pepper
- ¼ tsp. salt

Directions:

1. Whisk together the vinegar, honey, canola oil, gingerroot, paper, and salt.
2. Cut the mango and jicama into matchsticks.
3. Keep in a bowl.
4. Now toss with the lime juice.
5. Add the dressing and herbs. Combine well by tossing.

Preparation time: 10 minutes,
Cooking time: 10 minutes;
Servings: 2
Ingredients:

- 2 chicken breast halved, skinless
- ½ cup panko bread crumbs
- 4 cups spring mix salad greens
- 4 tsp. of sesame seeds
- ½ cup mushrooms, sliced

What you will need from the store cupboard:

- 1 tsp. sesame oil
- 2 tsp. of canola oil
- 2 tsp. hoisin sauce
- ¼ cup sesame ginger salad dressing

Directions:

1. Flatten the chicken breasts to half-inch thickness.
2. Mix the sesame oil and hoisin sauce. Brush over the chicken.
3. Combine the sesame seeds and panko in a bowl.
4. Now dip the chicken mix in it.
5. Cook each side of the chicken for 5 minutes.
6. In the meantime, divide the salad greens between two plates.
7. Top with mushroom.
8. Slice the chicken and keep on top. Drizzle the dressing.

Nutrition: Calories: 386; Carbohydrates: 29g; Cholesterol: 63mg; Fiber: 6g; Sugar: 1g; Fat: 17g; Protein: 30g; Sodium: 620mg

422.   Kale, Grape and Bulgur Salad

Preparation time: 10 minutes,
Cooking time: 15 minutes;
Servings: 6
Ingredients:

- 1 cup bulgur
- 1 cup pecan, toasted and chopped
- ¼ cup scallions, sliced
- ½ cup parsley, chopped
- 2 cups California grapes, seedless and halved

What you will need from the store cupboard:

- 2 tbsp. of extra virgin olive oil
- ¼ cup of juice from a lemon
- Pinch of kosher salt
- Pinch of black pepper
- 2 cups of water

Directions:

1. Boil 2 cups of water in a saucepan
2. Stir the bulgur in and ½ tsp. of salt.
3. Take out from the heat.
4. Keep covered. Drain.
5. Stir in the other ingredients.
6. Season with pepper and salt.

Nutrition: Calories: 289; Carbohydrates: 33g; Fat: 17g; Protein: 6g; Sodium: 181mg

423.   Strawberry Salsa

Preparation time: 10 minutes,
Cooking time: 5 minutes;
Servings: 4
Ingredients:

- 4 tomatoes, seeded and chopped
- 1-pint strawberry, chopped
- 1 red onion, chopped
- 2 tbsp. of juice from a lime
- 1 jalapeno pepper, minced

What you will need from the store cupboard:

- 1 tbsp. olive oil
- 2 garlic cloves, minced

Directions:

1. Bring together the strawberries, tomatoes, jalapeno, and onion in the bowl.

2. Stir in the garlic, oil, and lime juice.
3. Refrigerate. Serve with separately cooked pork or poultry.

Nutrition: Calories: 19; Carbohydrates: 3g; Fiber: 1g; Sugar: 0.2g; Cholesterol: 0mg; Total Fat: 1g; Protein: 0g

424.   Garden Wraps

Preparation time: 20 minutes,
Cooking time: 10 minutes;
Servings: 8
Ingredients:

- 1 cucumber, chopped
- 1 sweet corn
- 1 cabbage, shredded
- 1 tbsp. lettuce, minced
- 1 tomato, chopped

What you will need from the store cupboard:

- 3 tbsp. of rice vinegar
- 2 tsp. peanut butter
- 1/3 cup onion paste
- 1/3 cup chili sauce
- 2 tsp. of low-sodium soy sauce

Directions:

1. Cut corn from the cob. Keep in a bowl.
2. Add the tomato, cabbage, cucumber, and onion paste.
3. Now whisk the vinegar, peanut butter, and chili sauce together.
4. Pour this over the vegetable mix. Toss for coating.
5. Let this stand for 10 minutes.
6. Take your slotted spoon and place ½ cup salad in every lettuce leaf.
7. Fold the lettuce over your filling.

Nutrition: Calories: 64; Carbohydrates: 13g; Fiber: 2; Sugar: 1g; Cholesterol: 0mg; Total Fat: 1g; Protein: 2

425. Party Shrimp

Preparation time: 15 minutes,
Cooking time: 10 minutes;
Servings: 30
Ingredients:

- 16 oz. uncooked shrimp, peeled and deveined
- 1½ tsp. of juice from a lemon
- ½ tsp. basil, chopped
- 1 tsp. coriander, chopped
- ½ cup tomato

What you will need from the store cupboard:

- 1 tbsp. of olive oil
- ½ tsp. Italian seasoning
- ½ tsp. paprika
- 1 sliced garlic clove
- ¼ tsp. pepper

Directions:

1. Bring together everything except the shrimp in a dish or bowl.
2. Add the shrimp. Coat well by tossing. Set aside.
3. Drain the shrimp. Discard the marinade.
4. Keep them on a baking sheet. It should not be greased.
5. Broil each side for 4 minutes. The shrimp should become pink.

Nutrition: Calories: 14; Carbohydrates: 0g; Fiber: 0g; Sugar: 0g; Cholesterol: 18mg; Total Fat: 0g; Protein: 2g

426. Zucchini Mini Pizzas

Preparation time: 20 minutes,
Cooking time: 10 minutes;
Servings: 24
Ingredients:

- 1 zucchini, cut into ¼ inch slices diagonally
- ½ cup pepperoni, small slices
- 1 tsp. basil, minced
- ½ cup onion, chopped
- 1 cup tomatoes

What you will need from the store cupboard:

- 1/8 tsp. pepper
- 1/8 tsp. salt
- 3/4 cup mozzarella cheese, shredded
- 1/3 cup pizza sauce

Directions:

1. Preheat your broiler. Keep the zucchini in 1 layer on your greased baking sheet.
2. Add the onion and tomatoes. Broil each side for 1 to 2 minutes till they become tender and crisp.
3. Now sprinkle pepper and salt.
4. Top with cheese, pepperoni, and sauce.
5. Broil for a minute. The cheese should melt.
6. Sprinkle basil on top.

Nutrition: Calories: 29; Carbohydrates: 1g; Fiber: 0g; Sugar: 1g; Cholesterol: 5mg; Total Fat: 2g; Protein: 2g

427. Garlic-Sesame Pumpkin Seeds

Preparation time: 10 minutes
Cooking time: 20 minutes
Servings: 2
Ingredients:

- 1 egg white
- 1 tsp. onion, minced
- ½ tsp. caraway seeds
- 2 cups pumpkin seeds
- 1 tsp. sesame seeds

What you will need from the store cupboard:

- 1 garlic clove, minced
- 1 tbsp. of canola oil
- ¾ tsp. of kosher salt

Directions:

1. Preheat your oven to 350°F.

2. Whisk together the oil and egg white in a bowl.
3. Include pumpkin seeds. Coat well by tossing.
4. Now stir in the onion, garlic, sesame seeds, caraway seeds, and salt.
5. Spread in 1 layer in your parchment-lined baking pan.
6. Bake for 15 minutes until it turns golden brown.

Nutrition: Calories: 95; Carbohydrates: 9g; Fiber: 3g; Sugar: 0g; Cholesterol: 0mg; Total Fat: 5g; Protein: 4g

428. Dandelion Avocado Smoothie

Preparation time: 15 minutes
Cooking time: 0
Servings: 1
Ingredients:

- One cup of Dandelion
- One Orange (juiced)
- Coconut water
- One Avocado
- One key lime (juice)

Directions:

1. In a high-speed blender until smooth, blend the ingredients.

Nutrition: Calories: 160; Fat: 15g; Carbohydrates: 9g; Protein: 2g

429. Amaranth Greens and Avocado Smoothie

Preparation time: 15 minutes
Cooking time: 0
Servings: 1
Ingredients:

- One key lime (juice).
- Two sliced apples (seeded).
- Half avocado.
- Two cupsful of amaranth greens.
- Two cupsful of watercress.
- One cupful of water.

Directions:

1. Add all the ingredients together and transfer them into the blender. Blend thoroughly until smooth.

Nutrition: Calories: 160g; Fat: 15g; Carbohydrates: 9g; Protein: 2g

430. Lettuce, Orange and Banana Smoothie

Preparation time: 15 minutes
Cooking time: 0
Servings: 1
Ingredients:

- One and a half cupsful of fresh lettuce.
- One large banana.
- One cup of mixed berries of your choice.
- One juiced orange.

Directions:

1. First, add the orange juice to your blender.
2. Add the remaining recipes and blend thoroughly.
3. Enjoy the rest of your day.

Nutrition: Calories: 252.1; Protein: 4.1g

431. Delicious Elderberry Smoothie

Preparation time: 15 minutes
Cooking time: 0
Servings: 1
Ingredients:

- One cupful of Elderberry
- One cupful of Cucumber
- One large apple
- A quarter cupful of water

Directions:

1. Add all the ingredients together into a blender. Grind very well until they are uniformly smooth and enjoy.

Nutrition: Calories: 106; Carbohydrates: 26.68g

432. Peaches Zucchini Smoothie

Preparation time: 15 minutes
Cooking time: 0
Servings: 1
Ingredients:

- A half cupful of squash.
- A half cupful of peaches.
- A quarter cupful of coconut water.
- A half cupful of Zucchini.

Directions:

1. Add all the ingredients together into a blender and blend until smooth and serve.

Nutrition: Calories: 55; Fat: 0g; Protein: 2g; Sodium: 10mg; Carbohydrate: 14g; Fiber: 2g

433. Ginger Orange and Strawberry Smoothie

Preparation time: 15 minutes
Cooking time: 0
Servings: 1
Ingredients:

- One cup of strawberry.
- One large orange (juice)
- One large banana.
- Quarter small-sized ginger (peeled and sliced).

Directions:

2. Transfer the orange juice to a clean blender.
3. Add the remaining recipes and blend thoroughly until smooth.
4. Enjoy. Wow! You have ended the 9th day of your weight loss and detox journey.

Nutrition: Calories: 32; Fat: 0.3g; Protein: 2g; Sodium: 10mg; Carbohydrate: 14g; Fiber: 2g

434. Kale Parsley and Chia Seeds Detox Smoothie

Preparation time: 15 minutes
Cooking time: 0
Servings: 1
Ingredients:

- Three tbsp. chia seeds (grounded).
- One cupful of water.
- One sliced banana.
- One pear (chopped).
- One cupful of organic kale.
- One cupful of parsley.
- Two tbsp. of lemon juice.
- A dash of cinnamon.

Directions:

1. Add all the ingredients into a blender and pour the water before blending. Blend at high speed until smooth and enjoy. You may or may not place it in the refrigerator depending on how hot or cold the weather appears.

Nutrition: Calories: 75; Fat: 1g; Protein: 5g; Fiber: 10g

435. Watermelon Lemonade

Preparation time: 5 Minutes
Cooking time: 0 minutes
Servings: 6

When it comes to refreshing summertime drin lemonade is always near the top of the list. T Watermelon "Limenade" is perfect for using leftover watermelon or for those early fall days w stores and farmers are almost giving them away. Y can also substitute 4 cups of ice for the cold wate create a delicious summertime slushy.

Ingredients:

- 4 cups diced watermelon
- 4 cups cold water
- 2 tbsp. freshly squeezed lemon juice
- 1 tbsp. freshly squeezed lime juice

Directions:

1. In a blender, combine the watermelon, wa lemon juice, and lime juice, and blend fo minute.
2. Strain the contents through a fine-mesh si or nut-milk bag. Serve chilled. Store in refrigerator for up to 3 days.

Serving Tip: Slice up a few lemons or lime wedge serve with your Watermelon Limenade, or top it w a few fresh mints leaves to give it an extra-crisp, m flavor.

Nutrition: Calories: 60

436. Bubbly Orange Soda

Preparation time: 5 Minutes
Cooking time: 0 minutes
Servings: 4

Soda can be one of the toughest things to give up wl you first adopt a WFPB diet. That's partially beca refined sugars and caffeine are addictive, but it can a be because carbonated beverages are fun to drink! W sweetness from the orange juice and bubbliness fr the carbonated water, this orange "soda" is perfect assisting in the transition from SAD to WFPB.

Ingredients:

- 4 cups carbonated water
- 2 cups pulp-free orange juice (4 orang freshly squeezed and strained)

Directions:

1. For each serving, pour 2 parts carbona water and 1-part orange juice over ice ri before serving.
2. Stir and enjoy.

Serving Tip: This recipe is best made right before drinking. The amount of fizz in the carbonated water will decrease the longer it's open, so if you're going to make it ahead of time, make sure it's stored in an airtight, refrigerator-safe container.

Nutrition: Calories: 56

437.   Creamy Cashew Milk

Preparation time: 5 Minutes
Cooking time: 0 minutes
Servings: 8

Learning how to make your own plant-based milk can be one of the best ways to save money and ditch dairy for good. This is one of the easiest milk recipes to master, and if you have a high-speed blender, you can skip the straining step and go straight to a refrigerator-safe container. Large mason jars work great for storing plant-based milk, as they allow you to give a quick shake before each use.

Ingredients:

- 4 cups water
- ¼ cup raw cashews, soaked overnight

Directions:

1. In a blender, blend the water and cashews at high speed for 2 minutes.
2. Strain with a nut-milk bag or cheesecloth, then store it in the refrigerator for up to 5 days.

Variation Tip: This recipe makes unsweetened cashew milk that can be used in savory and sweet dishes. For a creamier version to put in your coffee, cut the amount of water in half. For a sweeter version, add 1 to 2 tbsp. maple syrup and 1 tsp. vanilla extract before blending.

Nutrition: Calories: 18

438.   Homemade Oat Milk

Preparation time: 5 Minutes
Cooking time: 0 minutes
Servings: 8

Oat milk is a fantastic option if you need nut-free milk or just want an extremely inexpensive plant-based milk. Making a half-gallon jar at home costs a fraction of the price of other plant-based or dairy milk. Oat milk can be used in both savory and sweet dishes.

Ingredients:

- 1 cup rolled oats
- 4 cups water

Directions:

1. Put the oats in a medium bowl, and cover with cold water. Soak for 15 minutes, then drain and rinse the oats.
2. Pour the cold water and the soaked oats into a blender. Blend for 60 to 90 seconds, or just until the mixture is a creamy white color throughout. (Blending any further may over blend the oats, resulting in gummy milk.)
3. Strain through a nut-milk bag or colander, then store in the refrigerator for up to 5 days.

Variation Tip: This recipe can easily be made into chocolate oat milk. Once you've strained the oat milk, return it to a blender with 3 tbsp. cocoa powder, 2 tbsp. maple syrup, and 1 tsp. vanilla extract, then blend for 30 seconds.

Nutrition: Calories: 39

439.   Lucky Mint Smoothie

Preparation time: 5 Minutes
Cooking time: 0 minutes
Servings: 2

As spring approaches and mint begins to once again take over the garden, "Irish"-themed green shakes begin to pop up as well. In contrast to the traditionally high-fat, sugary shakes, this smoothie is a wonderful option for sunny spring days. So next time you want to sip on something cool and minty, do so with a health-promoting Lucky Mint Smoothie.

Ingredients:

- 2 cups plant-based milk (here or here)
- 2 frozen bananas, halved
- 1 tbsp. fresh mint leaves or ¼ tsp. peppermint extract
- 1 tsp. vanilla extract

Directions:

1. In a blender, combine the milk, bananas, mint, and vanilla. Blend on high for 1 to 2 minutes, or until the contents reach a smooth and creamy consistency, and serve.

Variation Tip: If you like to sneak greens into smoothies, add a cup or two of spinach to boost the health benefits of this smoothie and give it an even greener appearance.

Nutrition: Calories: 152

440. Paradise Island Smoothie

Preparation time: 5 Minutes
Cooking time: 0 minutes
Servings: 2
Ingredients:

- 2 cups plant-based milk (here or here)
- 1 frozen banana
- ½ cup frozen mango chunks
- ½ cup frozen pineapple chunks
- 1 tsp. vanilla extract

Directions:

1. In a blender, combine the milk, banana, mango, pineapple, and vanilla. Blend on high for 1 to 2 minutes, or until the contents reach a smooth and creamy consistency, and serve.

Leftover Tip: If you have any leftover smoothies, you can put them in a jar with some rolled oats and allow the mixture to soak in the refrigerator overnight to create a tropical version of overnight oats.
Nutrition: Calories: 176

441. Apple Pie Smoothie

Preparation time: 5 Minutes
Cooking time: 0 minutes
Servings: 2

This smoothie is great for a quick breakfast or a cool dessert. Its combination of sweet apples and warming cinnamon is sure to win over children and adults alike. If the holidays find you in a warm area, this smoothie may just be the cool treat you've been looking for to take the place of pie at dessert time.

Ingredients:

- 2 sweet crisp apples, cut into 1-inch cubes
- 2 cups plant-based milk (here or here)
- 1 cup ice
- 1 tbsp. maple syrup
- 1 tsp. ground cinnamon
- 1 tsp. vanilla extract

Directions:

1. In a blender, combine the apples, milk, ice, maple syrup, cinnamon, and vanilla. Blend on high for 1 to 2 minutes, or until the contents reach a smooth and creamy consistency, and serve.

Variation Tip: You can also use this recipe for making overnight oatmeal. Blend your smoothie, mix it with 2 cups rolled oats, and refrigerate overnight for a premade breakfast for two.
Nutrition: Calories: 198

442. Choco-Nut Milkshake

Preparation time: 10 minutes
Cooking time: 0 minute
Servings: 2
Ingredients:

- 2 cups unsweetened coconut, almond
- 1 banana, sliced and frozen
- ¼ cup unsweetened coconut flakes
- 1 cup ice cubes
- ¼ cup macadamia nuts, chopped
- 3 tbsp. sugar-free sweetener
- 2 tbsp. raw unsweetened cocoa powder
- Whipped coconut cream

Directions:

1. Place all ingredients into a blender and blend on high until smooth and creamy.
2. Divide evenly between 4 "mocktail" glasses and top with whipped coconut cream, if desired.
3. Add a cocktail umbrella and toasted coconut for added flair.
4. Enjoy your delicious Choco-nut smoothie!

Nutrition: Carbohydrates: 12g; Protein: 3g; Calories 199

443. Pineapple & Strawberry Smoothie

Preparation time: 7 minutes
Cooking time: 0 minute
Servings: 2
Ingredients:

- 1 cup strawberries
- 1 cup pineapple, chopped
- ¾ cup almond milk
- 1 tbsp. almond butter

Directions:

1. Add all ingredients to a blender.
2. Blend until smooth.
3. Add more almond milk until it reaches your desired consistency.

4. Chill before serving.
Nutrition: Calories: 255; Carbohydrate: 39g; Protein: 5.6g

444. Cantaloupe Smoothie

Preparation time: 11 minutes
Cooking time: 0 minute
Servings: 2
Ingredients:

- ¾ cup carrot juice
- 4 cups cantaloupe, sliced into cubes
- Pinch of salt
- Frozen melon balls
- Fresh basil

Directions:

1. Add the carrot juice and cantaloupe cubes to a blender. Sprinkle with salt.
2. Process until smooth.
3. Transfer to a bowl.
4. Chill in the refrigerator for at least 30 minutes.
5. Top with the frozen melon balls and basil before serving.

Nutrition: Calories: 135; Carbohydrate: 31g; Protein: 4g

445. Berry Smoothie with Mint

Preparation time: 7 minutes
Cooking time: 0 minute
Servings: 2
Ingredients:

- ¼ cup orange juice
- ½ cup blueberries
- ½ cup blackberries
- 1 cup reduced-fat plain kefir
- 1 tbsp. honey
- 2 tbsp. fresh mint leaves

Directions:

1. Add all the ingredients to a blender.
2. Blend until smooth.

Nutrition: Calories: 137; Carbohydrate: 27g; Protein:

446. Green Smoothie

Preparation time: 12 minutes
Cooking time: 0 minute

Servings: 2
Ingredients:

- 1 cup vanilla almond milk (unsweetened)
- ¼ ripe avocado, chopped
- 1 cup kale, chopped
- 1 banana
- 2 tsp. honey
- 1 tbsp. chia seeds
- 1 cup ice cubes

Directions:

1. Combine all the ingredients in a blender.
2. Process until creamy.

Nutrition: Calories: 343; Carbohydrate: 14.7g; Protein: 5.9g

447. Banana, Cauliflower & Berry Smoothie

Preparation time: 9 minutes
Cooking time: 0 minute
Servings: 2
Ingredients:

- 2 cups almond milk (unsweetened)
- 1 cup banana, sliced
- ½ cup blueberries
- ½ cup blackberries
- 1 cup cauliflower rice
- 2 tsp. maple syrup

Directions:

1. Pour almond milk into a blender.
2. Stir in the rest of the ingredients.
3. Process until smooth.
4. Chill before serving.

Nutrition: Calories: 149; Carbohydrate: 29g; Protein: 3g

448. Berry & Spinach Smoothie

Preparation time: 11 minutes
Cooking time: 0 minute
Servings: 2
Ingredients:

- 2 cups strawberries
- 1 cup raspberries
- 1 cup blueberries
- 1 cup fresh baby spinach leaves

- 1 cup pomegranate juice
- 3 tbsp. milk powder (unsweetened)

Directions:
1. Mix all the ingredients in a blender.
2. Blend until smooth.
3. Chill before serving.

Nutrition: Calories: 118; Carbohydrate: 25.7g; Protein: 4.6g

449. Peanut Butter Smoothie with Blueberries

Preparation time: 12 minutes
Cooking time: 0 minute
Servings: 2
Ingredients:
- 2 tbsp. creamy peanut butter
- 1 cup vanilla almond milk (unsweetened)
- 6 oz. soft silken tofu
- ½ cup grape juice
- 1 cup blueberries
- Crushed ice

Directions:
1. Mix all the ingredients in a blender.
2. Process until smooth.

Nutrition: Calories: 247; Carbohydrate: 30g; Protein: 10.7g

450. Peach & Apricot Smoothie

Preparation time: 11 minutes
Cooking time: 0 minute
Servings: 2
Ingredients:
- 1 cup almond milk (unsweetened)
- 1 tsp. honey
- ½ cup apricots, sliced
- ½ cup peaches, sliced
- ½ cup carrot, chopped
- 1 tsp. vanilla extract

Directions:
1. Mix milk and honey.
2. Pour into a blender.
3. Add the apricots, peaches, and carrots.
4. Stir in the vanilla.
5. Blend until smooth.

Nutrition: Calories: 153; Carbohydrate: 30g; Protein: 32.6g

451. Tropical Smoothie

Preparation time: 8 minutes
Cooking time: 0 minute
Servings: 2
Ingredients:
- 1 banana, sliced
- 1 cup mango, sliced
- 1 cup pineapple, sliced
- 1 cup peaches, sliced
- 6 oz. nonfat coconut yogurt
- Pineapple wedges

Directions:
1. Freeze the fruit slices for 1 hour.
2. Transfer to a blender.
3. Stir in the rest of the ingredients except pineapple wedges.
4. Process until smooth.
5. Garnish with pineapple wedges.

Nutrition: Calories: 102; Carbohydrate: 22.6; Protein: 2.5g

452. Banana & Strawberry Smoothie

Preparation time: 7 minutes
Cooking time: 0 minute
Servings: 2
Ingredients:
- 1 banana, sliced
- 4 cups fresh strawberries, sliced
- 1 cup ice cubes
- 6 oz. yogurt
- 1 kiwi fruit, sliced

Directions:
1. Add banana, strawberries, ice cubes, a yogurt in a blender.
2. Blend until smooth.
3. Garnish with kiwi fruit slices and serve.

Nutrition: Calories: 54; Carbohydrate: 11.8g; Prote 1.7g

453. Cantaloupe & Papaya Smoothie

Preparation time: 9 minutes
Cooking time: 0 minute

Servings: 2

Ingredients:

- ¾ cup low-fat milk
- ½ cup papaya, chopped
- ½ cup cantaloupe, chopped
- ½ cup mango, cubed
- 4 ice cubes
- Lime zest

Directions:

1. Pour milk into a blender.
2. Add the chopped fruits and ice cubes.
3. Blend until smooth.
4. Garnish with lime zest and serve.

Nutrition: Calories: 207; Carbohydrate: 18.4g; Protein: 7.7g

454. Watermelon & Cantaloupe Smoothie

Preparation time: 10 minutes
Cooking time: 0 minute
Servings: 2

Ingredients:

- 2 cups watermelon, sliced
- 1 cup cantaloupe, sliced
- ½ cup nonfat yogurt
- ¼ cup orange juice

Directions:

1. Add all the ingredients to a blender.
2. Blend until creamy and smooth.
3. Chill before serving.

Nutrition: Calories: 114; Carbohydrate: 13g; Protein: 8g

55. Raspberry and Peanut Butter Smoothie

Preparation time: 10 minutes
Cooking time: 0 minute
Servings: 2

Ingredients:

- Peanut butter, smooth and natural [2 tbsp]
- Skim milk [2 tbsp]
- Raspberries, fresh [1 or 1 ½ cups]
- Ice cubes [1 cup]
- Stevia [2 tsp]

Directions:

1. Situate all the ingredients in your blender. Set the mixer to puree. Serve.

Nutrition: Calories: 170; Fat: 8.6g; Carbohydrate: 20g

456. Strawberry, Kale, and Ginger Smoothie

Preparation time: 13 minutes
Cooking time: 0 minute
Servings: 2

Ingredients:

- Curly kale leaves, fresh and large with stems removed [6 pcs]
- Grated ginger, raw and peeled [2 tsp]
- Water, cold [½ cup]
- Lime juice [3 tbsp]
- Honey [2 tsp]
- Strawberries, fresh and trimmed [1 or 1 ½ cups]
- Ice cubes [1 cup]

Directions:

1. Position all the ingredients in your blender. Set to puree. Serve.

Nutrition: Calories: 205; Fat: 2.9g; Carbohydrates: 42.4g

457.   Berry Mint Smoothie

Preparation time: 5 Minutes
Cooking time: 5 Minutes
Servings: 2
Ingredients:

- 1 tbsp. Low-carb Sweetener of your choice
- 1 cup Kefir or Low Fat-Yoghurt
- 2 tbsp. Mint
- ¼ cup Orange
- 1 cup Mixed Berries

Directions:

1. Place all of the ingredients in a high-speed blender and then blend it until smooth.
2. Transfer the smoothie to a serving glass and enjoy it.

Nutrition: Calories: 137; Carbohydrates: 11g; Protein: 6g; Fat: 1g; Sodium: 64mg

458.   Greenie Smoothie

Preparation time: 5 Minutes
Cooking time: 5 Minutes
Servings: 2
Ingredients:

- 1 ½ cup Water
- 1 tsp. Stevia
- 1 Green Apple, ripe
- 1 tsp. Stevia
- 1 Green Pear, chopped into chunks
- 1 Lime
- 2 cups Kale, fresh
- ¾ tsp. Cinnamon
- 12 Ice Cubes
- 20 Green Grapes
- ½ cup Mint, fresh

Directions:

1. Pour water, kale, and pear in a high-sp blender and blend them for 2 to 3 minutes u mixed.
2. Stir in all the remaining ingredients and bl until it becomes smooth.
3. Transfer the smoothie to a serving glass.

Nutrition: Calories: 123; Carbohydrates: 27g; Prot 2g; Fat: 2g; Sodium: 30mg

459. Coconut Spinach Smoothie

Preparation time: 5 Minutes
Cooking time: 5 Minutes
Servings: 2

Ingredients:

- 1 ¼ cup Coconut Milk
- 2 Ice Cubes
- 2 tbsp. Chia Seeds
- 1 scoop of; Protein: Powder, preferably vanilla
- 1 cup Spin

Directions:

1. Pour coconut milk along with spinach, chia seeds; Protein: powder, and ice cubes in a high-speed blender.
2. Blend for 2 minutes to get a smooth and luscious smoothie.
3. Serve in a glass and enjoy it.

Nutrition: Calories: 251; Carbohydrates: 10.9g; Protein: 20.3g; Fat: 15.1g; Sodium: 102mg

460. Oats Coffee Smoothie

Preparation time: 5 Minutes
Cooking time: 5 Minutes
Servings: 2

Ingredients:

- 1 cup Oats, uncooked & grounded
- 2 tbsp. Instant Coffee
- 3 cup Milk, skimmed
- 2 Banana, frozen & sliced into chunks
- 2 tbsp. Flax Seeds, grounded

Directions:

1. Place all of the ingredients in a high-speed blender and blend for 2 minutes or until smooth and luscious.
2. Serve and enjoy.

Nutrition: Calories: 251; Carbohydrates: 10.9g; Protein: 20.3g; Fat: 15.1g; Sodium: 102mg

461. Veggie Smoothie

Preparation time: 5 Minutes
Cooking time: 5 Minutes
Servings: 1
Ingredients:

- ¼ of 1 Red Bell Pepper, sliced
- ½ tbsp. Coconut Oil
- 1 cup Almond Milk, unsweetened
- ¼ tsp. Turmeric
- 4 Strawberries, chopped
- Pinch of Cinnamon
- ½ of 1 Banana, preferably frozen

Directions:

1. Combine all the ingredients required to make the smoothie in a high-speed blender.
2. Blend for 3 minutes to get a smooth and silky mixture.
3. Serve and enjoy.

Nutrition: Calories: 169; Carbohydrates: 17g; Protein: 2.3g; Fat: 9.8g; Sodium: 162mg

462. Avocado Smoothie

Preparation time: 10 Minutes
Cooking time: 0 Minutes
Servings: 2
Ingredients:

- 1 Avocado, ripe & pit removed
- 2 cups Baby Spinach
- 2 cups Water
- 1 cup Baby Kale
- 1 tbsp. Lemon Juice
- 2 sprigs of Mint
- ½ cup Ice Cubes

Directions:

1. Place all the ingredients needed to make the smoothie in a high-speed blender then blend until smooth.
2. Transfer to a serving glass and enjoy it.

Nutrition: Calories: 214; Carbohydrates: 15g; Protein: 2g; Fat: 17g; Sodium: 25mg

463. Orange Carrot Smoothie

Preparation time: 5 Minutes
Cooking time: 0 Minutes
Servings: 1
Ingredients:

- 1 ½ cups Almond Milk
- ¼ cup Cauliflower, blanched & frozen
- 1 Orange
- 1 tbsp. Flax Seed
- 1/3 cup Carrot, grated
- 1 tsp. Vanilla Extract

Directions:

1. Mix all the ingredients in a high-speed blender and blend for 2 minutes or until you get the desired consistency.
2. Transfer to a serving glass and enjoy it.

Nutrition: Calories: 216; Carbohydrates: 10g; Protein: g; Fat: 7g; Sodium: 25mg

464. Blackberry Smoothie

Preparation time: 5 Minutes
Cooking time: 0 Minutes
Servings: 1
Ingredients:

- 1 ½ cups Almond Milk
- ¼ cup Cauliflower, blanched & frozen
- 1 Orange
- 1 tbsp. Flax Seed
- 1/3 cup Carrot, grated
- 1 tsp. Vanilla Extract

Directions:

1. Place all the ingredients needed to make the blackberry smoothie in a high-speed blender and blend for 2 minutes until you get a smooth mixture.
2. Transfer to a serving glass and enjoy it.

Nutrition: Calories: 275; Carbohydrates: 9g; Protein: 11g; Fat: 17g; Sodium: 73mg

465. Key Lime Pie Smoothie

Preparation time: 5 Minutes
Cooking time: 0 Minutes
Servings: 1
Ingredients:

- ½ cup Cottage Cheese
- 1 tbsp. Sweetener of your choice
- ½ cup Water
- ½ cup Spinach
- 1 tbsp. Lime Juice
- 1 cup Ice Cubes

Directions:

1. Spoon in the ingredients to a high-speed blender and blend until silky smooth.
2. Transfer to a serving glass and enjoy it.

Nutrition: Calories: 180; Carbohydrates: 7g; Protein: 36g; Fat: 1g; Sodium: 35mg

466. Cinnamon Roll Smoothie

Preparation time: 5 Minutes
Cooking time: 0 Minutes
Servings: 1
Ingredients:

- 1 tsp. Flax Meal or oats, if preferred
- 1 cup Almond Milk
- ½ tsp. Cinnamon
- 2 tbsp.; Protein: Powder
- 1 cup Ice
- ¼ tsp. Vanilla Extract
- 4 tsp. Sweetener of your choice

Directions:

1. Pour the milk into the blender, followed by the Protein: powder, sweetener, flax meal, cinnamon, vanilla extract, and ice.
2. Blend for 40 seconds or until smooth.
3. Serve and enjoy.

Nutrition: Calories: 145; Carbohydrates: 1.6g; Protein: 26.5g; Fat: 3.25g; Sodium: 30mg

467. Strawberry Cheesecake Smoothie

Preparation time: 5 Minutes
Cooking time: 0 Minutes
Servings: 1
Ingredients:

- ¼ cup Soy Milk, unsweetened
- ½ cup Cottage Cheese, low-fat
- ½ tsp. Vanilla Extract
- 2 oz. Cream Cheese
- 1 cup Ice Cubes
- ½ cup Strawberries
- 4 tbsp. Low-carb Sweetener of your choice

Directions:

1. Add all the ingredients for making the strawberry cheesecake smoothie to a high-speed blender until you get the desired smooth consistency.
2. Serve and enjoy.

Nutrition: Calories: 347; Carbohydrates: 10.05g; Protein: 17.5g; Fat: 24g; Sodium: 45mg

468. Peanut Butter Banana Smoothie

Preparation time: 5 Minutes
Cooking time: 2 Minutes
Servings: 1
Ingredients:

- ¼ cup Greek Yoghurt, plain
- ½ tbsp. Chia Seeds
- ½ cup Ice Cubes
- ½ of 1 Banana
- ½ cup Water
- 1 tbsp. Peanut Butter

Directions:

1. Place all the ingredients needed to make the smoothie in a high-speed blender and blend to get a smooth and luscious mixture.
2. Transfer the smoothie to a serving glass and enjoy it.

Nutrition: Calories: 202; Carbohydrates: 14g; Protein: 10g; Fat: 9g; Sodium: 30mg

469. Avocado Turmeric Smoothie

Preparation time: 5 Minutes
Cooking time: 2 Minutes
Servings: 1
Ingredients:

- ½ of 1 Avocado
- 1 cup Ice, crushed
- ¾ cup Coconut Milk, full-fat
- 1 tsp. Lemon Juice
- ¼ cup Almond Milk
- ½ tsp. Turmeric
- 1 tsp. Ginger, freshly grated

Directions:

1. Place all the ingredients excluding the crushed ice in a high-speed blender and blend for 2 to 3 minutes or until smooth.
2. Transfer to a serving glass and enjoy it.

Nutrition: Calories: 232; Carbohydrates: 4.1g; Protein: 1.7g; Fat: 22.4g; Sodium: 25mg

470. Lemon Blueberry Smoothie

Preparation time: 5 Minutes
Cooking time: 2 Minutes
Servings: 2
Ingredients:

- 1 tbsp. Lemon Juice
- 1 ¾ cup Coconut Milk, full-fat
- ½ tsp. Vanilla Extract
- 3 oz. Blueberries, frozen

Directions:

1. Combine coconut milk, blueberries, lemo juice, and vanilla extract in a high-spee blender.
2. Blend for 2 minutes for a smooth and luscio smoothie.
3. Serve and enjoy.

Nutrition: Calories: 417; Carbohydrates: 9g; Prote 4g; Fat: 43g; Sodium: 35mg

471.   Matcha Green Smoothie

Preparation time: 5 Minutes
Cooking time: 2 Minutes
Servings: 2
Ingredients:

- ¼ cup Heavy Whipping Cream
- ½ tsp. Vanilla Extract
- 1 tsp. Matcha Green Tea Powder
- 2 tbsp.; Protein: Powder
- 1 tbsp. Hot Water
- 1 ¼ cup Almond Milk, unsweetened
- ½ of 1 Avocado, medium

Directions:

1. Place all the ingredients in the high-blender for one to two minutes.
2. Serve and enjoy.

Nutrition: Calories: 229; Carbohydrates: 1.5g; Protein: .1g; Fat: 43g; Sodium: 35mg

472.   Blueberry Smoothie

Preparation time: 10 minutes
Cooking time: 0 minutes
Servings: 2
Ingredients:

- 2 cups frozen blueberries
- 1 small banana
- 1½ cups unsweetened almond milk
- ¼ cup ice cubes

Directions:

1. Place all the ingredients in a high-speed blender and pulse until creamy.
2. Pour the smoothie into two glasses and serve immediately.

Nutrition: Calories: 158; Total Fat: 3.3g; Saturated Fat: 0.3g; Cholesterol: 0mg; Sodium: 137mg; Total Carbs: 34g; Fiber: 5.6g; Sugar: 20.6g; Protein: 2.4 g

473.   Beet & Strawberry Smoothie

Preparation time: 10 minutes
Cooking time: 0 minutes
Servings: 2
Ingredients:

- 2 cups frozen strawberries, pitted and chopped
- 2/3 cup roasted and frozen beet, chopped
- 1 tsp. fresh ginger, peeled and grated
- 1 tsp. fresh turmeric, peeled and grated
- ½ cup fresh orange juice
- 1 cup unsweetened almond milk

Directions:

1. Place all the ingredients in a high-speed blender and pulse until creamy.
2. Pour the smoothie into two glasses and serve immediately.

Nutrition: Calories: 258; Total Fat: 1.5g; Saturated Fat: 0.1g; Cholesterol: 0mg; Sodium: 134mg; Total Carbs: 26.7g; Fiber: 4.9g; Sugar: 18.7g; Protein: 2.9 g

474.   Kiwi Smoothie

Preparation time: 10 minutes
Cooking time: 0 minutes
Servings: 2
Ingredients:

- 4 kiwis
- 2 small bananas, peeled
- 1½ cups unsweetened almond milk
- 1–2 drops liquid stevia
- ¼ cup ice cubes

Directions:

1. Place all the ingredients in a high-speed blender and pulse until creamy.
2. Pour the smoothie into two glasses and serve immediately.

Nutrition: Calories: 228; Total Fat: 3.8g; Saturated Fat: 0.4g; Cholesterol: 0mg; Sodium: 141mg; Total Carbs: 50.7g; Fiber: 8.4g; Sugar: 28.1g; Protein: 3.8 g

475.   Pineapple & Carrot Smoothie

Preparation time: 10 minutes
Cooking time: 0 minutes
Servings: 2
Ingredients:

- 1 cup frozen pineapple
- 1 large ripe banana, peeled and sliced
- ½ tbsp. fresh ginger, peeled and chopped
- ¼ tsp. ground turmeric
- 1 cup unsweetened almond milk
- ½ cup fresh carrot juice
- 1 tbsp. fresh lemon juice

Directions:

1. Place all the ingredients in a high-speed blender and pulse until creamy.
2. Pour the smoothie into two glasses and serve immediately.

Nutrition: Calories: 132; Total Fat: 2.2g; Saturated Fat: 0.3g; Cholesterol: 0mg; Sodium: 113mg; Total Carbs: 629.3g; Fiber: 4.1g; Sugar: 16.9g; Protein: 2 g

476.   Oats & Orange Smoothie

Preparation time: 10 minutes
Cooking time: 0 minutes
Servings: 4
Ingredients:

- 2/3 cup rolled oats
- 2 oranges, peeled, seeded, and sectioned
- 2 large bananas, peeled and sliced
- 2 cups unsweetened almond milk
- 1 cup ice cubes, crushed

Directions:

1. Place all the ingredients in a high-speed blender and pulse until creamy.
2. Pour the smoothie into four glasses and serve immediately.

Nutrition: Calories: 175; Total Fat 3g; Saturated Fat: 0.4g; Cholesterol: 0mg; Sodium: 93mg; Total Carbs: 36.6g; Fiber: 5.9g; Sugar: 17.1g; Protein: 3.9 g

477.   Pumpkin Smoothie

Preparation time: 10 minutes
Cooking time: 0 minutes
Servings: 2

Ingredients:

- 1 cup homemade pumpkin puree
- 1 medium banana, peeled and sliced
- 1 tbsp. maple syrup
- 1 tsp. ground flaxseeds
- ½ tsp. ground cinnamon
- ¼ tsp. ground ginger
- 1½ cups unsweetened almond milk
- ¼ cup ice cubes

Directions:

1. Place all the ingredients in a high-speed blender and pulse until creamy.
2. Pour the smoothie into two glasses and serve immediately.

Nutrition: Calories: 159; Total Fat: 3.6g; Saturated Fat 0.5g; Cholesterol: 0mg; Sodium: 143mg; Total Carbs 32.6g; Fiber: 6.5g; Sugar: 17.3g; Protein: 3 g

478.   Red Veggie & Fruit Smoothie

Preparation time: 10 minutes
Cooking time: 0 minutes
Servings: 2
Ingredients:

- ½ cup fresh raspberries
- ½ cup fresh strawberries
- ½ red bell pepper, seeded and chopped
- ½ cup red cabbage, chopped
- 1 small tomato
- 1 cup water
- ½ cup ice cubes

Directions:

1. Place all the ingredients in a high-speed blend and pulse until creamy.
2. Pour the smoothie into two glasses and ser immediately.

Nutrition: Calories: 39 Cholesterol 0 mg Saturated F 0g; Sodium: 10mg; Total Carbs: 8.9g; Fiber: 3.! Sugar: 4.8g; Protein: 1.3 g; Total Fat: 0.4 g

479.   Kale Smoothie

Preparation time: 10 minutes
Cooking time: 0 minutes
Servings: 2
Ingredients:

- 3 stalks fresh kale, trimmed and chopped
- 1–2 celery stalks, chopped

- ½ avocado, peeled, pitted, and chopped
- ½-inch piece ginger root, chopped
- ½-inch piece turmeric root, chopped
- 2 cups coconut milk

Directions:
1. Place all the ingredients in a high-speed blender and pulse until creamy.
2. Pour the smoothie into two glasses and serve immediately.

Nutrition: Calories: 248; Total Fat: 21.8g; Saturated Fat: 12g; Cholesterol: 0mg; Sodium: 59mg; Total Carbs: 11.3g; Fiber: 4.2g; Sugar: 0.5g; Protein: 3.5 g

480. Green Tofu Smoothie

Preparation time: 10 minutes
Cooking time: 0 minutes
Servings: 2
Ingredients:
- 1½ cups cucumber, peeled and chopped roughly
- 3 cups fresh baby spinach
- 2 cups frozen broccoli
- ½ cup silken tofu, drained and pressed
- 1 tbsp. fresh lime juice
- 4–5 drops liquid stevia
- 1 cup unsweetened almond milk
- ½ cup ice, crushed

Directions:
1. Place all the ingredients in a high-speed blender and pulse until creamy.
2. Pour the smoothie into two glasses and serve immediately.

Nutrition: Calories: 118; Total Fat: 15g; Saturated Fat: 3g; Cholesterol: 0mg; Sodium: 165mg; Total Carbs: .6g; Fiber: 4.8g; Sugar: 3.4g; Protein: 10 g

481. Grape & Swiss Chard Smoothie

Preparation time: 10 minutes
Cooking time: 0 minutes
Servings: 2
Ingredients:
- 2 cups seedless green grapes
- 2 cups fresh Swiss chard, trimmed and chopped
- 2 tbsp. maple syrup

- 1 tsp. fresh lemon juice
- 1½ cups water
- 4 ice cubes

Directions:
1. Place all the ingredients in a high-speed blender and pulse until creamy.
2. Pour the smoothie into two glasses and serve immediately.

Nutrition: Calories: 176; Total Fat: 0.2g; Saturated Fat: 0g; Cholesterol: 0mg; Sodium: 83mg; Total Carbs: 44.9g; Fiber: 1.7g; Sugar: 37.9g; Protein: 0.7 g

482. Matcha Smoothie

Preparation time: 10 minutes
Cooking time: 0 minutes
Servings: 2
Ingredients:
- 2 tbsp. chia seeds
- 2 tsp. matcha green tea powder
- ½ tsp. fresh lemon juice
- ½ tsp. xanthan gum
- 8–10 drops liquid stevia
- 4 tbsp. coconut cream
- 1½ cups unsweetened almond milk
- ¼ cup ice cubes

Directions:
1. Place all the ingredients in a high-speed blender and pulse until creamy.
2. Pour the smoothie into two glasses and serve immediately.

Nutrition: Calories: 132; Total Fat: 12.3g; Saturated Fat: 6.8g; Cholesterol: 0mg; Sodium: 15mg; Total Carbs: 7g; Fiber: 4.8g; Sugar: 1g; Protein: 3 g

483. Banana Smoothie

Preparation time: 10 minutes
Cooking time: 0 minutes
Servings: 2
Ingredients:
- 2 cups chilled unsweetened almond milk
- 1 large frozen banana, peeled and sliced
- 1 tbsp. almonds, chopped
- 1 tsp. organic vanilla extract

Directions:
1. Place all the ingredients in a high-speed blender and pulse until creamy.
2. Pour the smoothie into two glasses and serve immediately.

Nutrition: Calories: 124; Total Fat: 5.2g; Saturated Fat: 0.5g; Cholesterol: 0mg; Sodium: 181mg; Total Carbs: 18.4g; Fiber: 3.1g; Sugar: 8.7g; Protein: 2.4 g

484. Strawberry Smoothie

Preparation time: 10 minutes
Cooking time: 0 minutes
Servings: 2
Ingredients:

- 2 cups chilled unsweetened almond milk
- 1½ cups frozen strawberries
- 1 banana, peeled and sliced
- ¼ tsp. organic vanilla extract

Directions:

1. Add all the ingredients to a high-speed blender and pulse until smooth.
2. Pour the smoothie into two glasses and serve immediately.

Nutrition: Calories: 131; Total Fat: 3.7g; Saturated Fat: 0.4g; Cholesterol: 0mg; Sodium: 181mg; Total Carbs: 25.3g; Fiber: 4.8g; Sugar: 14g; Protein: 1.6 g

485. Raspberry & Tofu Smoothie

Preparation time: 15 minutes
Cooking time: 0 minutes
Servings: 2
Ingredients:

- 1½ cups fresh raspberries
- 6 ounces firm silken tofu, drained
- 1/8 tsp. coconut extract
- 1 tsp. powdered stevia
- 1½ cups unsweetened almond milk
- ¼ cup ice cubes, crushed

Directions:

1. Add all the ingredients to a high-speed blender and pulse until smooth.
2. Pour the smoothie into two glasses and serve immediately.

Nutrition: Calories: 131; Total Fat: 5.5g; Saturated Fat: 0.6g; Cholesterol: 0mg; Sodium: 167mg; Total Carbs: 14.6g; Fiber: 6.8g; Sugar: 5.2g; Protein: 7.7 g

486. Mango Smoothie

Preparation time: 10 minutes
Cooking time: 0 minutes

Servings: 2
Ingredients:

- 2 cups frozen mango, peeled, pitted, and chopped
- ¼ cup almond butter
- Pinch of ground turmeric
- 2 tbsp. fresh lemon juice
- 1¼ cups unsweetened almond milk
- ¼ cup ice cubes

Directions:

1. Add all the ingredients to a high-speed blender and pulse until smooth.
2. Pour the smoothie into two glasses and serve immediately.

Nutrition: Calories: 140; Total Fat: 4.1g; Saturated Fat: 0.6g; Cholesterol: 0mg; Sodium: 118mg; Total Carbs: 26.8g; Fiber: 3.6g; Sugar: 23g; Protein: 2.5 g

487. Pineapple Smoothie

Preparation time: 10 minutes
Cooking time: 0 minutes
Servings: 2
Ingredients:

- 2 cups pineapple, chopped
- ½ tsp. fresh ginger, peeled, and chopped
- ½ tsp. ground turmeric
- 1 tsp. natural immune support supplement *
- 1 tsp. chia seeds
- 1½ cups cold green tea
- ½ cup ice, crushed

Directions:

1. Add all the ingredients to a high-speed blender and pulse until smooth.
2. Pour the smoothie into two glasses and serve immediately.

Nutrition: Calories: 152; Total Fat: 1g; Saturated Fat: 0g; Cholesterol: 0mg; Sodium: 9mg; Total Carbs: 30; Fiber: 3.5g; Sugar: 29.8g; Protein: 1.5 g

488. Kale & Pineapple Smoothie

Preparation time: 15 minutes
Cooking time: 0 minutes
Servings: 2
Ingredients:

- 1½ cups fresh kale, trimmed and chopped

- 1 frozen banana, peeled and chopped
- ½ cup fresh pineapple chunks
- 1 cup unsweetened coconut milk
- ½ cup fresh orange juice
- ½ cup ice

Directions:
1. Add all the ingredients to a high-speed blender and pulse until smooth.
2. Pour the smoothie into two glasses and serve immediately.

Nutrition: Calories: 148; Total Fat: 2.4g; Saturated Fat: 2.1g; Cholesterol: 0mg; Sodium: 23mg; Total Carbs: 31.6g; Fiber: 3.5g; Sugar: 16.5g; Protein: 2.8 g

489. Green Veggies Smoothie

Preparation time: 15 minutes
Cooking time: 0 minutes
Servings: 2
Ingredients:

- 1 medium avocado, peeled, pitted, and chopped
- 1 large cucumber, peeled and chopped
- 2 fresh tomatoes, chopped
- 1 small green bell pepper, seeded and chopped
- 1 cup fresh spinach, torn
- 2 tbsp. fresh lime juice
- 2 tbsp. homemade vegetable broth
- 1 cup alkaline water

Directions:
1. Add all the ingredients to a high-speed blender and pulse until smooth.
2. Pour the smoothie into glasses and serve immediately.

Nutrition: Calories: 275; Total Fat: 20.3g; Saturated Fat: 4.2g; Cholesterol: 0mg; Sodium: 76mg; Total Carbs: 24.1g; Fiber: 10.1g; Sugar: 9.3g; Protein: 5.3 g

490. Avocado & Spinach Smoothie

Preparation time: 10 minutes
Cooking time: 0 minutes
Servings: 2
Ingredients:

- 2 cups fresh baby spinach
- ½ avocado, peeled, pitted, and chopped
- 4–6 drops liquid stevia

- ½ tsp. ground cinnamon
- 1 tbsp. hemp seeds
- 2 cups chilled alkaline water

Directions:
1. Add all the ingredients to a high-speed blender and pulse until smooth.
2. Pour the smoothie into two glasses and serve immediately.

Nutrition: Calories: 132; Total Fat: 11.7g; Saturated Fat: 2.2g; Cholesterol: 0mg; Sodium: 27mg; Total Carbs: 6.1g; Fiber: 4.5g; Sugar: 0.4g; Protein: 3.1 g

491. Raisins—Plume Smoothie (RPS)

Preparation time: 10 minutes
Cooking time: 0 minutes
Servings: 1
Ingredients:

- 1 tsp. Raisins
- 2 Sweet Cherry
- 1 Skinned Black Plume
- 1 Cup Dr. Sebi's Stomach Calming Herbal Tea/ Cuachalate back powder,
- ¼ Coconut Water

Directions:
1. Flash 1 tsp. of Raisin in warm water for 5 seconds and drain the water completely.
2. Rinse, cube Sweet Cherry and skinned black Plum
3. Get 1 cup of water boiled; put ¾ Dr. Sebi's Stomach Calming Herbal Tea for 10–15minutes.
4. If you are unable to get Dr. Sebi's Stomach Calming Herbal tea, you can alternatively, cook 1 tsp. of powdered Cuachalate with 1 cup of water for 5–10 minutes, remove the extract, and allow it to cool.
5. Pour all the ARPS items into a blender and blend till you achieve a homogenous smoothie.
6. It is now okay, for you to enjoy the inevitable detox smoothie.

Nutrition: Calories: 150g; Fat: 1.2 g; Carbohydrates: 79g; Protein: 3.1 g

492. Nori Clove Smoothies (NCS)

Preparation time: 10 minutes
Cooking time: 0 minutes

Servings: 1
Ingredients:

- ¼ Cup Fresh Nori
- 1 Cup Cubed Banana
- 1 tsp. Diced Onion or ¼ tsp. Powdered Onion
- ½ tsp. Clove
- 1 Cup Dr. Sebi Energy Booster
- 1 Tbsp. Agave Syrup

Directions:

1. Rinse ANCS Items with clean water.
2. Finely chop the onion to take one tsp. and cut fresh Nori
3. Boil 1½ tsp. with 2 cups of water, remove the particle, allow to cool, measure 1 cup of the tea extract
4. Pour all the items inside a blender with the tea extract and blend to achieve homogenous smoothies.
5. Transfer into a clean cup and have a nice time with a lovely body detox and energizer.

Nutrition: Calories: 78g; Fat: 2.3 g; Carbohydrates: 5g; Protein: 6 g

493.   Brazil Lettuce Smoothies (BLS)

Preparation time: 10 minutes
Cooking time: 0 minutes
Servings: 1
Ingredients:

- 1 cup Raspberries
- ½ Handful Romaine Lettuce
- ½ Cup Homemade Walnut Milk
- 2 Brazil Nuts
- ½ Large Grape with Seed
- 1 Cup Soft jelly Coconut Water
- Date Sugar to Taste

Directions:

1. In a clean bowl rinse the vegetable with clean water.
2. Chop the Romaine Lettuce and cubed Raspberries and add other items into the blender and blend to achieve homogenous smoothies.
3. Serve your delicious medicinal detox.

Nutrition: Calories: 168g; Fat: 4.5 g; Carbohydrates: 31.3 g; Sugar: 19.2g; Protein: 3.6 g

494.   Apple—Banana Smoothie (Abs)

Preparation time: 10 minutes
Cooking time: 0 minutes
Servings: 1
Ingredients:

- I Cup Cubed Apple
- ½ Burro Banana
- ½ Cup Cubed Mango
- ½ Cup Cubed Watermelon
- ½ tsp. Powdered Onion
- 3 Tbsp. Key Lime Juice
- Date Sugar to Taste (If you like)

Directions:

1. In a clean bowl rinse the vegetable with clear water.
2. Cubed Banana, Apple, Mango, Watermelon and add other items into the blender and blend to achieve homogenous smoothies.
3. Serve your delicious medicinal detox.
4. Alternatively, you can add one tbsp. of finely dices raw red Onion if powdered Onion is no available.

Nutrition: Calories: 99g; Fat: 0.3g; Carbohydrate 23g; Protein: 1.1 g

495.   Ginger—Pear Smoothie (GPS)

Preparation time: 10 minutes
Cooking time: 0 minutes
Servings: 1
Ingredients:

- 1 Big Pear with Seed and Cured
- ½ Avocado
- ¼ Handful Watercress
- ½ Sour Orange
- ½ Cup Ginger Tea
- ½ Cup Coconut Water
- ¼ Cup Spring Water
- 2 Tbsp. Agave Syrup
- Date Sugar to satisfaction

Directions:

1. Firstly boil 1 cup of Ginger Tea, cover the c and allow it cool to room temperature.
2. Pour all the AGPS Items into your cle blender and homogenize them to smooth flu

3. You have just prepared yourself a wonderful Detox Romaine Smoothie.

Nutrition: Calories: 101g; Protein: 1 g; Carbs: 27g; Fiber: 6 g

496. Cantaloupe— Amaranth Smoothie (CAS)

Preparation time: 10 minutes
Cooking time: 0 minutes
Servings: 1
Ingredients:

- ½ Cup Cubed Cantaloupe
- ¼ Handful Green Amaranth
- ½ Cup Homemade Hemp Milk
- ¼ tsp. Dr. Sebi's Bromide Plus Powder
- 1 cup Coconut Water
- 1 tsp. Agave Syrup

Directions:

1. You will have to rinse all the ACAS items with clean water.
2. Chop green Amaranth, cubed Cantaloupe, transfer all into a blender and blend to achieve a homogenous smoothie.
3. Pour into a clean cup; add Agave syrup and homemade Hemp Milk.
4. Stir them together and drink.

Nutrition: Calories: 55 Fiber: 1.5 g; Carbohydrates: 8 g

97. Garbanzo Squash Smoothie (GSS)

Preparation time: 10 minutes
Cooking time: 0 minutes
Servings: 1
Ingredients:

- 1 Large Cubed Apple
- 1 Fresh Tomato
- 1 Tbsp. Finely Chopped Fresh Onion or ¼ tsp. Powdered Onion
- ¼ Cup Boiled Garbanzo Bean
- ½ Cup Coconut Milk
- ¼ Cubed Mexican Squash Chayote
- 1 Cup Energy Booster Tea

Directions:

1. You will need to rinse the AGSS items with clean water.
2. Boil 1½ Dr. Sebi's Energy Booster Tea with 2 cups of clean water. Filter the extract, measure 1 cup, and allow it to cool.
3. Cook Garbanzo Bean, drain the water, and allow it to cool.
4. Pour all the AGSS items into a high-speed blender and blend to achieve a homogenous smoothie.
5. You may add Date Sugar.
6. Serve your amazing smoothie and drink.

Nutrition: Calories: 82; Carbs: 22g; Protein: 2g; Fiber: 7 g

498. Strawberry— Orange Smoothies (SOS)

Preparation time: 10 minutes
Cooking time: 0 minutes
Servings: 1
Ingredients:

- 1 Cup Diced Strawberries
- 1 Removed Back of Seville Orange
- ¼ Cup Cubed Cucumber
- ¼ Cup Romaine Lettuce
- ½ Kelp
- ½ Burro Banana
- 1 Cup Soft Jelly Coconut Water
- ½ Cup Water
- Date Sugar.

Directions:

1. Use clean water to rinse all the vegetable items of ASOS into a clean bowl.
2. Chop Romaine Lettuce; dice Strawberry, Cucumber, and Banana; remove the back of Seville Orange and divide it into four.
3. Transfer all the ASOS items inside a clean blender and blend to achieve a homogenous smoothie.
4. Pour into a clean big cup and fortify your body with a palatable detox.

Nutrition: Calories: 298; Fat: 1g; Cholesterol: 2mg; Sodium: 73mg; Potassium 998mg; Carbohydrates: 68g; Fiber: 7g; Sugar: 50g

499.   Tamarind—Pear Smoothie (TPS)

Preparation time: 10 minutes
Cooking time: 0 minutes
Servings: 1
Ingredients:

- ½ Burro Banana
- ½ Cup Watermelon
- 1 Raspberry
- 1 Prickly Pear
- 1 Grape with Seed
- 3 Tamarind
- ½ Medium Cucumber
- 1 cup Coconut Water
- ½ Cup Distilled Water

Directions:

1. Use clean water to rinse all the ATPS items.
2. Remove the pod of Tamarind and collect the edible part around the seed into a container.
3. If you must use the seeds then you have to boil the seed for 15mins and add to the Tamarind edible part in the container.
4. Cubed all other vegetable fruits and transfer all the items into a high-speed blender and blend to achieve a homogenous smoothie.

Nutrition: Calories: 199; Carbohydrates: 47g; Fat: 1g; Protein: 6g

500.   Currant Elderberry Smoothie (CES)

Preparation time: 10 minutes

Cooking time: 0 minutes
Servings: 1
Ingredients:

- ¼ Cup Cubed Elderberry
- 1 Sour Cherry
- 2 Currant
- 1 Cubed Burro Banana
- 1 Fig
- 1 Cup 4 Bay Leaves Tea
- 1 Cup Energy Booster Tea
- Date Sugar to your satisfaction

Directions:

1. Use clean water to rinse all the ACES items
2. Initially boil ¾ tsp. of Energy Booster Tea with 2 cups of water on a heat source and allow boiling for 10 minutes.
3. Add 4 Bay leaves and boil together for another 4minutes.
4. Drain the Tea extract into a clean big cup and allow it to cool.
5. Transfer all the items into a high-speed blender and blend till you achieve a homogenous smoothie.
6. Pour the palatable medicinal smoothie into clean cup and drink.

Nutrition: Calories: 63g; Fat: 0.22g; Sodium: 1.1m; Carbohydrates: 15.5g; Fiber: 4.8g; Sugars: 8.25; Protein: 1.6g

28 DAY MEAL PLAN

	28 DAYS	BREAKFAST	LUNCH	DINNER	DESSERT
Week 1	Day 1	Bacon and Chicken Garlic Wrap	Cauliflower Rice with Chicken	Cauliflower Mac & Cheese	Peanut Butter Cups
	Day 2	Salty Macadamia Chocolate Smoothie	Turkey with Fried Eggs	Easy Egg Salad	Fruit Pizza
	Day 3	Buckwheat grouts breakfast bowl	Sweet Potato, Kale, and White Bean Stew	Baked Chicken Legs	Choco Peppermint Cake
	Day 4	Peach muesli bake	Slow Cooker Two-Bean Sloppy Joes	Creamed Spinach	Roasted Mango
	Day 5	Steel-cut oatmeal bowl with fruit and nuts	Lighter Eggplant Parmesan	Stuffed Mushrooms	Roasted Plums
	Day 6	Whole-grain dutch baby pancake	Coconut-Lentil Curry	Vegetable Soup	Figs with Honey & Yogurt
	Day 7	Mushroom, zucchini, and onion frittata	Stuffed Portobello with Cheese	Pork Chop Diane	Flourless Chocolate Cake
Week 2	Day 8	Berry-oat breakfast bars	Lighter Shrimp Scampi	Autumn Pork Chops with Red Cabbage and Apples	Lava Cake
	Day 9	Spinach and cheese quiche	Maple-Mustard Salmon	Chipotle Chili Pork Chops	Cheese Cake
	Day 10	Spicy Jalapeno Popper Deviled Eggs	Chicken Salad with Grapes and Pecans	Orange-Marinated Pork Tenderloin	Orange Cake
	Day 11	Blueberry breakfast cake	Roasted Vegetables	Homestyle Herb Meatballs	Madeleine
	Day 12	Lovely Porridge	Millet Pilaf	Lime-Parsley Lamb Cutlets	Waffles

	Day 13	Basil and Tomato Baked Eggs	Sweet and Sour Onions	Mediterranean Steak Sandwiches	Pretzels
	Day 14	Whole-grain pancakes	Sautéed Apples and Onions	Roasted Beef with Peppercorn Sauce	Cheesy Taco Bites
Week 3	Day 15	Whole-grain breakfast cookies	Zucchini Noodles with Portabella Mushrooms	Coffee-and-Herb-Marinated Steak	Nut Squares
	Day 16	Cinnamon and Coconut Porridge	Grilled Tempeh with Pineapple	Traditional Beef Stroganoff	Pumpkin & Banana Ice Cream
	Day 17	An Omelet of Swiss chard	Courgettes In Cider Sauce	Chicken and Roasted Vegetable Wraps	Brulee Oranges
	Day 18	Cheesy Low-Carb Omelet	Baked Mixed Mushrooms	Spicy Chicken Cacciatore	Frozen Lemon & Blueberry
	Day 19	Yogurt and Kale Smoothie	Spiced Okra	Scallion Sandwich	Peanut Butter Choco Chip Cookies
	Day 20	Grilled Chicken Platter	Lemony Salmon Burgers	Lean Lamb and Turkey Meatballs with Yogurt	Watermelon Sherbet
	Day 21	Parsley Chicken Breast	Caprese Turkey Burgers	Air Fried Section and Tomato	Strawberry & Mango Ice Cream
Week 4	Day 22	Mustard Chicken	Pasta Salad	Cheesy Salmon Fillets	Sparkling Fruit Drink
	Day 23	Balsamic Chicken	Chicken, Strawberry, And Avocado Salad	Salmon with Asparagus	Quinoa Porridge
	Day 24	Greek Chicken Breast	Lemon-Thyme Eggs	Shrimp in Garlic Butter	Apple Quinoa
	Day 25	Chipotle Lettuce Chicken	Spinach Salad with Bacon	Cobb Salad	Kamut Porridge
	Day 26	Stylish Chicken-Bacon Wrap	Pea and Collards Soup	Seared Tuna Steak	Hot Kamut With Peaches, Walnuts, And Coconut
	Day 27	Healthy Cottage Cheese Pancakes	Spanish Stew	Beef Chili	Overnight "Oats"
	Day 28	Avocado Lemon Toast	Creamy Taco Soup	Greek Broccoli Salad	Blueberry Cupcakes

CONCLUSION

Diabetes is a life-threatening disease caused by a lack of insulin. Insulin is a hormone that is required for the body's healthy functioning. The cells in a person's body do not respond to insulin effectively when they acquire diabetes. As a result, the cells do not get the energy and nutrients they require, and they begin to die.

Being diagnosed with diabetes will bring some major changes in your lifestyle. From the time you are diagnosed with it, it would always be a constant battle with food. You need to become a lot more careful with your food choices and the quantity that you ate. Every meal will feel like a major effort. You will be planning every day for the whole week, well in advance. Depending upon the type of food you ate, you have to keep checking your blood sugar levels. You may get used to taking long breaks between meals and staying away from snacks between dinner and breakfast.

Food would be treated as a bomb like it can go off at any time. According to an old saying, "When the body gets too hot, then your body heads straight to the kitchen."

Managing diabetes can be a very, very stressful ordeal. There will be many times that you will mark your glucose levels down on a piece of paper like you are plotting graph lines or something. You will mix your insulin shots up and then stress about whether or not you are giving yourself the right dosage. You will always be over-cautious because it involves a LOT of math and a really fine margin of error. But now, those days are gone!

With the help of technology and books, you can stock your kitchen with the right foods, like meal plans, diabetic-friendly dishes, etc. You can also get an app that will even do the work for you. You can also people-watch on the internet and find the know-how to cook and eat right; you will always be a few meals away from certain disasters, like plummeting blood sugar level. Always carry some sugar in your pocket. You won't have to experience the pangs of hunger but if you are unlucky, you will have to ration your food and bring along some simple low-calorie snacks with you.

This is the future of diabetes.

As you've reached the end of this book, you have gained complete control of your diabetes and this is where your expedition towards a better, healthier life starts. I hope I was able to inculcate some knowledge into you and make this adventure a little bit less of a struggle.

I would like to remind you that you're not alone in having to manage this disease and that nearly 85% of the new cases are 20 years old or younger.

Regardless of the length or seriousness of your diabetes, it can be managed! Take the information presented here and art with it!

Preparation is key to having a healthier and happier life.

Is helpful to remember that every tool at your disposal can help in some way.

Printed in Great Britain
by Amazon